BRINGING DOWN THE BANKING SYSTEM

Bringing Down the Banking System

Lessons from Iceland

Gudrun Johnsen

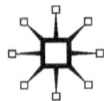

BRINGING DOWN THE BANKING SYSTEM

Grateful acknowledgment is made for the permissions to reprint the following previously published images:

(1) Figure (10.2) and Front Cover—Cross-ownership of firms with more than 500 million ISK in assets (Icel. Eignatengsl fyrirtækja með yfir 500 milljónir króna í eignir), SIC report, Appendix 2, Figure 6,

(2) Figure 10.3—Cross-ownership of firms with more than 500 million ISK in assets, 10% minimum cross-ownership (Icel. Eignatengsl fyrirtækja með yfir 500 milljónir í eignir, 10% lámarks eignatengsl), SIC report, Appendix 2, Figure 7,

(3) Figure 10.4—Related parties with Baugur Group hf as the main party (Icel. Hópur tengdra aðila þegar Baugur Group hf er aðalaðili), SIC report, Appendix 2, Figure 15,

(4) Figure 11.6—Total Lending to Baugur Group and related parties as percentage of capital base shown as a function of 2007 year-end minimum shareholding (Icel. Hlutfall heildarútlána Baugur Group og tendra aðila sem hlutfall af eiginfjárgrunni og sem fall af lágmarkseignarhlut við áramótin 2007/2008), SIC report, Appendix 2, Figure 30,

previously published in Bjarnadottir and Hansen, 2010, "Investigation into the cross ownership and bank credit to related parties," SIC Report, Volume 9 (Title in Icelandic: Rannsókn á krosseignartengslum og útlánum bankanna til tengdra aðila), Special Investigation Commission, Reykavik.

All quotations and illustrations from the Special Investigation Commission fall under the public domain and are not protected by copyrights.

First published in 2014 by
PALGRAVE MACMILLAN®
in the United States—a division of St. Martin's Press LLC,
175 Fifth Avenue, New York, NY 10010.

Where this book is distributed in the UK, Europe and the rest of the world, this is by Palgrave Macmillan, a division of Macmillan Publishers Limited, registered in England, company number 785998, of Houndmills, Basingstoke, Hampshire RG21 6XS.

Palgrave Macmillan is the global academic imprint of the above companies and has companies and representatives throughout the world.

Palgrave® and Macmillan® are registered trademarks in the United States, the United Kingdom, Europe and other countries.

ISBN: 978–1–137–35819–6

Library of Congress Cataloging-in-Publication Data

Johnsen, Gudrun.
    Bringing down the banking system : lessons from Iceland / Gudrun Johnsen.
      pages cm
    ISBN 978–1–137–35819–6 (hardback)
      1. Bank failures—Iceland—History—21st century. 2. Banks and banking—Corrupt practices—Iceland—History—21st century. 3. Bank management—Iceland—History—21st century. I. Title.

HG3154.J66 2013
332.1094912—dc23   2013025082

A catalogue record of the book is available from the British Library.

Design by Newgen Knowledge Works (P) Ltd., Chennai, India.

First edition: January 2014

To my mother
Stefania Valdis Stefansdottir
for her everlasting help, support, and encouragement
and
to my kindred spirit, husband, and editor in chief,
Thorarinn R. Einarsson

Contents

Figures

Tables

Acknowledgments

Writing a book like this one requires the knowledge, experience, and hard work of many individuals. First of all, it would not have been possible without the amazing work of Iceland's Special Investigation Commission (SIC). Pall Hreinsson, Tryggvi Gunnarsson, and Sigridur Benediktsdottir, and their employees and contractors, put in over 80-hour weeks for several months in order to deliver the SIC's 2,400-page report on April 12, 2010. I would like to thank them all for their contribution and for generously sharing their wisdom and knowledge with me, especially Sigridur Benediktsdottir, Bjarni Kristinn Torfason, Ludvik Eliasson, Margret Bjarnadottir, Olafur Gudmundsson, and Gudmundur Axel Hansen. They are my dream team to work with—enthusiastic, hardworking, intelligent, and kindhearted.

Seminar participants at central banks, financial supervisory authorities, and universities on both sides of the Atlantic must be thanked. They inspired me with their excellent questions, and encouraged me to get the story out, especially Oz Shy at the Boston Federal Reserve, Zac Rolnik, publisher, and Rick Wicks, who was then at Göteborg Universitet.

I would also like to thank the members of my personal editorial team. Andrew Nobel at UNC-Chapel Hill asked many great questions that provided guidance on how to focus in on the most important issues and thus tell the story in less than a thousand pages. Marcia Walker provided many helpful suggestions and opened my eyes to new possibilities. Meredith Blackwelder Kinder made corrections and suggestions. Ed Connell meticulously scrutinized countless details and provided great feedback. Rick Wicks—an economist who is also a wonderfully skilled freelance copy editor—volunteered to read the final draft very carefully and provided hundreds of helpful suggestions.

Many friends have provided great support in so many ways, such as by babysitting my daughters; listening to excerpts from the book; providing professional feedback, and even a country cottage in which to get much needed peace and quiet to write. They include Elfa and Stefan, Anthony and Birna, Bjorn Johannesson, Ragna Gardarsdottir, and my cousin Snaebjorn Gunnsteinsson, as well as Sigridur and Orn Steinar.

Stefan Andri Stefansson deserves many thanks for his excellent job working on the data while I was busy writing the last part of the book. He was instrumental in the final weeks so that I could deliver the project on time.

My family provided all the support that I could ask for. My brother Valdemar read over the first few chapters and provided much-needed encouragement in the early stages. My mother put countless hours into this project by taking care of our daughters, letting us stay at her place when we needed to, cooking dinners for the family, and, of course, encouraging me to keep going just when I needed it. My cousin and dear friend Laufey also took care of our girls and cooked countless (and delicious) dinners for our family.

Finally, I have to thank the one person who stood by my side every step of the way—my darling husband, Thorarinn. He took on the role of editor in chief, reading through every single chapter, making suggestions and changes, and extending encouragement with diplomacy and grace. Without him, the book would have been finished sometime in the next decade, or not at all.

Characters

Name	Title	Employer
Gudni Adalsteinsson	VP of Treasury	Kaupthing
Sigurjon Arnason	Chief Executive Officer	Landsbanki
Fridrik Mar Baldursson	Professor of Economics	Reykjavik University
Johannes Baldursson	VP of Capital Markets	Glitnir
Thorsteinn Mar Baldvinsson	Chairman of the Board	Glitnir
Sigridur Benediktsdottir	Member, Special Investigation Commission	Icelandic State
Johan Bergendahl	Consultant	J.P. Morgan
Bjorgolfur Thor Bjorgolfsson	Chairman of the Board Owner	Novator Partners Samson Group
Sturla Bodvarsson	Speaker of Parliament	Icelandic State
Bolli Thor Bollason	Permanent Secretary of the Prime Ministry	Icelandic State
Marc Dobler	Member of the Special Resolution Unit	Bank of England
Sigurdur Einarsson	Chairman of the Board	Kaupthing
Thordur Fridjonsson	Permanent Secretary of the Ministry of Commerce and Industry (1999–2006)	Icelandic State
Ingimundur Fridriksson	Deputy Governor	Central Bank of Iceland
Ingibjorg Solrun Gisladottir	Minister for Foreign Affairs	Icelandic State
Axel Gislason	Chief Executive Officer	VIS Insurance Ltd. (Vátryggingafélag Íslands hf.)
Ottar Gudjonsson	Member of SEB Negotiating Team	Skandinaviska Enskilda Banken, Stockholm

Continued

Name	Title	Employer
Baldur Gudlaugsson	Permanent Secretary of the Ministry of Finance	Icelandic State
Bjorgolfur Gudmundsson	Chairman of the Board	Landsbanki
Eirikur Gudnason	Deputy Governor	Central Bank of Iceland
Tryggvi Gunnarsson	Member, Special Investigation Commission	Icelandic State
Lars Gustavsson	Leader of SEB Negotiating Team	Skandinaviska Enskilda Banken, Stockholm
Geir H. Haarde	Prime Minister (2006–2009)	Icelandic State
Hordur Felix Hardarson	VP of Legal Affairs	Glitnir
Tryggvi Thor Herbertsson	Economic advisor to the prime minister	Icelandic State
Pall Hreinsson	Chairman, Special Investigation Commission	Icelandic State
Finnur Ingolfsson	Minister of Commerce and Industry (1995–1999)	Icelandic State
Greta Ingthorsdottir	Assistant to the Prime Minister	Icelandic State
Jon Asgeir Johannesson	CEO	Baugur Group
Jonas Fr. Jonsson	Director General	FME—Financial Supervisory Authority of Iceland (FME)
Yngvi Orn Kristinsson	VP of Capital Markets	Landsbanki
Halldor Kristjansson	Deputy CEO	Landsbanki
Jonina Larusdottir	Permanent Secretary of the Ministry of Commerce	Icelandic State
Sigridur Logadottir	General Counsel	Central Bank of Iceland
Arni Mathiesen	Minister of Finance	Icelandic State
David Oddsson	Governor (2005–2009) Prime Minister (1991–2004)	Central Bank of Iceland Icelandic State
Olafur Olafsson	Businessman	Kjalar
Jon Pain	Staff Member	Financial Services Authority (UK)
Sturla Palsson	Director of Market Operations	Central Bank of Iceland
Tryggvi Palsson	Director of Financial Stability	Central Bank of Iceland
Thorarinn G. Petursson	Economist	Central Bank of Iceland
Michael Ridley	Consultant	J.P. Morgan
Hector Sants	Chief Executive Officer	Financial Services Authority (UK)

Name	Title	Employer
Elin Sigfusdottir	VP of Corporate Banking	Landsbanki
Steingrimur J. Sigfusson	Opposition Leader in Parliament	Icelandic State
Arnor Sighvatsson	Chief Economist	Central Bank of Iceland
Johanna Sigurdardottir	Minister for Social Affairs	Icelandic State
Bjorgvin Sigurdsson	Minister of Commerce	Icelandic State
Hreidar Mar Sigurdsson	Chief Executive Officer	Kaupthing
Jon Sigurgeirsson	Economist	Central Bank of Iceland
Sturla Sigurjonsson	Staff Member at the Prime Ministry	Icelandic State
Ossur Skarphedinsson	Minister of Industry	Icelandic State
Petur Snaeland	Author's friend's grandfather	Petur Snaeland hf.
Skarphedinn Berg Steinarsson	Staff Member, Committee on Privatization	Icelandic State
Jon Steinsson	Associate Professor of Economics	Columbia University
Jon Thor Sturluson	Advisor to the Minister of Commerce	Icelandic State
Stefan Svavarsson	Certified Public Accountant	Central Bank of Iceland
Valgerdur Sverrisdottir	Minister of Commerce and Industry (1999–2006)	Icelandic State
Magnus Thorsteinsson	Business Associate of Bjorgolfur Thor Bjorgolfsson and his father	Samson Group
Vilhelm Mar Thorsteinsson	VP of Treasury	Glitnir
Armann Thorvaldsson	Chief Executive Officer	Kaupthing Singer and Friedlander
Tinna	Author's friend	N/A
Arni Tomasson	Special Advisor	FME—Financial Supervisory Authority of Iceland (FME)
Gary Weiss	Consultant	J.P. Morgan
Larus Welding	Chief Executive Officer	Glitnir
Karl Wernersson	Chairman of the Board	Milestone Group

Timeline of Relevant Events

Iceland	Year	United States and Europe
Dec: Samson purchases Landsbanki.	2002	Nov: US Federal funds rate reduced to 1.25%.
Jan: S-group purchases Bunadarbanki. Dec. Total bond issues of the three largest banks in Iceland reach 2.6 billion euros, or 25% of Iceland's GDP that year.	2003	June: US Federal funds rate reduced to 1%, the lowest value in 45 years.
The three Icelandic banks issue over 7 billion euros worth of bonds.	2004	June: US Federal funds rate is increased by 0.25% to 1.25%, the first tightening in over 4 years. Aug: US Federal funds rate is increased to 1.5%. Sep: US Federal funds rate is increased to 1.75%. Nov: US Federal funds rate is increased to 2.0%. Dec: US Federal funds rate is increased to 2.25%.
The Icelandic banks issue over 14 billion euros worth of bonds.	2005	Feb: US Federal funds rate is increased to 2.5%. Mar: US Federal funds rate is increased to 2.75%. May: US Federal funds rate is increased to 3%. July: IMF working paper on credit growth. Dec: US Federal funds rate is increased from 4% to 4.25%.
Feb: Rating agencies express an increasingly negative view toward the Icelandic banks.	2006	Jan: US Federal funds rate is increased to 4.5%.

Continued

Iceland	Year	United States and Europe
Mar: Merrill Lynch warns of frontloaded funding in 2007 in the amount of 1.7 times Iceland's GDP. Mar: A report from Danske Bank launches the Geyser Crisis. The banks issue over 10 billion euros worth of bonds.		Mar: US Federal funds rate is increased to 4.75%. May: US Federal funds rate hits 5%.
Feb: Moody's increases the rating of the banks to Aaa. Apr: Moody's lowers the rating of the banks to Aa3. CDS premiums rise sharply. REPOs with the Central Bank of Iceland exceed 5 billion euros.	2007	Aug: Subprime crisis enters spotlight. Sept: Northern Rock receives liquidity support from the Bank of England.
Jan: Collateralized lending at the Central Bank of Iceland doubles. Apr: ECB governor, Jean-Claude Trichet, contacts the Central Bank of Iceland because of "*abnormal, artificial*" bonds used as collateral. May: David Oddsson, governor of the Central Bank of Iceland describes the bonds issued by the three Icelandic banks as "*foam*," referring to them as "*love letters*" of the banks, and explains them to the cabinet. Sept. 25: Glitnir requests a loan of last resort. Sept. 29: Iceland's government announces purchase of 75% of shares in Glitnir. Oct. 6: Prime Minister of Iceland delivers "God Bless Iceland" speech. The emergency law is passed. Oct. 7: Landsbanki and Glitnir fall. Oct. 9: Kaupthing falls.	2008	Feb: Northern Rock is nationalized by UK government. Mar: Bear Stearns is sold to J.P. Morgan Chase for $2 a share. Sept. 15: Lehman Brothers files for bankruptcy. Sept. 16: AIG receives an emergency loan from the government. Sept. 18: Lloyds TSB is taken over by HBOS in the UK.

Part I

From Prosperity to Panic

Chapter 1

Illusion of Prosperity

I have always had considerable respect for those who pursue their entrepreneurial vision, risking their money and foregoing consumption during the first few years of their business with the hope of future gains. This is what I used to think of as the fundamental element of capitalism.

I had several role models who contributed to this respect. One of them, Petur Snaeland, the grandfather of one of my best childhood friends, began with a small auto garage in the 1940s. Through careful management and kindness to his employees, many of whom were former convicts, he managed to support his family of six. But things didn't always go as planned for Snaeland. One day, his garage burned to the ground, leaving the family with no assets and no livelihood. In an attempt to comfort his wife, Snaeland gave her a big hug and said: "*Don't worry honey, nobody lost anything on this, except for us.*"

With little but his name and mechanical skills, Snaeland got started again, this time with an equipment rental business he built up by restoring obsolete machinery he bought as scrap from the US military base in Keflavik, Iceland. Business was good in the postwar years and in 1952 he opened one of the first rubber factories in Scandinavia. As the years went by, his business grew and in 1968 he added a foam production factory. By the 1980s, his company was among the best-known brands in Iceland, bearing his name "Petur Snaeland hf."

When capital controls were lifted in Iceland in the 1980s, competition in the furniture production industry got tougher, and in 1988, Snaeland, having overextended himself with an additional investment in a new production plant, was forced to file for bankruptcy. By the time he was ready to retire, he had not only lost his business and his pension, but also his wonderful family home, inherited by his wife from her father, the former mayor of Reykjavik.

In my view, Petur Snaeland was one of those capitalists who form the pillars of a great society—who keep the wheels of the economy turning. They get ideas, invest their savings, work hard, and either reap the rewards, or fail. And this is how it has been for centuries.

I used to think that all entrepreneurs were like Petur Snaeland. It was a naïve view that changed over time, but never did I imagine how far we could stray from these fundamental aspects of capitalism. In 2009, however, I came to see just how far, when serving as senior researcher for Iceland's Special Investigation Commission. The Commission was set up to investigate the causes and events leading to the fall of the three largest banks in Iceland in October 2008. It issued its 2.400-page report on April 12, 2010.

One of the main discoveries of the investigation was a complex ownership structure: a cobweb of holding companies. This complex structure (*see front cover image*) was used to avoid consolidated accounting, to accumulate dividend payments through off-shore special purpose vehicles (SPVs), and to successfully tunnel money out of the banking system through easy access to risky borrowing. Under such structures, there is no limit to how much risk owners are willing to take. They have little or no skin in the game. In the case of the fallen systemically important Icelandic banks, creditors and the rest of society bore most of the risk. In a remarkably short period of time after privatization, the Icelandic banking system collapsed, with severe consequences for the Icelandic nation. Most of those responsible for the collapse, however, escaped serious financial and legal repercussions and, unlike Petur Snaeland, can comfortably say to their significant other: "*Don't worry honey, everybody lost, except for us.*"

Iceland—the Yardstick of Luxury

"*Wow, have you seen the bathrooms in this place? They are so nice they could be in Iceland,*" my friend Tinna said as she came walking out of the restroom at the Zaytinya restaurant in downtown Washington, DC in January 2006. She and her husband were visiting DC for the first time, and in an attempt to be a good host, I had put together a small itinerary, a list of the must-sees in Washington, DC. I wanted to impress them with everything the US capital had to offer, but I never considered putting the restroom at Zaytinya on the list.

Tinna's comment, however, underscored the state of affairs in my home country of Iceland, which had been experiencing outstanding economic growth for several years and had been recognized in my research at the International Monetary Fund (IMF) as having too rapid a growth of credit. Tinna wasn't one to be caught by the latest fad, or to be swept by a wave of lavish spending; so if the bathrooms of Zaytinya were catching her attention, something in Iceland truly must have changed.

A few months later, my husband and I moved back to Iceland, to our 80-year-old, 750-square-foot apartment in downtown Reykjavik, and since the original kitchen cabinets were about to fall apart, we decided to install new ones we found at a good price at IKEA. Unfortunately, every trip to IKEA took at least a couple of hours, no matter what the purpose. It wasn't that IKEA was far away, but rather that everybody else was renovating as well.

The transformation of Iceland was obvious, and the crowds were not limited to IKEA. Designer furniture stores were busy too, and so were car dealers, and carpenters building summer cottages, and travel agents, and fashion boutiques, and the list goes on.

By December 2006, after seven months in Iceland, I wrote to my former colleagues at the IMF trying to describe life in Iceland:

> As you probably know, the economy has been piping hot, hence it has been a challenge not to immerse oneself into the Hollywood type of rat-race that is going on. The Icelandic consumers are not constrained by the question of whether to buy a car or not, or a house or not, but rather whether to buy a brand new Porsche Cayenne, Jeep, or Range Rover...!

The credit boom was evident all around Reykjavik, from banks to building cranes to the BMW dealership. It was as if Iceland had discovered a new oil field. Unfortunately, it had only discovered access to, and appetite for, easy credit. Iceland was indeed headed for a world-record credit boom.

Credit Boom

A credit boom is defined as rapid expansion of credit to the private sector, accompanied by rising asset prices. The boom is often followed by a bust, consisting of risk aversion on the part of the financial sector as asset prices fall again to sustainable levels, marked by unwillingness to lend under this price level uncertainty. This in turn causes a reduction in investment and consumption, and often results in a recession.

It is difficult to estimate a normal level of credit growth, especially in the case of underdeveloped countries that are on the path of structural changes to spur economic growth. One rule of thumb, derived from empirical work, points to a possible danger at a 17 percent real growth of credit, since that is the average annual real growth of credit during episodes that are associated with excessive cyclical movements in credit that have not been sustainable and have eventually collapsed.[1] Any given country could thus be considered to be going through a credit boom if bank credit to the private sector rises by around 50 percent in a three-year period. This is not hard to grasp—since our economies, when healthy, grow no more than 4–6 percent in real terms over one year. If our banks extend credit to the private sector at a rate twice or three times that of the growth of the economy, chances are that safe investment opportunities, which yield high rates of return to cover the cost of credit and leave something on the table for the investors, become harder and harder to find. As Pierre-Olivier Gourinchas and his coauthors put it:

> During a lending boom, the typical story goes, credit to the private sector rises quickly. Leverage increases, and financing is extended to projects with low—possibly even negative—net present value, either because monitoring becomes difficult when the volume of lending increases rapidly, which increases the likelihood of fraud (including looting, self-lending, and evergreening[[2]]), or because domestic borrowers' net worth increases. As lending expands, the quality of funded projects goes from bad to worse, exposure increases, and the banking sector becomes more vulnerable.[3]

During a credit boom, financial markets participants have a distorted notion of risk. While it is difficult for bankers to assess the correlation of losses across borrowers and lenders over time, risk also tends to be underestimated during booms and overestimated in recessions.[4] Moreover, assessment of the viability of investments by the market is distorted by implicit or explicit guarantees made by the government sector. Entrepreneurs and lenders price new projects under the best possible scenario, taking into account a government bailout in the worst-case scenario, and begin reaching for the bottom of the barrel to continue supporting the good times.[5]

To prevent the possible bad consequences of rapid credit growth, it is important for policy makers to identify the origin of the episode. While it is important to avoid "crying wolf" when credit growth may be the result of a simple catching-up process, it would be too optimistic to assume that rapid credit growth is simply the result of the system reaching a new and much higher "equilibrium level" of credit without any risks or need for action. In fact, such behavior on the part of policy makers can only be categorized as regulatory gambling, considering the devastating consequences faced by all citizens in the worst-case scenario.

When it comes to the possible causes of credit growth, the same medicine cannot be applied to all maladies. Financial stability instruments such as reserve requirements, dynamic provisioning, elevated equity ratio requirements, and tightening collateral requirements are among those measures that can be found in the policy toolbox to contain credit growth, in addition to a host of other prudential policy instruments, thoroughly documented in an IMF working paper by Hilbers and his coauthors, including myself, from 2005.[6]

Considering the credit growth numbers from Iceland (see Table 1.1), it should have been easy to build a case for a public policy response. The numbers warrant a pause to think about the difference between what science knows and what government does in its duties to protect the interests of its citizens. According to the early warning

Table 1.1 Credit to the private sector by deposit money banks and other credit institutions as share of Iceland's GDP 1990–2010

Year	Private credit / GDP	Growth y.o.y. (%)	3-year cum. growth (%)
1990	41.3		
1991	41.5	0.39	
1992	45.2	8.96	
1993	46.5	2.98	12.33
1994	44.3	−4.95	6.98
1995	44.7	1.08	−0.90
1996	45.9	2.52	−1.35
1997	55.6	21.26	24.86
1998	61.8	11.16	34.95
1999	66.1	6.99	39.42
2000	82.3	24.49	42.65
2001	93.3	13.30	44.79
2002	100.3	7.49	45.28
2003	116.3	16.01	36.80
2004	130.8	21.07	44.57
2005	197.2	40.04	77.11
2006	269.3	36.54	97.64
2007	272.8	1.3	77.88
2008	184.3	−32.45	5.39
2009	118.9	−35.45	−66.59
2010	109.3	−8.14	−76.04

Source: Martin Cihák, Asli Demirgüç-Kunt, Erik Feyen, and Ross Levine, "Benchmarking Financial Development Around the World." *Policy Research Working Paper 6175, World Bank, Washington, DC, August 2012.*

signs and the rules of thumb described above, there was ample evidence to push for a policy response against the buildup of credit in the Icelandic system, at least from 2003, if not already in 2000. To be completely fair, it does take time to assemble statistics such as these, but that does not excuse the inaction on the part of the regulators, who had reasons to act over a five- to seven-year period before the system finally collapsed.

Credit Growth Research

My interest in the strategic behaviors of financial institutions began when I was working as a broker at the newly formed Icelandic Investment Bank (FBA) in 1999. A year earlier, I had been working as an analyst at the financially conservative Nordic Investment Bank (NIB) in Helsinki, keeping track of the performance measurements of the bank's mark-to-market portfolio. NIB had never encountered a default and had only bought bonds with a rating of AA- or better. The culture at NIB at that time could be described as professional, conservative, and cautious. The employees were meticulous professionals, with a solid track record and a diverse international experience from leading financial institutions. NIB's credit rating of AAA was, in those days, as rare for financial institutions as a black swan, and was mostly held by sovereign states. The risk profile of FBA, however, was quite different. It was a brand new institution, which was focused on growth and increasing profits and staffed with young and relatively inexperienced professionals with recent college or postgraduate degrees.

The Icelandic financial market was going through reorganization, including the privatization of financial institutions, and incentivizing tools such as bonuses were introduced. Times were looking up, particularly for the employees of FBA, who quickly became labeled as high-income individuals—the new privileged few. I remember a sign at a local theater in 2000 explaining the price of admission. It read something like:

Children	400 kr.
Adults	1,500 kr.
Senior Citizens	900 kr.
FBA employees	24,000 kr.

Iceland was going through a transition, with economic indicators improving after several years of missteps. There was optimism in the air, a sense of increased prosperity.

Like my coworkers, I was pleased to have a decent job, being able to make my first investment in real estate. At the same time, I became curious to study the relationship between the incentives and the different economic outcomes they might yield, both for financial institutions and for other firms.

That opportunity came when I was hired by RAND Corporation in California after graduating from the University of Michigan in 2003. RAND allowed me to focus my research on the pay-for-performance relationship by scrutinizing the interaction between different incentivizing tools readily available to discipline managers. This work eventually brought me to the IMF in 2004, where I narrowed down on the compensation structures of financial institutions and the impact they could have on operations such as lending practices, potentially leading to rapid credit growth. One of my projects was to identify those countries that were likely to experience a financial crisis as a result of too-rapid credit growth. The results were published in the aforementioned IMF working paper.

In addition to identifying countries in Central and Eastern Europe that were under the threat of too-rapid credit growth, my group's task at the IMF was to explain how to react to the threat, and how to alleviate it. To accomplish this, the team used univariate analysis on bank credit to the private sector in relation to GDP, a method developed by Gourinchas et al. (2001), who had successfully shown how it worked for Latin American countries in the 1990s. Using this method on the benchmark countries, the team could identify credit booms that had already happened, and, when applying it to the focus group, could identify those countries where credit booms were in progress. Needless to say, one of those countries was Iceland.

Although the method isn't perfect, it turned out to be very successful. All of the countries identified in the paper in 2005 as being under threat of unsustainable rapid growth are now recognized as having had a financial crisis as a result—all except one. Lebanon was identified as a rapid-credit-growth country, but managed to steer away from a crisis. The other countries in the focus group have already begun dealing with the consequences, and most of them are even under an IMF program as a result.

Findings as Foes

In 2005, I visited the Central Bank of Iceland, figuring that economists at the bank would be aware of the issue and would appreciate further evidence that a crisis was building, and in particular, ideas how to avoid it. Surprisingly, they had limited interest. I then contacted the prime ministry of Iceland, but received the response that I was too technical and too theoretical. I finally approached the director general of the financial supervisory authority of Iceland, FME, sent him the credit growth paper, and asked to speak with him about it. I received a response from the Human Resources manager, who said that I would first have to take a test to prove my proficiency, and that I would be allowed access to Microsoft Word and the Internet in doing so. I politely declined.

Perhaps it was my blonde hair, but slowly it dawned on me that the message I was carrying about the risks of rapid credit growth and how it was developing in Iceland put me in the position of someone who was there to stop the party. Nobody wanted to entertain the idea that the good times would not last, not to mention that they might even come to a sudden and painful end.

When working in science, it is not enough to have made the discovery; we must also have the means and the organization to make effective use of our knowledge.

At a meeting at the OECD in May 2009, Svein Andresen, secretary general of the Financial Stability Board, the global financial stability body set up by the G20 earlier that year, explained that the IMF had an "Early Warning System," which had described the risks to the global financial system in detail in "a fine report."[7] When the audience asked what happened to the report, Andresen replied: "Well, the report was circulated internally to Central Banks and to key financial ministries, but nobody acted on it." He added that the Financial Stability Board's predecessor, the Financial Stability Forum, had no power, except to convene meetings.

In Iceland, the problem was further exacerbated by the fact that policy makers were simply not willing to listen to warnings while the economy was experiencing an illusion of prosperity. On the contrary, Icelandic policy makers were very active in speeding up the train. Nobody wanted to be responsible for stepping on the brakes, and they certainly didn't want to know what the data were telling us. Fortunately, however, when I teach my class on Financial Markets, it is immensely important to be able to prove to my students that economists did warn of the impending crisis. If nothing else, it helps maintain the students' confidence and appreciation for science.

Worst-Case Scenario

During 2000–2007, while credit in Iceland consistently grew too fast, warnings of a potential worst-case scenario for Iceland were few and far between. Icelandic economists risked being ridiculed and dismissed. Furthermore, there are those who would acknowledge the existence of rapid credit growth and simply accept the eventual consequences: lack of credit and falling asset prices, reduction in investment and consumption, and recession. After all, the economy moves in cycles and our political ideology drives our view of how much we should intervene in those cycles. Without intervention, we risk excessive economic cycles with financial instability and a difficult working environment for businesses, but if we intervene too much, we risk holding back economic growth and job creation.

Political ideology aside, however, the 2005 IMF working paper on assessing and managing credit growth provides a clear warning when describing potential outcomes and discussing the need to consider macroeconomic stability. It points out the impact that rapid credit growth has on the external current account balance, inflation, and currency stability, and clearly states that "a continued deterioration in the current account deficit may in turn trigger a cutback of external credit lines and foreign liquidity and thus lead to a deterioration of the condition of the banking system, bringing about a full-fledged financial and economic crisis."[8]

Unfortunately for my beloved home country, Iceland, this worst-case scenario became a reality in October 2008, when three of its largest banks collapsed, bringing down roughly 97 percent of its banking system.

Chapter 2

Collapse

August 8, 2007–Subprime Crisis Enters the Spotlight

It seemed like any ordinary August day in New York City, although a bit hot for a tourist from Iceland. The occasional rain showers helped keep us cool as my husband and I strolled through the city with my mother and our elder daughter. We were just spending a few days there, getting ready to visit friends in North Carolina where my husband had been working for many years. It was a memorable time for us in many ways, but I will always remember those New York City days in August 2007 as the time when news coverage of the subprime mortgage crisis gained international attention and the most serious financial crisis since the Great Depression officially began.

From an economic standpoint, the story of the world financial crisis begins many years earlier, of course, and so does the particularly Icelandic story in this book. In fact, the threads of these two stories are often woven together, and many of the lessons we can draw from them are the same. The lessons from Iceland, however, benefit from a thorough and unique 15-month-long autopsy of the Icelandic financial system following the collapse of Iceland's three largest banks in 2008; an autopsy, performed by Iceland's Special Investigation Commission (SIC), for which I served as Senior Researcher.

The case of Iceland also represents extremes in both directions: the largest credit boom the world has seen so far, and the largest collapse of a banking system so far, proportionally speaking of course. Add to that the manageable size of the Icelandic system and you've got an example exceptionally well suited for learning.

Understandably, some academics, scholars, and business professionals have dismissed the lessons from Iceland, simply calling them another bubble as so many before, but as the story in this book will show, the devil surely lurks in the details. The findings of the SIC investigation provide us an unprecedented view of the events occurring throughout the Icelandic credit boom–bust cycle. In fact, in my presentations at central banks and other financial institutions around the world, in front of some of the most experienced financial markets experts of our time, I am yet to find an audience that wasn't surprised and even shocked by the details of the Icelandic story. I thank these audiences for encouraging me to write this book and for providing great feedback that helped guide the story.

*   *   *

October 6, 2008—God Bless Iceland

As I left my university office on October 6, 2008, many of my colleagues were looking for conference rooms to watch the just-announced television broadcast at 4 p.m. by the prime minister of Iceland. The previous two weeks, from late September 2008 and into October, had been particularly turbulent, with one of the three largest banks in Iceland, Glitnir, going to the Central Bank and requesting a loan of last resort, but ending up being partially nationalized. The controversial 600 million euros share purchase by the government reduced the share of previous owners to 25 percent and provided the government full control with a 75 percent share in the bank.

The governor of the Central Bank, David Oddsson, as well as the prime minister, Geir H. Haarde, tried to convince the public that the investment had been made to protect the assets of deposit holders as well as the country's financial stability, and that, in due time, the government would sell its shares and hopefully even make a profit on the transaction.[1]

The events of the previous weeks gave little reason to be optimistic though. The banks were in trouble; that was now public knowledge. The question was only how deep. While most people were anxious, they were also relieved that Prime Minister Haarde was going to address the nation. Many Icelanders expected a broadcast that would calm the situation and even bring people ease. Very few were in a position to extrapolate the elusive effects of contagion and consider how much worse things could get.

With my mother living near the university, my husband and I decided to meet at her place to watch the broadcast. We arrived just before 4 p.m. Within a couple of minutes, Prime Minister Haarde appeared, sitting at a desk in the National Broadcasting Service studio with a dark blue background fading into black behind him and the Icelandic coat of arms up to the left. The studio setup seemed darker than usual when the prime minister spoke. Already we had a sense of national emergency. Then Prime Minister Haarde began speaking:

Fellow Icelanders.

I have requested to speak to you at this moment, now that the Icelandic nation is facing great difficulties. The entire world is now going through a serious financial crisis, and its effects on the world's banking system can be considered an economic disaster. Large and solid banks on both sides of the Atlantic have fallen prey to the crisis, and governments in many countries are desperately trying to salvage as much as possible domestically. In a situation like this, each nation must of course focus first and foremost on its own interests. Even the largest economies in the world are having difficulty dealing with the consequences of the crisis.

Just like other international banks, the Icelandic banks have not been spared from this serious financial crisis, and their position is now very grave. The growth and success of the Icelandic banks in recent years have been phenomenal. As access to funding in the international markets peaked, the banks, as well as other Icelandic enterprises, seized the opportunity to fund further expansion beyond our shores.

During this time, the Icelandic banks have grown enormously, and their obligations are now equivalent to Iceland's GDP many times over. Under normal circumstances, large banks would be more likely to weather a temporary storm, but the economic disaster unfolding around the world today is of a different kind, and the current size of the banks in relation to the Icelandic economy is now their biggest weakness.

When the world financial crisis began just over a year ago, with the collapse of the US real estate market and the resulting chain reaction due to the so-called sub-prime loans, the position of the Icelandic banks was considered solid, since they had not participated in such lending to any extent. However, the consequences of that chain reaction have proven to be more serious and far-reaching than anyone could have imagined.

In the last few weeks, the world financial system has suffered enormous blows. Some of the largest investment banks in the world have been swallowed by the crisis, and the liquidity in the market has essentially dried up. Consequently, large international banks have ceased funding other banks, and total mistrust has materialized amongst banks. The position of the Icelandic banks has therefore seriously deteriorated over the last several days.

Fellow Icelanders.

The Government of Iceland, the Central Bank, and the financial supervisory authority have over the last few days and weeks worked very hard, in good cooperation with the banks, to resolve the grave difficulties facing the Icelandic banks. Many stakeholders have been involved, including pension funds and unions. The Government has strongly emphasized that the Icelandic banks sell their foreign assets and reduce their operations so that the Icelandic State, small in comparison to the Icelandic banks, can support them. Let us keep in mind, in this context, that the enormous package decided on by US authorities to save their financial system constitutes about 5% of their GDP. The balance sheet of the Icelandic banks, however, is many times the GDP of Iceland.

The decision to put together a wide-ranging rescue package to save the Icelandic banks is therefore not a question of temporarily increasing the taxpayers' burden; it pertains instead to the long-term position of the entire Icelandic nation.

The Government has announced that it will do everything in its power to strengthen the Icelandic banking system. To that end, several important achievements have been attained over the last few weeks and months. In the alarming situation now prevailing in global financial markets, extending a lifeline to the banks entails great risk for the entire Icelandic nation. This must be kept in mind when addressing foreign borrowing by the National Treasury, amounting to thousands of billions of Icelandic kronas, for defending the banks in the rough seas they now find themselves in. The risk is real, fellow Icelanders, that the Icelandic economy would, in the worst-case scenario, be sucked together with the banks into the violent surge of the financial crisis and consequently into national bankruptcy. No responsible government jeopardizes the future of its nation to such an extent, even if the nation's banking system itself is at stake. We, the elected officials, simply do not have permission to do so. The Icelandic nation and its future are our top priority.

We have been meeting nearly non-stop over the weekend regarding the current state of the financial system. I can assure you that everyone involved has put their utmost effort into ensuring that the banks and financial institutions continue operating today as normal. The outcome of this weekend's work gave us reason to believe that the banks would be able to get funding for the short term. I therefore said last night that it was my and the Government's assessment that there was no reason for special measures on our part. No responsible government introduces far-reaching actions regarding its nation's banking and financial system unless there is no other option.

Today, the situation has taken a sharp turn for the worse. Significant credit lines for the banks have closed, and a decision was made this morning to suspend trading with banking institutions in the Iceland Stock Exchange.

It is time for swift and responsible action. In a few moments, I will introduce a bill in parliament enabling the National Treasury to respond to the current situation on the financial markets. I have today discussed this with the leadership of the Opposition and have received reassurance that the bill will be passed into law today. I thank them for their cooperation.

This new law enables us to adjust the banking system to Icelandic circumstances and rebuild foreign trust in banking and financial activities in Iceland. Assuming the bill is passed today, these authorizations will go into effect immediately thereafter.

I wish to clearly emphasize that the deposits of Icelanders and retirement savings in all Icelandic banks are guaranteed, and the National Treasury will see to it that these assets are available in full to their owners. No one needs to doubt that. The Government will furthermore see to it that businesses have access to capital and financial services as much as possible.

Fellow Icelanders.

I fully realize that the situation is a shock to many, causing all of us fear and anguish. Under these circumstances it is imperative that the authorities, businesses, organizations, parents, and others who can help, make every effort to ensure that our daily routine is not affected.

If there ever was need for the Icelandic people to stick together and show serenity in the face of difficulty—that time has come. I encourage you all to safeguard that which is most precious in the life of every individual, safeguard the life values that can weather the current storm. I encourage families to talk to one another and not let despair gain the upper hand, despite the dark outlook of many. We need to explain to our children that the world is not coming to an end, and we must, each and every one of us, find the courage within to look ahead.

Despite these great setbacks, the future of our nation is both secure and bright. Most importantly, the foundation of our society and our economy is solid, even though other parts of the social superstructure are giving way under the shock that has hit us. We have natural resources, both in the sea and on land, which will provide us great means, no matter what. The education level of our nation and our human capital are no less enviable in the eyes of other nations than our natural resources. By the same token, we have an opportunity to rebuild the financial system. We have learned from the mistakes made during the high-growth years, and this experience will be valuable to us going forward. Our united effort and our characteristic optimism will bring us through these difficulties and allow us to launch a new and energetic beginning.

Fellow Icelanders.

The Government's task in the coming days is clear: to prevent chaos should the Icelandic banks become non-operational to any extent. For that purpose, the Government has various options at its disposal, and they will be utilized. In the political arena, as well as elsewhere, it is important to bury the hatchet during this crisis. It is important that we remain calm and restrained in the coming difficult days, that we not lose hope but rather support each other as best we can. That is how, armed with our Icelandic optimism, serenity, and solidarity, we will weather the storm.

God bless Iceland.[2]

We were stunned. The words "chaos" and "national bankruptcy"[3] echoed in our heads, and the final words underscored the severity of the situation.

Over the years, I have watched many State of the Union addresses in the United States and I have grown used to hearing "God bless America" at the end of each one of them. On October 6, 2008, however, I heard "God bless Iceland" in Icelandic for the first time from an Icelandic elected official.[4] It was a historic moment. Every nation has her historic moments where each citizen can remember where he or she was located at the time. For Icelanders, this was such a moment. The last three words of the speech have not only become some of the most defining words of that prime minister's time in office, they have also become defining words of the financial-system collapse in the minds of Icelanders.[5]

The prime minister's speech did not calm the situation–it raised the stakes. People were surprised, shocked, and alarmed; and for Icelanders looking to their elected leader to set their minds at ease, the broadcast did nothing of the sort. On the other hand, the entire nation was now on the same page–just as alarmed as the prime minister himself had been for several weeks.

The pleasant August days in New York City in 2007 were suddenly put into a new and more personal perspective. My own country, Iceland, had become the canary in the coalmine of the world financial crisis.

Chapter 3

Panic

Changing Financial Markets

On September 15, 2008, the day when Lehman Brothers filed for bankruptcy, one of the three Icelandic banks, Glitnir, was already in a precarious situation, with a total of 550 million euros of loan repayments scheduled for October 13 and 15,[1] amounting to roughly 50 percent of its equity[2] and 3.2 percent of its total outstanding bond issues.[3] In addition, Glitnir was due on payments of 1.2 billion euros during the first quarter of 2009, roughly 44 percent of the Icelandic state budget, and 14 percent of Iceland's GDP in 2008. Glitnir had been working on securing funds for the repayment in several ways, including selling assets of its subsidiary in Norway to Nordea bank.

The following day, September 16, the US government provided emergency funds to insurance giant AIG, and, two days later, the British bank Lloyds TSB took over the operations of HBOS. In a matter of a few days, Glitnir's outlook for funding therefore took a sharp turn for the worse, with each additional day adding more alarming news from international financial markets and further exacerbating Glitnir's situation.

In this chapter, we will walk through the events in Iceland of the final two weeks before the collapse of Glitnir, Landsbanki, and Kaupthing, showing the escalating panic of Icelandic bankers and politicians in the final days. Through these events, we can glean knowledge and experience, as well as their intentions, and ultimately assess the quality of their decisions under these very stressful circumstances.

Prelude to a Collapse

Tuesday, September 23, 2008

Glitnir receives the news that Nordea will not purchase the assets of Glitnir's subsidiary in Norway. On the same day, Bayerische Landesbank in Germany rejects Glitnir's request to extend two loans totaling 150 million euros, stating that Bayerische Landesbank has reached its "Iceland limit" after lending the Icelandic government 300 million euros shortly before.[4]

Wednesday, September 24, 2008

The young and relatively new CEO of Glitnir, Larus Welding, talks to a senior person at JP Morgan, who says that the investment bank can lend a billion pounds sterling to Iceland within 24–48 hours, but that they will only lend it to the Central Bank.[5] The contact adds hat the Central Bank of Iceland cannot stand and watch any longer, that it is time for them to support their financial system just like other central banks around the world are doing. On the same day, the chairman of Glitnir, Icelandic fishing business tycoon Thorsteinn Mar Baldvinsson, requests a meeting with the governor of the Central Bank of Iceland, David Oddsson.[6] The meeting is scheduled for noon the next day.

Thursday, September 25, 2008

The meeting between the tall, slender, and self-assured Baldvinsson and the confident, politically savvy, and often comedic Oddsson begins with one-on-one discussions of Glitnir's problems before Oddsson invites the two deputy governors of the Central Bank to enter the meeting: the reserved Eirikur Gudnason and Ingimundur Fridriksson.

Baldvinsson expresses his concerns about Glitnir's October payments and explains that even if they can make it through October, the bank may still only survive until Christmas, or perhaps into January.[7] Baldvinsson mentions 600 million euros as a possible loan request, but views the meeting primarily as an opportunity for information sharing.[8]

In the afternoon, Glitnir's VP of Capital Markets, Johannes Baldursson, and Glitnir's VP of Treasury, Vilhelm Mar Thorsteinsson, arrive at the Central Bank to meet with the Central Bank's Director of Market Operations, Sturla Palsson, and an economist from the

Governor's office, Jon Sigurgeirsson. Although the meeting is conducted informally, Glitnir makes a specific request to the Central Bank for a loan of 500 million euros.[9]

Amidst growing concerns about the future of the Icelandic banks, the Board of Directors of Kaupthing meets and decides to make employees who have borrowed money to buy shares in the bank exempt from personal liability on those loans, citing the risk to the bank if those employees were to start selling their shares.[10]

Friday, September 26, 2008

Glitnir's chairman, Baldvinsson, and Glitnir's CEO, Welding, meet with Governor Oddsson. The governor steps out during the meeting to call Iceland's prime minister, Geir H. Haarde, who is in New York City at the time. Governor Oddsson explains to Prime Minister Haarde that Glitnir is facing problems and that he had better return from New York immediately. The calm and composed Haarde then contacts the Minister for Foreign Affairs, Ingibjorg Solrun Gisladottir, also in New York at the time (for medical reasons), and explains to her that the financial markets are shaky.[11]

Unable to attend meetings regarding Glitnir, Gisladottir calls a member of her extended family, Minister of Industry, Ossur Skarphedinsson, and asks him to attend on her behalf.[12] The burly Skarphedinsson is caught off guard, standing naked at a local health club and about to enter the shower when he receives the phone call.[13] He tells Gisladottir that he is neither the right person for the job nor does he have any knowledge of these matters. He therefore suggests that she call Minister of Commerce Bjorgvin Sigurdsson, the minister responsible for the banking system, but Gisladottir decides to leave Sigurdsson out of it.[14]

On the same day, the Board of Governors of the Central Bank meets with Jonas Fr. Jonsson, director general of the financial supervisory authority, FME, and his deputy director. In accordance with the Icelandic law regarding lending of last resort, the Central Bank requests an assessment of Glitnir's equity.[15]

Governor Oddsson also meets with Minister of Finance Arni Mathiesen, who was unaware of Glitnir's problems up to this point. During the meeting, Mathiesen learns that Governor Oddsson has in fact decided not to grant Glitnir a loan of last resort, but rather to buy shares in the bank.[16] Meanwhile, Glitnir employees examine the bank's loan books looking for collateral to be used for a loan of last resort.

At 7 p.m., FME director general Jonsson meets with Glitnir CEO Welding, who is still optimistic that Glitnir will receive a loan. Jonsson asks him whether a merger with Landsbanki is an option, and Welding indicates that he is ready to consider it.[17]

Saturday, September 27, 2008

Prime Minister Haarde arrives from New York City early in the morning.[18] Shortly thereafter, FME director general Jonsson meets with the CEOs of all three Icelandic banks, Glitnir, Kaupthing, and Landsbanki, for informal talks and asks them if they are considering mergers. The CEO of Kaupthing, Hreidar Mar Sigurdsson, comments how funding is drying up. Before the end of the meeting, Sigurdsson asks the others: "Is anybody having a problem now? If anybody is having problems now then you have to tell me, we have to know."[19] Welding, however, decides not to share Glitnir's problems with the other bankers.

Glitnir CEO Welding and Chairman Baldvinsson then meet with the prime minister and his economic advisor, explaining that after the fall of Lehman Brothers, funding has become very difficult.[20]

At noon, the Board of Governors of the Central Bank meets with FME director general Jonsson and his deputy director.[21] The Governors express their doubts about the collateral that Glitnir is offering, but the FME directors express indifference as to which option should be chosen—a loan of last resort or a share purchase. At Glitnir's headquarters, the legal department examines the legal issues of a loan of last resort and introduces new asset-backed securities as collateral.[22]

That afternoon, the Minister of Commerce, Bjorgvin Sigurdsson, on a trip outside Reykjavik with some of his staff, has still not been notified of Glitnir's problems. Around 4 p.m., when the media reports a meeting in the prime ministry with the Board of Governors attending, the advisor to the Minister of Commerce, Jon Thor Sturluson, calls the prime minister's economic advisor, Tryggvi Thor Herbertsson, asking if anything is going on. Herbertsson replies: "No, no, nothing happening. Just going over the situation with the banks." Being on good terms with Herbertsson, the minister and his advisor conclude that everything is fine.[23]

That Saturday evening, Sturla Palsson, the Central Bank's director of Market Operations, and Jon Sigurgeirsson, the economist from the Central Bank Governor's office, prepare the first draft of a memo outlining the possible options in response to Glitnir's problems.

Palsson later explained that the memo was not about making suggestions, but rather "a description of whether you want to be crucified, hanged, or shot."[24] He added that there were no concrete solutions on the table. The system had collapsed. That evening the first draft of the memo was delivered to Governor Oddsson.

Sunday, September 28, 2008

Palsson and Sigurgeirsson meet with the Board of Governors in the morning to go over the memo outlining options regarding Glitnir, which Governor Oddsson had finalized the night before. The goals are described as follows: (1) protect deposit holders, (2) reduce systemic risk, (3) protect the operation of payment systems, (4) protect the operation of international transactions, and (5) increase confidence in the Icelandic financial system, domestically and abroad. The memo also proposes several options, the first one being the nationalization of Glitnir.[25]

One of the negative consequences listed in the memo is a run on both Landsbanki and Kaupthing, both with deposit holders in the UK and in the Netherlands. The memo therefore suggests seeking assistance from the Bank of England and the UK's Financial Services Authority, FSA. The Board of Governors of the Central Bank of Iceland, however, decides not to seek such assistance.[26]

At noon, Glitnir's VP of Treasury, Thorsteinsson, calls Sturla Palsson regarding the collateral for a loan of last resort, describing the value of the collateral as 1.3 billion euros and thus sufficient for the Central Bank. Palsson responds that he is on his way to a meeting and will try to look over the information.[27]

At 3 p.m., the Central Bank receives a proposal from Landsbanki about merging Landsbanki with Glitnir as well as Straumur-Burdaras investment bank, whose main shareholder is Bjorgolfur Thor Bjorgolfsson, also the largest shareholder of Landsbanki. The proposal stipulates that the government would provide a 660 million euro equity infusion (roughly USD 1 billion at the time) for Glitnir before it is merged with Landsbanki and Straumur-Burdaras. In addition, Landsbanki should receive a 2–3 billion euro credit line from the Central Bank of Iceland after the merger.[28]

Later that afternoon, Prime Minister Haarde, Minister of Finance Arni Mathiesen, permanent secretary of Finance Baldur Gudlaugsson, permanent secretary of the Prime Ministry Bolli Bollason, the prime minister's economic adviser Tryggvi Thor Herbertsson, as well as the Board of Governors of the Central Bank, meet in a small building near the Ministry of Finance. The meeting begins with the Central Bank's memo being handed out and read out loud by the Governor. When he is done reading, the prime minister's economic adviser, Herbertsson, points out that with the proposed share purchase, the real estate conglomerate Stodir hf. will go bankrupt.[29] He further explains that this will, in turn, have a tremendous effect on both Kaupthing and Landsbanki as they are Stodir's major creditors. He adds that Glitnir's shares held by Kaupthing and Landsbanki as collateral will plummet, and many, if not all, of those pledging those shares will be unable to respond to margin calls at this time. His conclusion is therefore that the government's purchase of Glitnir will lead to "a domino effect that nobody could explain how would end" and that most likely "the whole system would collapse."[30] Governor Oddsson reacts angrily to the analysis, and the two have a sharp debate. Oddsson also calls the economic advisor's presence at the meeting inappropriate as he is a former CEO of a financial company, currently on leave to assist Prime Minister Haarde.

Around 6 p.m., Halldor J. Kristjansson, Deputy CEO of Landsbanki, calls Governor Oddsson to inquire about the Central Bank's view of the proposal to merge Landsbanki, Glitnir, and Straumur-Burdaras investment bank. Governor Oddsson replies that he can get the Board of Governors to accept the proposal on one condition. When Kristjansson asks what the condition is, Governor Oddsson facetiously replies that it involves getting himself on the board of the flower and gift store company Blomaval. Kristjansson then asks: "Is it that outrageous?" to which Governor Oddsson replies: "Yes, it is that outrageous."[31]

Around dinnertime, the Central Bank's General Counsel, Sigridur Logadottir, is called into work. She arrives at the bank as a meeting is starting in the board room, attended by everybody who has anything to do with the financial system, including the Board of Governors, the Governor's economic advisor, the Central Bank's Director of Market Operations, the Prime Minister, the permanent secretary of the Prime Ministry, the permanent secretary of the Ministry of Finance, the Minister of Finance, the Minister for Foreign Affairs, the advisor to the Minister of Commerce, the Prime Minister's economic advisor, the Director General of the FME, and the Deputy Director of the FME. Conspicuously absent is Minister of Commerce Bjorgvin Sigurdsson, the minister responsible for the banking system.[32]

At the beginning of the meeting, Minister of Industry, Skarphedinsson, clears his throat and remarks that he has absolutely no knowledge of banking.[33] After the meeting, everybody runs in different directions making phone calls since the "Glitnir guys" are about to arrive at the Central Bank. Logadottir later described the meeting as "short," one without a clear indication that any decision was being made, but added that apparently there was one.[34]

Prime Minister Haarde later testified that no numerical analysis had been carried out regarding the impact that the Glitnir decision would have on the other banks. In addition, there was no sound financial basis for the government's share evaluation of Glitnir—the 600 million euros for a 75 percent stake. In testimony, Bolli Bollason, the permanent secretary of the Prime Ministry, added: "I remember the calculations of the share price, how this was calculated. It was introduced to us on a board. [One of the governors] wrote the numbers and showed us how...well, nobody understood how he derived his answer, neither before or after, so it really didn't make much of a difference."[35]

At 8:09 p.m., the chairman of the holding company Milestone, Karl Wernerson, a significant shareholder in Glitnir, sends an email to Governor Oddsson's economic advisor introducing his ideas of how the Government and the Central Bank could support the financial system, indicating that the news of Glitnir's serious problems had spread to its major shareholders.[36]

Around 9 p.m., Minister for Social Affairs Johanna Sigurdardottir calls Minister of Commerce Bjorgvin Sigurdsson asking if he knows what is happening with Glitnir. Sigurdsson, almost equally unaware, immediately calls his advisor and finds out that he is already at the Central Bank.[37]

At 10 p.m., the decision to purchase shares in Glitnir is introduced to the Board of Directors of FME. In the meeting notes, the FME board concludes that "if the government is willing to put 600 million Euros into Glitnir than that will of course strengthen the bank."[38]

At 10:30 p.m., Glitnir Chairman Baldvinsson, Glitnir CEO Welding, Glitnir VP of Legal Affairs Hardarson, and their attorney, enter the Central Bank through a crowd of journalists to meet Prime Minister Haarde and Governor Oddsson. Oddsson and Haarde introduce the government's plan to purchase a 75 percent share in Glitnir for 600 million euros, but the Glitnir team receives neither documentation nor a draft of the offer and understands the purchase as being made by the Central Bank, not the government.[39]

After a recess to notify others at Glitnir, the meeting continues with the addition of the Minister of Industry, Skarphedinsson, the permanent secretary of the Ministry of Finance, Gudlaugsson, and the permanent secretary of the Prime Ministry, Bollason.[40] Glitnir's chairman Baldvinsson expresses his displeasure with the proposal, but Governor Oddsson then points out that if Baldvinsson doesn't accept, the Central Bank will be obligated to notify the FME that Glitnir cannot meet a payment on October 15. Governor Oddsson adds, however, that he is pleased with the work of the CEO and the chairman and that they can remain in their current positions at Glitnir after the purchase.[41]

Shortly before 11 p.m., the prime minister's economic advisor, Herbertsson, tells Prime Minister Haarde that the share purchase is a bad idea. After a brief discussion, they agree that Herbertsson bring it up with Governor Oddsson. Herbertsson then goes into Oddsson's office to explain his view where, according to Herbertsson, Oddsson becomes furious on hearing his opinion, accusing him of undermining Oddsson's authority, adding: "The Prime Minister is out there, shaking like a leaf in the wind and can't make a decision. He listens to you and you are undermining this. If this plan doesn't go through, I will personally see to it that you will not be able to live in Iceland for the rest of your life."[42]

Governor Oddsson has not confirmed these strong words, but instead claims that he told Herbertsson that he would be removed from the building and never allowed back in. Governor Oddsson also explained that he had always been unhappy that Herbertsson was involved, given his ties with the Milestone holding company, a major shareholder of Glitnir, as well as Askar Capital investment bank.[43] Herbertsson was, at the time, on leave from Askar Capital, where he had been CEO.

At 11 p.m., representatives from the opposition parties show up at the Central Bank and are told about the plan to purchase shares in Glitnir. The governors explain that Glitnir is essentially bankrupt and that it needs to be nationalized as a result. They also explain that they will only purchase a 75 percent share in order to keep things "humane," sort of a friendly gesture.[44] The opposition representatives ask about the impact the plan will have on the other banks and are told that Kaupthing is fine, but that Landsbanki may end up in trouble too.[45]

Government Announces Purchase of Glitnir Shares

Monday, September 29, 2008

At 15 minutes past midnight, Glitnir's Board of Directors meets to go over the plan and the possible consequences. After considering their options, they decide to reject the purchase. Between 2 a.m. and

3 a.m., Glitnir's VP of Treasury, Thorsteinsson, calls the Central Bank's Director of Market Operations, Palsson, only to find out that a loan isn't an option and never really was, except perhaps for a brief period on Saturday, when it was "seriously looked at."[46]

The Glitnir Board of Directors meets again at 5 a.m., but with no new developments and no other solutions on the horizon, Chairman Baldvinsson suggests a shareholder meeting to accept the Central Bank's offer.[47]

Before 6 a.m., Minister of Commerce Sigurdsson and his advisor meet with Glitnir's Chairman Baldvinsson and one of the major shareholders. The Minister and his advisor are told that the Central Bank's decision is very serious, not just for Glitnir, but also for the other banks, and are asked whether the share percentage being purchased can be lowered. The Minister of Commerce, in an attempt to get involved in the rescue, agrees to attempt to lower the share percentage in order to reduce the impact on Glitnir's share price.[48]

Around the same time, one of the deputy governors of the Central Bank receives a call that Glitnir's Board will make a decision very soon. Moments later, Minister of Commerce Sigurdsson and his advisor arrive at Prime Minister Haarde's home to discuss whether the share percentage can be reduced. Prime Minister Haarde is open to the idea, but then receives information that Glitnir's Board has accepted the offer.[49]

The Icelandic nation wakes up to the news that the Government has purchased a 75 percent share in Glitnir. While there had been plenty of news about the banks over the weekend, the government's purchase is still a shock to most of the country, not least to the Chief Economist of the Central Bank and the Deputy Chief Economist, who both find out about the purchase that morning on the news. As to why they had not been involved, one of the deputy governors of the Central Bank later testified that there had been "no time for economic analysis."[50] The Central Bank's director of Market Operations added, "Well, we probably figured that they didn't have much to add at that point since we are…this is actually not a complicated issue."[51]

The markets react quickly to the news as Standard & Poor's lowers the credit ratings of both Glitnir and the state of Iceland. During the Icelandic National Broadcasting Service news (RUV) in the evening, Governor Oddsson is interviewed about the Glitnir decision and explains: "When this storm is over, because every storm ends at some point of course, then this bank will be in good shape and then I fully expect the state to sell its share and then I expect that the state, and therefore taxpayers, will make a profit on the whole thing."[52]

Many of Glitnir's customers rush to its branches around the country to ask questions about their deposits and to withdraw funds, while others frantically try to get through to customer service by telephone.[53] Before noon, Glitnir is forced to shut down access to money market accounts.[54]

The CEO of Kaupthing is interviewed on a popular national news show about the status of Kaupthing and explains why Kaupthing is not at risk due to the very popular Kaupthing Edge savings accounts and its strong equity position.[55]

Tuesday, September 30, 2008

Glitnir customers rush to the bank as it opens to ask questions about their accounts and withdraw funds, but several types of money market accounts remain closed.[56] Customers react angrily and security is inconspicuously increased.

Moody's lowers the credit rating of Glitnir and the new rating immediately begins having an effect on some of Glitnir's loans. Creditors DZ Bank and Sumitomo Bank call two loans worth a total of 425 million euros, due to the lowered credit rating, as stipulated by loan covenants.[57] The FME appoints Arni Tomasson as a special advisor for Glitnir.[58]

The government cabinet meets and agrees to allow Governor Oddsson to attend the meeting to explain the situation of the banks. Oddsson tells the cabinet that he believes the Icelandic financial system will collapse in two to three weeks. One of the ministers replies, "There is no need to dramatize the issue here," to which Oddsson replies, "I just told you that the entire Icelandic financial system was about to collapse. You can't dramatize that."[59]

The largest shareholder of Glitnir, bohemian business tycoon Jon Asgeir Johannesson, tells the newspaper *Frettabladid* that the government's share purchase is the largest bank robbery in Icelandic history. He also claims that the purchase is part of a larger feud he has been having with Governor Oddsson.[60]

Net outflow from Kaupthing Edge savings accounts at Kaupthing subsidiary Kaupthing Singer & Friedlander reaches 37 million pounds in a day, while deposits stand at roughly 2.8 billion pounds.[61]

The Central Bank assembles a liquidity crisis task force consisting of Tryggvi Palsson, director of Financial Stability at the Central Bank; attorney Karl Axelsson; Ragnar Onundarson, a local business consultant; and Stefan Svavarsson, Certified Public Accountant.[62] The task force subsequently meets with the government's Coordination Group, consisting of representatives from the Prime Ministry, Ministry of Finance, Ministry of Commerce, FME, and the Central Bank.[63]

Wednesday, October 1, 2008

At 8:30 a.m., the government's liquidity crisis task force meets for the second time. The decision is made to create a backup plan with the goal of checking whether it is possible to separate the banks along the lines of their domestic versus foreign operations.[64]

At 11:30 a.m., Central Bank staff members meet with the FME directors, permanent secretaries of the Ministry of Finance and the Prime Ministry, and others. According to the meeting minutes, Director General Jonsson of the FME explains: "[We] need to think about communications abroad after this. [We] need to think about the future. Maybe we need to put heavy pressure on Landsbanki to switch to subsidiaries," referring to the fact that Landsbanki is operating its foreign branches under the Icelandic company, and not a foreign subsidiary, making the Icelandic Depositors' and Investors' Guarantee Fund (FDIC equivalent) responsible for deposits at Landsbanki abroad.[65] Permanent secretary of the Ministry of Finance Baldur Gudlaugsson replies, "Isn't that taken care of already?"

The Asset Liability Committee (ALCO) report at Glitnir describes the effects of the lower credit rating and expects a 1 billion euro credit line from Deutsche Bank to be shut down. Margin calls also begin coming in due to the reduced value of collateral used in repurchase agreements (REPOs).[66]

Thursday, October 2, 2008

At 8:30 a.m., the liquidity crisis task force meets for the third time. The Central Bank's Director of Financial Stability Tryggvi Palsson, who had been on a golfing trip in Spain the previous weekend and therefore not involved in the Glitnir decision, reports that contagion is beginning to spread and that the coming weekend will be crucial. He adds that a plan of action is needed and suggests that the group meet in three subgroups.[67]

At 8:56 a.m., a subgroup from the previous meeting discusses the "Irish way" as the first step to the "Swedish way."[68]

Later that day, after Glitnir asks for written confirmation from the government that it is bound by the agreement, the government coordination group meets and discusses the upcoming Glitnir shareholder meeting. Tryggvi Palsson comments that the government may not be bound by the agreement due to the changing conditions.[69] They discuss involving the pension funds as shareholders since rating agency Moody's had viewed the government's involvement negatively. Later in the meeting, the permanent secretary of the Ministry of Commerce, Jonina Larusdottir, comments that if the government backs out of the deal with Glitnir, then "everything will tumble."[70] Director of Financial Stability Palsson replies, "Everything is tumbling anyway."

Armann Thorvaldsson, CEO of Kaupthing Singer & Friedlander, Kaupthing's subsidiary in London, meets with the UK's Financial Services Authority (FSA) in London and is asked if he can request a 1-billion-pound transfer of funds from the parent company, Kaupthing, as stipulated in the liquidity contract between the parent and the subsidiary. Thorvaldsson replies that he believes he can only get 300–400 million pounds.[71]

At 3:38 p.m., Fridrik Mar Baldursson, professor at Reykjavik University, contacts Prime Minister Haarde by email to offer his assistance, saying: "Please excuse my forwardness in writing you, but I cannot contain myself and thus want to offer the following food for thought."[72] He explains to the prime minister that it is now a matter of life and death for the Icelandic economy to separate the foreign and domestic operations of the banks and move the headquarters out of the country. Prime Minister Haarde answers the professor by email 7 minutes later thanking him for the suggestion.[73]

The Central Bank agrees to lend Kaupthing 73 million euros to assist with Kaupthing's acquisition of a small domestic credit union that had previously been facing bankruptcy.[74] Meanwhile, the total payments of Kaupthing Singer & Friedlander to cover margin calls of its parent company, Kaupthing, exceed 500 million pounds.[75]

By the end of the day, credit default swaps (CDS) quotes for the three Icelandic banks reach new heights, 1821 points for Glitnir, 1752 points for Kaupthing, and 1593 points for Landsbanki.[76]

Friday, October 3, 2008

At 8:19 a.m., assistant professor of economics at Columbia University Jon Steinsson, a personal friend of Prime Minister Haarde, sends the prime minister an email explaining that it is paramount for the government and the Central Bank to provide funds for the banks.

Steinsson says that he has just arrived from the USA that morning and would like to offer his assistance. Prime Minister Haarde replies and sets up a meeting for 2 p.m.[77]

The government coordination group meets and discusses Glitnir's request for a formal declaration from the government about the share purchase, as Glitnir had stated that it could not announce a shareholder meeting without a formal declaration of the government's intention. The permanent secretary of the Ministry of Finance, Baldur Gudlaugsson, tells the other members of the government coordination group that Glitnir is now realizing that the government may not uphold the agreement, and advises not to issue a formal declaration of the government's share purchase.[78]

At 9:30 a.m., the government cabinet meets and discussions quickly heat up regarding Governor Oddsson's comments at the cabinet's previous meeting that an emergency interim cabinet should be installed. Minister of Industry Skarphedinsson emphasizes that Governor Oddsson should step down as a result, and Minister of Commerce Sigurdsson files a complaint that he, the minister responsible for the banking system, had not been kept in the loop.[79]

The Central Bank's liquidity crisis task force meets for the fourth time. Tryggvi Palsson, Director of Financial Stability, comments that it is now too late to split the system into domestic and foreign operations—the banks must be given an ultimatum. The group then discusses what will happen to payment systems if the banks go bankrupt. One member comments that the payment system might be down for up to a week, and adds that it could have a negative impact on Iceland's reputation.[80]

Jon Pain, an employee of the UK's FSA, sends an email to FME Director General Jonsson, saying:

> Our guidelines required KSF [Kaupthing Singer & Friedlander] to maintain at least 95% of the instant access retail deposits amounting to circa 2 billion pounds to be maintained in cash or near cash equivalents. [...] As at today these funds only amount to 500 million pounds. It's therefore clear to us that KSF has breached our liquidity guidelines and in its reporting has substantially overstated the true liquidity position. Additionally KSF has used its liquidity position to fund circa 500 million pounds of margin calls of its parent, this again is in clear breach of our guidelines.[81]

The FSA then requests that Kaupthing transfer 1,600 million pounds to KSF before close of business on Monday, October 6, 2008, in order to avoid being shut down.[82]

At 1 p.m., Prime Minister Haarde meets with the chairman of Kaupthing, Sigurdur Einarsson, and the chief executive officer, Hreidar Mar Sigurdsson. During the meeting, Alistair Darling, UK's Chancellor of the Exchequer, contacts Prime Minister Haarde and tells him that, according to UK authorities, the Kaupthing subsidiary Kaupthing Singer & Friedlander has transferred 600 million pounds out of the UK. Chancellor Darling considers the issue so serious that the FSA will shut down KSF that evening if the funds are not returned.[83]

The FSA then requests that Kaupthing Singer & Friedlander place all deposits that have come in on October 2 and 3 into a special account at the Bank of England. Furthermore, any transactions above 250 thousand pounds require the approval of the FSA, and the bank is no longer allowed to provide the parent company any assistance without a written notice to the FSA three days in advance.[84]

At 2 p.m., an anxious and overstressed Haarde meets with Columbia economist Jon Steinsson and tells him that the Kaupthing guys are in the next room and that he has just finished a conversation with Alistair Darling. According to Steinsson, the Prime Minister appeared on the brink of a nervous breakdown.[85] Steinsson then visits his colleagues at the Central Bank who tell him that the entire economics department of the Central Bank has been left out in the cold. They explain that the Board of Governors isn't taking any advice from the economists and that Governor Oddsson is referring to Prime Minister Haarde as an idiot.[86]

At 5 p.m., FME's director general Jonsson meets with Kaupthing Chairman Einarsson and CEO Sigurdsson, as well as Kaupthing's VP of Treasury Gudni Adalsteinsson, regarding the FSA's claim that Kaupthing Singer & Friedlander has been funding margin calls of parent company Kaupthing. Despite the recent information from the UK's FSA, the Kaupthing bankers manage to convince the boyish-looking Jonsson that they have not illegally transferred funds from KSF to Kaupthing.[87]

The situation begins having an impact on the daily lives of Icelanders. An Icelandic business newspaper reports that the CEO of one of the largest oil companies in Iceland is concerned that the country may run out of oil in a month or so due to a lack of foreign currency. Furthermore, the CEO of a major grocery store chain adds that the country may run into food shortages. People therefore begin rushing to stock up on essentials such as food, gasoline, and pharmaceutical products.[88]

By the end of the day, Glitnir margin calls total approximately 1.1 billion euros, approximately 100 percent of the bank's equity,[89] and 6.1 percent of total outstanding bond issues.[90]

Saturday, October 4, 2008

Kaupthing and KSF bankers work on a plan to sell some of KSF's assets to raise funds to meet FSA's demands.[91]

After several threats are made against ministers by telephone, Icelandic authorities assign body guards from the Icelandic State Police Special Operations team to guard Prime Minister Haarde and several other ministers as well as Governor Oddsson of the Central Bank.[92]

At 8:45 a.m., the government cabinet meets with the Central Bank Board of Governors. Oddsson announces that Glitnir's situation is worse than expected and explains how loan covenants have been activated due to the reduced credit rating. He further reveals that the largest shareholder of Glitnir is also the largest borrower. A memo from the meeting then says: "Glitnir will go bankrupt on Monday."[93]

At 11:30 a.m., Jon Steinsson arrives for a meeting in the Prime Ministry, where he is told that the government's coordination group for financial stability is essentially paralyzed due to a deep disagreement with the Central Bank and that the Prime Ministry will now be working according to its own plan. He is specifically told that the Central Bank should not be kept in the loop.[94]

The Prime Ministry's new group begins working on its own plan, without any documentation or data from the government coordination group. They have no designated office or meeting room in government buildings and therefore move over to Reykjavik University, where they begin by printing out the annual reports and quarterly reports of the three banks. Next they move over to the headquarters of the financial supervisory authority, FME, and request access to privileged information about the banks. By 4 p.m. that day, the three banks have all granted access to their privileged information. The group then continues working into the night and the following morning.[95]

Landsbanki sends a memo to the government, the FME, and the Central Bank stating that its liquidity position has deteriorated significantly and that the bank may have a liquidity problem within the next few weeks if things continue at the current rate. The memo also explains that the bank has forward contracts with Icelandic pension funds worth 500 million euros that are overdue but that the bank is not able to collect on them.[96]

Sunday, October 5, 2008

The Prime Ministry's new group presents its plan to government ministers. The plan, referred to as "Emergency plan for the Icelandic financial system" includes steps to create a financial system for Iceland of a "manageable" size that can be launched in the event that all three banks fail. It explains the need for a new law that would allow the FME to take control of a financial institution under particular circumstances, and outlines three possible options at this stage:[97]

A. The branch option.
   Glitnir sells its foreign operations and buys the domestic branches from Kaupthing and Landsbanki. The government provides an equity infusion to Glitnir as needed but does not assist the other banks.

B. The domestic option.
   Glitnir sells its foreign operations and buys the domestic operations from the other two banks, Kaupthing and Landsbanki, aside from loans to holding companies. The government provides an equity infusion to Glitnir to support these transactions but does not assist the other banks.

C. The "do nothing" option.
   The banks go bankrupt without any attempt to intervene by the government, rendering payments systems defunct. A new law is required so that deposit holders receive primary claims to the bankrupt-estates.

The size of the banking system for each option is estimated at 1.2 times GDP for option A, at 1.9 times GDP for option B, and at 12.8 times GDP for C. The economists recommend option B, but one of them is told that the Central Bank recommends option C.[98]

The members of the group argue the options as increasing panic marks the meeting. The prime minister's economic advisor, Tryggvi Thor Herbertsson, argues with the two outside economists, Jon Steinsson and Fridrik Mar Baldursson, over whether to mention the International Monetary Fund (IMF) in the presentation slides. The two economists push hard for including the IMF, but Herbertsson considers it very harmful for Iceland to contact the IMF due to the harsh conditions imposed by an IMF program.[99]

After the meeting, Prime Minister Haarde and Minister of Industry Skarphedinsson meet privately to discuss the options. When they return, Skarphedinsson grabs the two economists and light-heartedly says, "I don't think this is constitutional at all what you guys are proposing," thereby concluding discussion about the three options.[100]

At 10:30 a.m., the ministers meet with representatives from Landsbanki about the bank's liquidity issue, the Icesave deposits, and the outlook for the next few days. Yngvi Orn Kristinsson, VP of Capital Markets at Landsbanki, comments that, without assistance, the bank will not be able to open the next day.[101]

At 11:30 a.m., the government ministers meet with Glitnir's representatives to discuss the outlook for Monday. CEO Welding explains that the bank will need 425 million euros on Tuesday, October 7, and a further 600 million euros to pay a margin call from the European Central Bank.[102]

The Central Bank's CPA, Stefan Svavarsson, reports on his assessment of Glitnir's accounts and concludes that the liquidity problems of Glitnir can quickly turn into a serious equity problem.[103]

Around noon, three JP Morgan consultants arrive from London at the Central Bank's request and spend the day and the evening working at the Central Bank. The consultants had previously worked for the bank and are therefore quite familiar with the Icelandic financial system.[104]

At 5 p.m., the government ministers meet with representatives from both Kaupthing and Landsbanki and discuss how to split Glitnir between the two remaining banks. The plan is that Kaupthing, on behalf of both Kaupthing and Landsbanki, take over the general operations of Glitnir but that Glitnir's assets (loan books) be equally split between Kaupthing and Landsbanki. Furthermore, the Central Bank is to immediately provide 500 million euros to Kaupthing and 1 billion euros to Landsbanki in the form of REPOs. The ministers also discuss moving the so-called Icesave deposits expeditiously into Heritable Bank, a Landsbanki subsidiary in the UK.[105]

Growing mistrust complicates the discussions with the bankers. Minister of Finance Arni Mathiesen later testified that the bankers repeatedly lied to the ministers and could not be counted on. "And the worst one was Bjorgolfur [Thor Bjorgolfsson, the main shareholder of Landsbanki]," Mathiesen said. "He was lying to the others as well and then they just showed up again in the evening and said, 'You can't believe a word this man says'."[106]

Bjorgolfur Thor Bjorgolfsson had been trying to convince the ministers that Landsbanki could be rescued, and several ministers described how he prevented the CEO of Landsbanki, Sigurjon Arnason, from expressing his opinion. Minister of Industry Skarphedinsson described the meeting:

> [The Landsbanki guys] came to present us with a great offer. And he [Bjorgolfsson] sat there in his nice clothes, great seller, selling what sounded like a deal where they would get Glitnir for free and get all kinds of other things and then most of the foreign exchange reserves [of the Central Bank] and some guarantee on top of that. And [the Deputy CEO of Landsbanki] just sat there like a beaten dog and didn't have anything to add. Then the meeting was over, [the CEO of Landsbanki] was there, there were donuts on the table, cut into two, big donuts. [The CEO] has a big mouth, literally, and he is a big guy, and when everybody had left the room and he was there by himself, he grabbed half a donut, shoved it in his face and mumbled: 'I don't have faith in this, I don't have faith in this', but then this arm with a golden watch just suddenly appeared and yanked him out of there.[107]

Shortly after 6 p.m., the government ministers meet with the two economists, Jon Steinsson and Fridrik Mar Baldursson, as well as the prime minister's economic advisor, Tryggvi Thor Herbertsson, and the advisor to the Minister of Commerce, Jon Thor Sturluson, along with a few others. The economists express their concerns about the plan introduced by the leaders of Kaupthing and Landsbanki and point out that the plan is only half an offer since there is no obligation on the part of the banks to take action that would avoid a total collapse within days. The government would therefore be taking a big risk with 1.5 billion euros of taxpayer money. The ministers interrogate the economists about other options and the group eventually comes to the conclusion that "something very drastic" needs to be done, such as passing an emergency law.[108]

After the meeting, the two economists and Sturluson continue their discussions, but now more optimistic than before. "I remember that I felt really good after the meeting," said Jon Steinsson. "I felt that we had had some impact and perhaps we had helped convince the ministers not to lend the banks 1.5 billion Euros."[109]

Around dinnertime, Gordon Brown, Prime Minister of the United Kingdom, calls Prime Minister Haarde. The purpose of the call is to encourage Haarde to request assistance from the International Monetary Fund. Brown even offers to personally contact the IMF's managing director. He also says that the UK authorities consider Kaupthing Singer & Friedlander in violation of British law for transferring 1.6 billion pounds out of the UK, not 600 million as previously thought. Prime Minister Haarde replies that Kaupthing is already in agreement with the UK's FSA on how to solve the issue. They continue their conversation, but unfortunately the remainder of the conversation with Prime Minister Brown remains a mystery due to an audio recording error in Iceland.[110]

After the call, Haarde finds the economists again, as they are still in the building, and enters their room ecstatic. He tells them that he has just had a conversation with Gordon Brown, who has told him that the European Central Bank was not going through with a margin call against the Icelandic banks. The situation was therefore turning out to be manageable.[111]

At 10 p.m., Haarde introduces a formal announcement to the rest of the cabinet regarding deposit insurance and suggests that it be sent to the media. He also brings up the question of whether to contact the IMF. The Deputy Governor of the Central Bank, Ingimundur Fridriksson, is at the meeting and explains the process by which a country applies for a loan from the IMF. Fridriksson then leaves the meeting and the ministers continue discussing an IMF loan application without reaching a consensus. Only Minister of Finance Arni Mathiesen and Minister of Commerce Bjorgvin Sigurdsson seem to be ready to contact the IMF. Mathiesen later testified that before his trip to Washington, DC, later that week, Governor Oddsson had called him and said something along the lines of: "Arni my boy, by all means, never go to the IMF."[112]

At 11 p.m., journalists finally manage to get a quick interview with Prime Minister Haarde. As the eye of the storm moves through, Haarde concludes that the worst is over and makes a short statement to journalists: "This weekend has brought us to the conclusion that we no longer consider it necessary to put together a special package [for the banks]."[113]

Only a few hours earlier, he had suggested an emergency cabinet to be headed by Governor Oddsson. Other ministers had reacted angrily, and to Haarde's great disappointment, Minister of Industry Skarphedinsson had threatened to resign, which would have ended coalition government. Others suggested the newly appointed FME Chairman of the Board, Jon Sigurdsson, as the best candidate to lead an emergency cabinet. Sigurdsson had formerly served as Minister of Industry as well as Governor of the Central Bank of Iceland in the 1990s. Ultimately, the idea appeared to die because of the refusal to accept Governor Oddsson for the leading role.[114]

Monday, October 6, 2008

At 2 a.m., the JP Morgan consultants, who had been working at the Central Bank, meet with Prime Minister Haarde, Minister of Finance Mathiesen, Minister of Commerce Sigurdsson, Minister of Industry Skarphedinsson, permanent secretary of the Prime Ministry Bollason, and permanent secretary of the Ministry of Finance Gudlaugsson. The consultants, Michael Ridley, Johan Bergendahl, and Gary Weiss, explain that the experiment is over, referring to the government's policy of making Iceland an international financial center. The only option now is to intervene. The banks need to be taken over and split into good banks and bad banks—the so-called Washington Mutual approach. Everybody in the meeting is shocked, and it finally dawns on the ministers that the system really is going to collapse after all. Skarphedinsson described the moment: "These were really nice guys and fun to talk to and they gave it to us right between the eyes. […] They just said it plainly that everything was going to collapse, all the banks were going to collapse, and that maybe it might have been possible to save Kaupthing at some point."[115] Minister of Commerce Sigurdsson described Michael Ridley's presentation: "It was a strange moment, suddenly it became crystal clear, the man just drew it up on the board. Just suddenly, it was like the moment of truth after this insane roller coaster weekend, which was probably more or less based on wishful thinking."[116]

On February 17, 2006, a joint task force of the Central Bank, the FME, the Ministry of Finance, the Ministry of Commerce, and the Prime Ministry had issued a memo covering legal changes regarding operations of financial institutions and their oversight. As a result of the memo, the FME began drafting a new bill to address shortcomings. The work was later passed on to the Ministry of Commerce.[117]

In early 2008, the draft of the bill had become known as the emergency law bill, a law that would be passed in the event of a catastrophic failure of the Icelandic banking system. The work was conducted by several individuals in different places within the government and its agencies, including Runar Gudmundsson, financial supervisor at the FME; Aslaug Arnadottir, acting permanent secretary to the Ministry of Commerce; Jonina Larusdottir, permanent secretary to the Ministry of Commerce; Sigridur Rafnar Petursdottir, attorney at the Ministry of Commerce; and Johannes Karl Sveinsson, outside counsel. This group understood the need to have one last card to play if everything else should fail.[118] The IMF had also pointed out legal shortcomings in its preliminary assessment issued on April 14, 2008, in which it said: "On bank resolution, however, the authorities' legal powers appear relatively weak, as the supervisory agency does not have the power to intervene and take over a bank."[119]

Recognizing the imminent need for the law during the weekend of October 4, 2008, the group works intensely to get the bill done that weekend, along with the members of staff of the FME; Iris Hreinsdottir, lawyer; and Arni Huldar Sveinbjornsson, also a lawyer; and additional staff members from the Ministry of Commerce, Valgerdur R. Benediktsdottir and Thora M. Hjaltested. After the cabinet's meeting with the JP Morgan consultants in the middle of the night, the group finally gets the word; the bill is needed, right away. They immediately go to work to finalize it and deliver the bill by morning.[120]

The only public recognition that this group has received for their important contribution came when the Chief Justice of Landsdomur, Markus Sigurbjornsson, declared Article 6 of the bill "the savior of Iceland." The article included a provision reordering claims to banks' bankrupt estates, giving deposit holders primary claim to their assets.[121]

At 8:30 a.m., Minister of Commerce Sigurdsson introduces the new emergency law bill to the cabinet, which decides that Prime Minister Haarde should present the bill to parliament. The government then issues a formal declaration that all deposits of Icelandic banks in branches in Iceland are fully insured. By noon, the rate of withdrawals has slowed.[122]

At 11:52 a.m., Hector Sants, the chief executive officer of the UK's FSA, sends an email to the Kaupthing CEO, Hreidar Mar Sigurdsson, regarding a possible purchase by Barclays of Kaupthing Singer & Friedlander assets. The CEO replies at 12:32 p.m. that Kaupthing is going through with its plan to reduce KSF's debt and increase liquidity with more than 700 million pounds coming that same day, although some of it won't be available for 2–3 days. The CEO also adds that Kaupthing is not aware of a run on Kaupthing Edge accounts, but that Kaupthing welcomes any interest by Barclays.[123]

At 1:34 p.m., the Ministry of Commerce receives a message that an additional article is needed in the emergency law bill to provide the Central Bank of Iceland the authority to own and operate financial institutions. The permanent secretary of Commerce, Jonina Larusdottir, then contacts the Central Bank to find out why such an unusual clause needs to be in the law. She is told that the Central Bank has just granted Kaupthing a 500 million euro loan and has accepted shares in the Danish bank FIH as collateral. The work on the emergency law bill therefore continues that afternoon.[124]

At 4 p.m., Prime Minister Haarde delivers his "God Bless Iceland" speech, calling on the nation to remain calm and restrained in the next few days, to not lose hope, and to support each other. That evening, the offices of the London branch of Landsbanki close for the last time.[125]

At 9:08 p.m., Haarde receives an email from Sturla Sigurjonsson, a staff member at the Prime Ministry, titled: "British demand an explanation." Sigurjonsson explains that the UK Ambassador to Iceland has notified him that British authorities need further explanations from Icelandic authorities in order to be able to prepare for the opening of financial markets the next day.[126] The UK Ambassador had also stated that he needs to get in touch with the Minister of Finance or the permanent secretary of the Ministry of Finance at the request of Chancellor Alistair Darling.

At 9:38 p.m., Sigurjonsson sends another email to Haarde, as well as permanent secretary of the Prime Ministry Bollason, permanent secretary of the Ministry of Finance Gudlaugsson, and assistant to the prime minister, Greta Ingthorsdottir, titled: "British very unhappy," saying that the UK Ambassador had just called and that Alistair Darling was waiting for a report from Reykjavik. The Ambassador had further stated that if Icelandic authorities did not respond that night, it would have very negative implications for bilateral relations between the two countries and would constitute a breach of trust.[127]

At 10:08 p.m., permanent secretary of the Ministry of Finance Gudlaugsson replies that, if everything works out, the next day will present an entirely new situation, and adds: "We are not looking for any special treatment or flexibility on the part of the British at this point in time so there is no reason to give them a chance to squeeze us any more about deposit insurance. Can't you find some way to explain that nobody is available here and now?"[128] Sigurjonsson replies at 10:12 p.m. saying that he has just told the UK Ambassador that a call would come from Iceland the next morning. The UK Ambassador then asks if he can expect the call before the markets open, but Sigurjonsson replies that he can't promise it. Sigurjonsson then asks Gudlaugsson to make a call to the Ambassador but Gudlaugsson replies: "I don't know if or when I can get to it."[129]

At 10:37 p.m., Sigurjonsson sends an email to Haarde titled: "Darling wants to call [the Prime Minister]." At 10:44 p.m., Haarde's assistant, Greta Ingthorsdottir, replies that it would be more appropriate for Chancellor Darling to talk to Minister of Finance Mathiesen. She provides a number and a time; 9:15 a.m. the next morning.[130]

At 11:18 p.m. that night, the Icelandic Parliament passes law number 125/2008, also known as the emergency law, providing the government the authority to react to special circumstances in financial markets by assuming control of financial institutions. An official copy of the law is delivered to the National University Hospital for the signature of the president of Iceland, who is at the time about to undergo heart surgery.[131]

The emergency law allowed the Icelandic financial supervisory authority to put all three banks into receivership and reorder primacy of claims, putting deposit holders in front of bondholders.[132]

Landsbanki and Glitnir Fall
Tuesday, October 7, 2008

At 6:45 a.m., Governor Oddsson receives a call from the Russian Ambassador to Iceland about a possible loan from Russia. Just over an hour later, the Central Bank announces that Vladimir Putin has confirmed Russian plans for a loan to Iceland in the amount of 4 billion euros for 3–4 years, bearing low interest. Later that morning, however, Governor Oddsson tells Bloomberg that he had misunderstood the Russians. The loan had not been confirmed, but the Russians were willing to meet for discussions.[133]

Arnor Sighvatsson, Chief Economist of the Central Bank, returns from a meeting with the Board of Governors after being told that the bank will fix the exchange rate. "Because the bank was honestly just out of control, totally out of control, that was just it," said Central Bank economist Thorarinn G. Petursson, describing the situation at the bank at the time. "I am talking about the fixing of the exchange rate and the Russian loan. [...] I will never forget this day."[134]

Petursson asked Sighvatsson about the meeting with the Board: "This number, he told me, was just [...] decided based on nothing... it was just arbitrarily picked and some numbers just thrown out, and then that was the decision. [Governor Oddsson] was very enthusiastic about the Central Bank announcing the Russian loan ahead of the Ministry of Finance, he jumped the gun of course, there was no basis for it.... I think this is the low point.... Or the high point of no control but a low point.... It was absolutely horrible..."[135]

As Kaupthing Singer & Friedlander opens for business, its liquidity position is 396 million pounds.[136] During the day, however, net outflow from Kaupthing Edge savings accounts exceeds 95 million pounds.[137]

As Landsbanki's foreign currency liquidity deteriorates to the point where it will no longer be able to meet its upcoming obligations, the Icelandic financial supervisory authority, FME, steps in and takes control of the bank, dismisses the board and the CEO and appoints a resolution committee.[138] Only a week earlier, a company owned by its largest shareholder, Bjorgolfur Thor Bjorgolfsson, had borrowed 153 million euros to meet a margin call from Deutsche Bank, further deepening Landsbanki's foreign currency liquidity crisis.[139]

The Board of Governors of the Central Bank meets with Kaupthing CEO Sigurdsson and Chairman Einarsson, who tells the Board of Governors: "Everybody is squeezing money out of us," and "FSA is on our back and the demands are continuously changing. Faith is gone."[140]

Chancellor Alistair Darling calls Minister of Finance Mathiesen and asks about deposits at Landsbanki in the UK. Mathiesen points out that Iceland has implemented the Deposit Insurance Fund according to the European Union directive for deposit insurance. Chancellor Darling than asks if the 16,000 pound insurance will be paid out to each British deposit holder and Mathiesen replies that he hopes so, but that he cannot confirm or guarantee it at this point—the issue is being worked on. Darling then says that he has heard that the government of Iceland is going to fully guarantee the deposits of Icelanders and Mathiesen confirms that all deposits in Icelandic branches are guaranteed. Darling then asks if this is not in breach of European Economic Area rules, and Mathiesen replies that he doesn't think so.[141]

At 12:05 p.m., FSA's chief executive officer, Hector Sants, emails Kaupthing CEO Sigurdsson and reiterates that if funds are not transferred to KSF, the bank will not be allowed to continue operations.[142] Sigurdsson replies 50 minutes later and asks that either Hector Sants or Jon Pain call him. Two minutes later, he sends Hector Sants another email saying that earlier that day Kaupthing had closed a deal on its shares in Mitchells & Butlers Ltd. worth 130 million pounds. He further explains that Ravi from the investment firm J.C. Flowers will be arriving that evening and that Kaupthing will likely be able to announce a deal with J.C. Flowers the next morning.[143]

At 5:35 p.m., Jon Pain sends Sigurdsson an email to explain the FSA's assessment of KSF. The first point is that the FSA is seeing increasing outflow from KSF's deposit accounts, putting the bank at risk of going under. The FSA will, however, delay further action until

7:30 a.m. the next morning to provide Kaupthing an opportunity to close a deal with J.C. Flowers. To continue operations, Kaupthing needs to notify the FSA by 6:30 a.m. the next morning whether negotiations with J.C. Flowers result in a deal or not. Kaupthing also needs to confirm that J.C. Flowers will provide KSF with funds that same day. It also needs to present a clear plan to the FSA on how it intends to fund the bank during this period.[144]

At 6:57 p.m., Sigurdsson replies that the Central Bank of Iceland has provided Kaupthing a loan of 600 million pounds earlier that day and that it will be available the next day. He also states that the three largest pension funds in Iceland will sell foreign assets and transfer the funds to Kaupthing in the next three days amounting to 500 million to one billion euros. In addition, he says that Kaupthing is still in talks with the government of Iceland and the Central Bank regarding a possible purchase of Glitnir's operations, which he says would strengthen Kaupthing. Finally, he outlines recent deals amounting to roughly 500 million euros and explains that the goal of the meeting with J.C. Flowers is to sell them the operations of KSF, allowing Kaupthing to get through this difficult period.[145]

Finally the Icelandic financial supervisory authority, FME, takes control of Glitnir on the basis of the new emergency law, dismisses the board and the CEO, and appoints a resolution committee.[146]

Kaupthing Falls

Wednesday, October 8, 2008

At 3 minutes past midnight, Kaupthing CEO Sigurdsson notifies Hector Sants that negotiations with J.C. Flowers have not been successful owing to the limited time J.C. Flowers had to familiarize themselves with KSF operations. On the other hand, Kaupthing intends to provide KSF with over 500 million pounds that day, and more in the coming few days.[147]

At 7 a.m., the UK Government announces the Credit Guarantee Scheme, including the Bank Recapitalization Fund with 500 billion pounds, to be made available to support the UK financial system.[148]

At 7:11 a.m., Hector Sants emails Sigurdsson and says that the liquidity situation of KSF is becoming very serious, requiring substantial funds in the next few days and weeks. Sants also explains that the Kaupthing Edge accounts are now at 2.8 billion pounds and the bank should expect significant outflows from those accounts in the coming days.[149]

Sigurdsson replies at 7:49 a.m., expressing his interest in the UK government's new bank recapitalization plan, and indicating that he considers KSF to be eligible for support from the UK government. He also requests instructions on how the bank can participate in the plan. At 8:19 a.m. he adds that Kaupthing is "chasing" the Central Bank of Iceland with the intention of transferring 300 million pounds as soon as possible.[150]

On BBC Radio 4, Chancellor Alistair Darling explains that the previous day the Government of Iceland had told him that it is not going to honor its obligations in the UK, referring to his conversation with Minister of Finance Arni Mathiesen.[151]

Around 10 a.m., the FSA formally prohibits KSF from receiving any further deposits, effective at 1:30 p.m. that day.[152]

At 10:10 a.m., the UK authorities freeze the assets of Landsbanki, as well as related assets of the Government of Iceland, using the power afforded to them by the Anti-terrorism, Crime and Security Act of 2001. They also take control of the Landsbanki branch in London and the Landsbanki subsidiary Heritable Bank. The Landsbanki freezing order includes the following explanation:[153]

> The Icelandic authorities have announced that Landsbanki has been placed into receivership but have not given any indication as to how overseas creditors will be dealt with. The Icelandic Government has also announced a guarantee of all depositors in Icelandic branches. However, overseas depositors have not been covered by the guarantee. This exclusion on grounds of nationality is discriminatory and unlawful under the rules governing the European Economic Area. The UK Government is taking action to ensure that Landsbanki assets are not transferred from the UK until the position of UK creditors becomes clearer. The UK authorities are seeking to work constructively with the Icelandic authorities to ensure a speedy resolution.[154]

Prime Minister Gordon Brown and Chancellor Alistair Darling hold a press conference, in which Prime Minister Brown explains:

> These decisions are the best way of providing long-term security for depositors and savers. And as people will now know, we are taking legal action against the Icelandic authorities to recover the money lost to people who deposited in UK branches of this bank. The Chancellor is saying today that he will stand behind the deposits of these customers.[155]

At 2:49 p.m., the UK Treasury puts Kaupthing Singer & Friedlander into liquidation, after earlier that day having moved the

Kaupthing Edge deposit accounts, totaling 3.2 billion pounds, to the Dutch bank ING Direct N.V.[156]

Thursday, October 9, 2008

During the night, the Board of Directors of Kaupthing resigns and the Icelandic financial supervisory authority, FME, takes control of the bank and appoints a resolution committee.[157]

With the three largest banks in Iceland having collapsed, and many other financial institutions running into difficulties as a result, constituting a 97 percent collapse of the Icelandic banking system in terms of assets, the government of Iceland is forced to bail out the Central Bank with new equity amounting to roughly 20 percent of GDP. The bailout brings the government's debt-to-GDP ratio from an enviable level of 38.42 percent in January 2008 to 80.81 percent at year-end 2008.[158]

Friday, October 10, 2008

Minister of Finance Mathiesen travels to Washington, DC for the annual meeting of the IMF and the World Bank, but a formal request for IMF assistance is still not on the agenda. The same day, however, many foreign banks stop trading the Icelandic currency, the Krona. As a result, Icelandic businesses begin running into difficulties paying foreign invoices, and Icelanders living abroad experience difficulties withdrawing funds from ATMs. In London, newspaper headlines begin reflecting British anger toward Iceland, with headlines such as: "Give us our money back."[159] One newspaper reads: "COLD WAR!" across the entire front page.[160]

Saturday, October 11, 2008

The first protest of many to come is held next to the Icelandic Parliament at Austurvollur Square, downtown Reykjavik. The public begins demanding elections, a new cabinet, and punishment for the bankers. Prime Minister Haarde begins referring to "a white book" intended to reveal the truth about the operations of the fallen banks.

Many questions were unanswered. Were the banks simply victims of the subprime crisis and the resulting recession? Was their collapse a case of strong banks in a small country being treated unfairly by international financial markets? Or were the operations of the three largest banks in Iceland simply not sustainable?

Who was primarily at fault? Was it the government for not keeping up with the financial system with its oversight? Was financial supervision in Iceland a case of "regulatory capture"? Did the Central Bank disregard its responsibility for managing systemic risk? Or did government officials drive the banking system off the edge with their cheerleading for the Icelandic "economic wonder"? How could the collapse have been avoided? The public demanded answers.

Chapter 4

Investigation

Installment of the Special Investigation Commission

On December 12, 2008, with constantly beating drums and blazing fires outside, the Icelandic parliament (Althingi), beset by the angry Icelandic public, passed legal act number 142/2008 installing the Special Investigation Commission (SIC). The parliament granted the Commission exceptional investigative powers in order to appease the demonstrators and to meet the public's demand for answers as to why their three largest banks, Glitnir, Landsbanki, and Kaupthing, had collapsed.

On December 30, Althingi appointed three members to the Commission, set a timetable of ten months, and provided the Commission with an initial budget of 100 million Icelandic kronas (ISK), equivalent to approximately 826,000 US dollars at the time. The appointees were people with impeccable reputation—Icelandic Supreme Court Justice and former law professor Pall Hreinsson, Sigridur Benediktsdottir, associate chair of the Economics Department at Yale University; and Althingi's ombudsman, Tryggvi Gunnarsson. The SIC officially began its work few days later, on Monday, January 5, 2009.

From early October, thousands of people, sometimes more than 2 percent of the entire population of Iceland, had gathered in front of parliament on Austurvollur square on Saturdays, calling for new parliamentary elections and the resignation of Prime Minister Haarde and his cabinet. The effort became known as the Kitchenware Revolution (Icelandic: *Búsáhaldabyltingin*) since protesters used pots, pans, ladles, and other kitchenware to keep the drumbeat going. The effort climaxed on January 25, 2009, with the resignation of Prime Minister

Haarde along with the entire cabinet. An interim government was established under the leadership of Johanna Sigurdardottir, and elections were held three months later, on April 25, 2009. Sigurdardottir served as prime minister of Iceland until April 2013.

Authority and Mandate of the SIC

According to the law on the SIC, the mandate of the Commission was to "seek the truth behind the events leading to, and the causes of, the downfall of the Icelandic banks in October 2008, and related events." The Commission was to "assess whether mistakes or negligence occurred in the course of the implementation of the laws and other rules regulating and providing for control of the Icelandic financial sector," and, in addition, "what persons may be responsible."[1]

To achieve its goals, the SIC was given exceptional investigative powers. The stakes were high, the Icelandic political situation volatile: Downtown Reykjavik was on the brink of deadly riots one Saturday after another, perhaps only prevented by riot police's exceptional patience in a standoff with demonstrators. In modern times, no country had seen 97 percent of its banking sector come crumbling down in a of few days. To stay intact, Althingi therefore had to show that it was capable of responding to the crisis with a serious investigation.

Althingi's response, an investigation commission with practically unlimited investigative powers, may have come as a surprise to many, but those powers, as it would turn out, were instrumental in allowing the SIC to perform a true autopsy of the failed financial system, thus allowing it to be successful in fulfilling its mandate.

To fully comprehend the uniqueness of the Icelandic parliament's SIC, one must consider it from at least three perspectives.

First of all, it is both historically and politically unique that a government that had so completely failed in its duties was nevertheless willing to launch an investigation into its own performance, an investigation that ultimately led to a conclusion unraveling government failures so severe on the part of that same government that four charges were brought against the prime minister. The charges resulted in one conviction; the world's first conviction of a political leader following the 2008 world financial crisis.

The SIC legal act specifically asked the Commission to spell out who was personally responsible for fraud or failure—a bold request considering the 18-year rule of the Independence Party, the party of such key figures as Prime Minister Haarde, Minister of Finance

Mathiesen, Central Bank Governor Oddsson, and FME director general Jonsson, to name a few.

After 18 years in power, the party had enough officials throughout the system to easily provide an impediment to an honest investigation. The installment of the SIC therefore clearly put party members at risk, and this may in turn have contributed to the common early opinions of the SIC that its final report would end up being a whitewash of Independence Party members. Such views were echoed in the Icelandic media for over a year, until the SIC report was finally released on April 12, 2010. Fortunately, and perhaps amazingly so, there was little evidence in the final report to support arguments of a whitewash. The report turned out to be a detailed description of failure, incompetence, and mishandling, often with shocking direct quotes from SIC interrogations of major government figures or business leaders.

The SIC work is also unique from a government administrative and organizational point of view. It is unprecedented that data from so many government agencies were brought into a single data warehouse for detailed analysis, when all over the world many of these same types of agencies are intentionally insulated from each other with "Chinese walls." The structure and content of the data warehouse will be discussed later in the chapter.

Finally, and perhaps most surprising (and exciting) to researchers, are the details of the SIC's authority. The Commission had powers to subpoena witnesses, search all premises, and seize all evidence it considered necessary for the purpose of the investigation. All contractual or legal confidentiality of all employees, government officials, or other individuals toward the SIC and its employees, was lifted although attorneys and accountants did not need to disclose confidential information under attorney/client privilege unless the client approved. Failing to comply with duties of providing information to the Commission could result in a fine, or imprisonment for up to two years.[2] All testimony was recorded, and the SIC could use direct quotes from people as evidence to back up statements in the report, as well as to capture the sentiment at the time the banks collapsed.

These investigative powers provided the Commission the ability to cross-reference its facts, challenge testimony, and provided witnesses with an incentive to stick to the truth. In return for these powers, the Commission had to report any suspicion of criminal conduct to a Special Prosecutor for the banking collapse.

During its investigation the SIC interrogated 147 witnesses. Among them was a designated group set up by the Government in

2006 including permanent secretaries of ministries and top government officials, responsible for financial oversight, to form a task force to gather information and formalize the Government's response to a possible financial crisis. During interrogations the members of the task force and ministers alike pointed the finger to one another, when asked who was responsible for taking action as the risk in the system was building up. Not a single one of them admitted to having made mistake.[3] Legal ambiguity aside, the members of the SIC were up against a well-known human characteristic—the motive for self-enhancement.

Humans have an innate bias toward positive self-regard and have acquired a myriad of cognitive functions or strategies to protect the self. One of them is self-serving bias, the tendency to take credit for success, and deny any responsibility for failure. We are also inclined to believe positive things about ourselves in order to avoid regret or other negative feelings we might otherwise have to deal with.[4]

The task of the SIC was particularly challenging in this regard, since highly intelligent people, many of whom were interrogated by the SIC, are even more prone to such biases simply because they are better at finding reasoning to support their self-enhancement and other such motivated reasoning, albeit unintentionally. All statements in the SIC report were therefore supported by data or documented evidence, as well as by people's testimony, if it supported other evidence. As a rule of thumb, statements in the report had to be supported by at least two types of evidence, if not simply unbiased data retrieved from the fallen estates, data that could not be disputed.

From the researcher's perspective, it is imperative to have such extensive investigative powers in order to be able to meet those challenges and deliver the requested work. It is, however, not as evident why a governing body would extend such exceptional investigative powers to an independent commission investigating it. For that, the Icelandic government and the opposition parties deserve praise.

At the time of their collapse, the three failed banks constituted 97 percent of the Icelandic financial system in terms of assets. Their combined failure is therefore the failure of the system as a whole, and, in such cases, normal rules don't apply. The situation calls for emergency measures and out-of-the-box thinking. It was this systemic nature of the failure in Iceland that called for the exceptional investigative powers of the SIC.

The Icelandic nation had, for several years, been misguided by illusions of prosperity built on credit, and then, in a relatively short time, been thrown off its high horse of abundance. Icelanders had enjoyed the boom with full employment (less than 1 percent unemployment), purchasing power never before seen on this harsh-natured island, quality healthcare, and education for all, while under only a modest tax regime. Suddenly—with 12 percent unemployment, the Icelandic krona at half of its previous value, inflation at 18 percent, and assets frozen in Britain so that no currency transfers could be made from Iceland, whether to purchase pharmaceuticals, oil, or send money to students studying abroad—the nation swung from a trusting society to one full of mistrust. Iceland was now at the mercy of its neighbors and international institutions. The poster child of alleged financial sector success was suddenly trying to figure out the firmness and even hostility it perceived toward it among its neighbors and allies.

Fortunately, the parliament managed to vote for the setup of the SIC under the leadership of the speaker of the parliament, Sturla Bodvarsson, and pressure from opposition leaders such as Steingrimur J. Sigfusson, who later became the Minister of Finance under a new government.

The SIC was given ten months to perform a postmortem on the fallen Icelandic banks. The law on the SIC offered the potential to provide a truly unique insight into the workings of financial institutions never possible before, given the level of confidentiality associated with financial information. It was up to the individuals appointed to the task, however, to deliver it. The outcome was out of the hands of parliament. In fact, according to the law on the SIC, any outside interference with the operation of the Commission would be reported and could be punished.

Building the Team

The SIC began by meeting with all parties with important evidence and data, in order to safeguard the material and secure the Commission's access to it. The Commission also held sessions with academic staff, mainly with people within Economics and Finance, and used these sessions to spot potential staff members, since one of the initial challenges of the Commission was to assemble a qualified team of experts quickly: individuals who would be capable of carrying out the necessary analysis as well as doing so without bias or inappropriate influence due to their previous jobs, social standing, or family relations. This was a particularly delicate task in Iceland, given the small and close-knit population of roughly 320,000. The risk of hiring an individual with a conflict of interest was therefore large, regardless of how well-motivated they might be.

During its time of operation, the Commission hired 48 employees or contractors to contribute to the investigation for longer or shorter terms and to write the report. Given the time pressure to get the project going, recruitment had to move quickly. Every new expert identified and recruited provided an extension to the professional network of the Commission, and thus to the pool of additional experts who could be interviewed and evaluated. While the pool of experts in Iceland is limited, owing to the small population and the lack of individuals with the education and experience to carry out such work, the Commission benefitted from the unusually high number of graduates from world-class universities, many with extensive work experience abroad. The SIC was therefore able to assemble well-functioning teams of people in various fields who had been tested elsewhere by their peers, both domestically and internationally, and were free of conflicts of interest.

The Commission's work was divided among five professional teams: the legal team (10 contributors, 5 full-time staff), whose main focus was administrative law, government bodies, the legal foundation of the Icelandic financial market, the introduction of European Directives into Icelandic legal acts, and more; a team of auditors (5 full-time staff) who developed case studies of lending by the banks to the 50 largest business groups in Iceland during 2004–2008; an ethics group (2 contributors) researched the collapse from social psychology, sociology, political science, and media-study perspectives; a team of quantitative analysts (14 contributors, 6 full-time staff with background in economics, finance, statistics, and engineering) completed the numerical and financial analysis of the project, the work that this book is largely based on.

The quantitative group identified and collected the data necessary to describe the financial operations of the banks, as well as to reveal the vast, complex cross-ownership structure of all Icelandic firms, information which had been specifically requested by the parliament. In all, the quantitative group covered the funding of the banking system, loan portfolios, contracts and incentive structures, stock market data, the foreign exchange market, mutual funds, market risk, and cross-ownership.

Prior to the establishment of the Commission, many people worried that qualified experts to carry out the investigation couldn't be found in Iceland, and thought that the Commission should be staffed mostly, or even exclusively, by foreign experts. Partly as a response to this concern, seven foreign experts were hired by the Commission for short-term consultation and/or research, among them Mark Flannery, professor of finance at the University of Florida, and Eric Talley, professor of law at the University of California, Berkeley. The foreign experts proved to be very important members of the team, providing both expert analysis and professional guidance and support to the rest of the team.

Scope of Research

The bankruptcy of the three Icelandic banks, with a combined total balance sheet of USD 180 billion, is the third largest bankruptcy in history, after Lehman Brothers (USD 691 billion) and Washington Mutual (USD 328 billion). It is almost three times larger than Enron, which, incidentally, could have been a lesson for Icelandic regulators and oversight institutions. The cross-ownership structure of the Icelandic banks and their major shareholders and related companies is reminiscent of the vast array of Enron offshore companies and Special Purpose Vehicles (SPVs) formed in order to falsify the Enron balance sheet.

The SIC had to conduct many different investigations at once. It had to look into the operations of three banks, Glitnir, Kaupthing, and Landsbanki, as well as all governmental bodies responsible for surveillance activities toward the banking sector. Pillar institutions such as the Central Bank, FME (financial supervisory authority), and the Government Coordination Group established to react to materializing systemic risk were also under investigation. Furthermore, the Commission impounded data from the Prime Ministry, the Ministry of Finance, and the Ministry of Commerce.

The Data Warehouse

Guided by economic and financial theory, the quantitative team laid out the questions that were important to be answered in the course of the investigation, in light of what had happened. The team got a unique chance to test some of the most prevalent theories in economics and how they materialized in the case of Iceland, such as the theory of market manipulation, and incentive theory. Theory was therefore the foundation on which the Commission's data warehouse was built. It took about six months to assemble. The data warehouse took full advantage of the power of the Commission to seek data, covering the five years leading up to the collapse, 2004–2008.

The SIC data warehouse contained six main types of data: bank operational data, stock market data, foreign exchange data, enterprise registry data, tax records, and contractual data.

Operational data consisted of data on the funding of the banks, including all bonds, domestic and foreign issues, all securitized debt obligations issued and their underlying assets, all collateralized loans from central banks, all deposits, monthly stocks and weekly flows, all derivatives contracts, and entire bank loan portfolios, including all loans extended by the banks' parent companies in Iceland: a total of over 6 million records.

The stock market data was particularly interesting. A truly unique dataset was compiled, including all stock market trades in the market for a four-year period, down to the individual investor. At any point in time, when a trade had occurred in the market, the team could trace it to which investor or investors were behind the trade. Since the team had managed to link the trade data from the stock market with data from the securities registry, and also had access to bank data, it could reveal who was behind all trades in the custodial accounts of the banks, thereby revealing an old trick intended to hide ownership, at least for the shorter term.

Information on foreign exchange trades was available as high-frequency data, and the enterprise registry provided shareholders of each enterprise over a five-year period, including ownership changes. This dataset was rather fragmentary, but thanks to access to qualitative documents of the banks, the team could track down changes in ownership and fill in the gaps where the public data collection agency had failed in its task.

Data collected from the Icelandic tax authorities included income statements as well as balance sheet items of Icelandic households and firms, but data regarding tax reporting of individuals was coded and could thus not be combined with other datasets. However, the SIC received all information on tax reporting of firms reporting in Iceland, including dividend payments of domestic and foreign entities.

In the spirit of the famous quote attributed to John Paul Getty: "If you owe the bank one hundred dollars, it's your problem. If you owe the bank one hundred million dollars, that's the bank's problem," all credit extended to individuals related to the banks, politics, or media exceeding 100 million ISK (or approximately 1 million USD) was disclosed in the SIC report. The ten largest dividend payment recipients, at both individual and firm level, as well as amounts paid as dividends, were disclosed in the report for each year from 2003 to 2008.[5]

Finally, to map out the incentives laid before the bankers during the five years leading up to the collapse of the banks, the Commission impounded all compensation information from the banks: both fixed and variable salaries, including bonuses, profits from exercised options, all option grants, stock ownership, and debt issued by bankers and funded by the banks. In addition, it obtained copies of all employ-ment contracts and loan contracts of all staff, including C-level staff.

The SIC Report

On April 12, 2010, the Commission issued a nine-volume report cov-ering roughly 2,400 pages. Another 800 pages were published online, including authored papers in applied analysis of academic disciplines such as history, social psychology, finance, and others.

Althingi had formulated the mandate of the Commission with a fair amount of detail, asking for specific questions to be addressed. However, Althingi did not impose constraints on the Commission as to how the investigation should be conducted, or what topics to address apart from those specifically requested. But Althingi had installed a separate investigative group in parallel, which was to answer the ques-tion whether the collapse could be attributed to poor governance and/or ethics standards. The Ethics Group was staffed by Vilhjalmur Arnason, professor of philosophy at the University of Iceland; Salvor Nordal, director of the Center for Ethics Studies at the University of Iceland; and Kristin Astgeirsdottir, director of the Center for Gender Equality. The Ethics Report was issued on April 12, 2010, along with the SIC report, and was widely considered to be an excellent analysis of the lapse in ethics that had occurred in Iceland prior to the collapse.

Much to the surprise of the Icelandic public, the SIC report received great reviews, and stayed at the top of the best-seller list at one of the largest bookstores in Reykjavik for many weeks. A Gallup survey revealed that 87 percent of the public were pleased with the report, 12 percent indifferent to it, and only 1 percent unhappy with it.[6] It was quickly pointed out that the Icelandic public had never before agreed on anything so resoundingly.

The SIC Main Findings

When a systemically important bank, in a financially mature mar-ket, grows faster than the economy, it is a signal of a possible dete-rioration of its assets, that is, primarily the loan book, because the number of reliable borrowers is not growing at the same rate as the bank, as explained in chapter 1. Consequently, the SIC had two main leads to follow at the beginning of its investigation, namely, the rapid growth of credit, and the size of the three banks at their collapse, in relation to GDP.

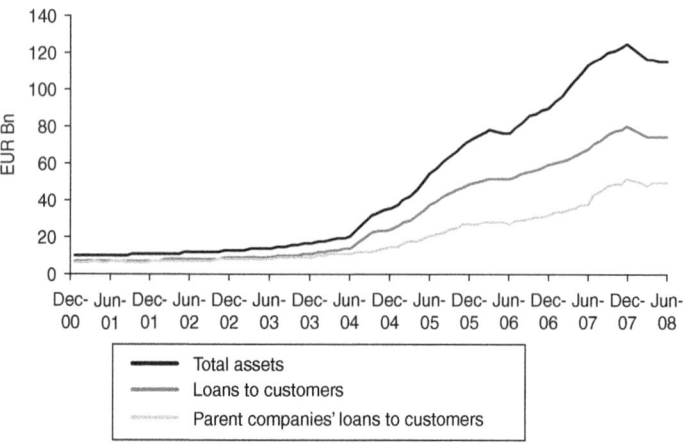

Figure 4.1   Aggregate assets of the three banks

Source: Central Bank of Iceland, Glitnir, Kaupthing and Landsbanki and SIC Report, Volume 7, Chapter 21, p. 177.

The combined assets of the three banks before the collapse were 115 billion euros (USD 180 billion), which was roughly ten times Iceland's GDP.[7] They had grown at an average rate of 70 percent from 2002 to 2007, from 12 billion euros (see Figure 4.1).[8] This brings up three fundamental questions:

1. How was it possible to expand to ten times GDP a banking sector that, in terms of assets, was just 65 percent of GDP only seven years before the collapse?
2. Given the enormous risk this strategy entailed, why would anyone want to pursue it?
3. Given the devastating consequences this strategy had on so many, why didn't somebody stop this development?

The remaining chapters draw on the findings of the SIC in an attempt to answer these three questions for a wider audience than the roughly 320,000 Icelandic speakers who can read the detailed 2,400 page report of the Icelandic parliament's Special Investigation Commission.

In the final chapter, I lay out what I consider to be the most important lesson of the Icelandic banking system meltdown, and what implications it should have for the world of finance and financial oversight.

Part II

How Did the Bankers Do It?

Chapter 5

Financial Liberalization

Before we look at the first question, how was it possible to expand a banking sector so much in a 7-year period, we need to be aware of who the bank owners are, what background and experience they had, and, even more importantly, how they came to be there. Getting acquainted with the owners helps explain some of the unusual decisions made throughout the 7-year period leading up to the collapse.

Financial liberalization has the potential of positively transforming a stagnant economy, providing funding for new ventures, creating jobs, and improving economic diversity. On the other hand, if not carefully carried out, it also has the potential to be laden with political favoritism and back-room deals—common occurrences when countries privatize some of their largest state-holdings—thus resulting in an outcome that is unlikely to be beneficial in the long run. That was certainly the case for Iceland.

The Special Investigation Commission, with its broad investigative assignment and limited time, focused its attention on specific aspects of the privatization process, and who was involved in the preparations before the sale, and in the decisions during the sale, of large portions of shares in Landsbanki and Bunadarbanki in 2002. The latter became Kaupthing after a merger with a small brokerage firm. Relevant aspects of privatization included (1) the law allowing for the sale of the banks, (2) requirements regarding buyers and share-size, (3) requirements regarding financial services experience, (4) changes in the requirements during privatization, and (5) general strategic planning and decision-making during the sale of the banks.[1]

Privatization—Part I

When Iceland's Independence Party and the Progressive Party formed a coalition government in April 1995, they announced their intention to create a privatization plan and begin selling state holdings. This would include assets such as the national telephone company, the state-owned banks, investment funds, and other state-owned companies competing with private firms.[2] A memo from the Ministry of Commerce to the Committee on Privatization (CoP), dated June 15, 1998, described the government's intentions:[3]

> It is proposed to sell the shares both in Iceland and abroad, and to register at least one of the banks at London Stock Exchange and possibly elsewhere. There are two main reasons. One is that the scope of the sale is probably greater than the domestic market is capable of handling adequately in a single year. The other is the desirability of attracting foreign investors to participate in providing financial services in Iceland.

One of the first steps in the privatization process was the merger of several government-owned investment funds in 1997 to form the Icelandic Investment Bank (FBA), later Glitnir, which opened its doors as a government-owned investment bank on January 1, 1998, and was set for an initial public offering later that year.[4]

Following the Commerce Ministry's June 15 memo, Skandinaviska Enskilda Banken (SEB) of Sweden expressed interest in buying a one-third share in Landsbanki. Negotiations took place late in the summer of 1998 and covered future changes in ownership. SEB wanted an option to buy another 17 percent in the bank, but the Icelandic government was reluctant to let a foreign bank hold the majority of shares. The government also had ideas about adding VIS, one of the largest insurance companies in Iceland, to the deal, in which Landsbanki and VIS would be owned by a holding company, referred to as LFG, and SEB would own one-third in LFG, instead of directly holding shares in Landsbanki. This made the SEB negotiators nervous. They worried that the rest of the process would leave them as a minority shareholder with little power over the course of the bank. "That is what we were most worried about, because the original document is rather political, the splitting of assets, mergers with various firms, or in other words, so much was going to be done at the same time that we got worried that we would somehow be tricked," said Ottar Gudjonsson, an Icelandic member of the SEB negotiating team.[5]

Furthermore, when the SEB representatives met with Axel Gislason, the CEO of VIS, and his colleagues, they were told that VIS wanted to be involved in the approval of SEB candidates for the board of Landsbanki. Understandably, the SEB team was quite puzzled by the request. During the lunch that followed, Lars Gustavsson, the leader of the SEB team, asked his colleague, Ottar Gudjonsson: "What was that? I mean,…are these guys all right?" Gudjonsson couldn't explain it, and simply apologized for the behavior of his countrymen.[6]

On August 11, 1998, JP Morgan delivered an estimate of Landsbanki's price, and by early September, SEB had finished its due diligence work. According to the SEB representatives, the Swedes were still interested, and well on their way to making the deal. But then came the word from Iceland: The deal was off, completely surprising SEB.[7]

Prime Minister David Oddsson testified before the SIC that it was his decision to stop the sale, explaining that the privatization of state holdings was under his jurisdiction. He further explained that, up to that point, the Minister of Commerce, Finnur Ingolfsson, and the permanent secretary of the Ministry of Commerce, Thordur Fridjonsson, had primarily driven the sales process. Prime Minister Oddsson did not consider it proper to deal exclusively with one potential buyer, and wanted a more open and transparent sales process. The Minister of Finance at the time, Geir Haarde, also pointed out that the price that SEB was offering was simply not high enough.[8]

In the fall of 1998 the government floated 15 percent of the shares of Landsbanki and Bunadarbanki, and in November it floated 49 percent of the FBA shares.[9] Landsbanki then had a total of 12,112 shareholders, Bunadarbanki over 93,000 shareholders, and FBA 10,734 shareholders.

In November 1999 the government sold the rest of its shares in FBA. A month later, 55 thousand subscribers participated in a public offering when the government sold more of its shares in Landsbanki and Bunadarbanki, leaving it with a 72 percent share in the banks after the sale. At that point, privatization was put to rest for almost three years due to unfavorable market conditions.[10]

Privatization—Part II

On May 18, 2001, the Icelandic parliament passed law 70/2001, permitting the sale of all remaining shares in both Landsbanki and Bunadarbanki. The law included only two short articles and did not provide a framework for how the sales should be carried out nor any specific guidance or rules. It therefore left the execution of the remaining privatization steps wide open.[11]

Aside from political statements that the state should not be involved in running financial services, there were no specific reasons given for selling both banks at that time. Parliament therefore left it to the Committee on Privatization to make all major decisions on how and when the banks would be sold. The CoP alone could decide how many shares to sell, to what types of investors, and at what price. The CoP would also decide on buyer requirements, how much financial services experience they would need to have, and, in general, what type of conditions should be met for the sale to go through. Furthermore, the CoP would decide whether to sell one bank first, or both at the same time.[12]

Prime Minister Oddsson testified that it was simply a majority decision to give the CoP that much authority, and admitted that the plan was wide open, explaining that "perhaps it was so at that time that people hadn't formed any ideas on how this should be carried out."[13]

On May 23, 2001, the CoP issued a memo on the sale of the banks, recommending that they be sold separately. It recommended the sale of Landsbanki first, followed by Bunadarbanki. The memo prompted the Minister of Commerce to formally announce to the Icelandic Stock Exchange on June 26 that preparations for the sale of a large share of Landsbanki, up to 33 percent, would commence. One of the conditions was that the sale would lead to increased competition in the Icelandic financial market.[14]

The sale was targeted for later that year and, on August 17, 2001, it was announced that the British bank HSBC had been hired as advisor for the sale.[15]

HSBC and the CoP searched for buyers for a controlling share in Landsbanki in the fall of 2001, primarily aiming to find a foreign investor. The effort was unsuccessful, and on December 21, after approaching approximately 20 foreign investors and financial services companies, the CoP announced that the sale of Landsbanki would be delayed due to difficult market conditions.[16]

On June 14, 2002, privatization continued with a small step, however, when the government conducted a public offering of 20 percent of the shares in Landsbanki, where no single investor could buy more than a 4 percent share.[17]

Controlling Shareholders Emerge

Soon after the June 14 public offering of Landsbanki shares, the CoP received a letter from three individuals, dated June 27, 2002, expressing interest in buying a 33.3 percent share in Landsbanki. The trio, which came to be known as the Samson group, consisted of Bjorgolfur Gudmundsson, his son Bjorgolfur Thor Bjorgolfsson, and their business associate, Magnus Thorsteinsson.[18] The CoP then issued a memo to the Minister of Commerce regarding the sales process and its current status, announcing the interest from the Samson group.

Three days later, the Ministry of Commerce replied, modifying the memo to say that Bunadarbanki should be sold at the same time.[19] No reasoning was provided for this change in plans. The Minister of Commerce at the time, Valgerdur Sverrisdottir of the Progressive Party, testified before the SIC that the government's term was nearing completion and that the plan had always been to sell both banks. Sverrisdottir, as well as Prime Minister Oddsson, admitted that the government knew that the market conditions were not favorable for such a sale, but pointed out that advertising a sale is by no means an obligation to sell.[20]

Oddsson also testified that members of the Progressive Party wanted both banks on the table, while Independence Party members thought it would be best to sell one at a time. Finally, the Independence Party members decided to give in to the pressure in order to maintain good relations within the coalition government.[21]

The Samson group claimed that they had not been planning on buying a bank. Bjorgolfur Gudmundsson, of the Samson group, testified that shortly after they finished a deal in Russia, his son, Bjorgolfur Thor, and their business associate, Magnus Thorsteinsson, were at a cocktail party in London when they met a man from HSBC who mentioned that HSBC still had a mandate from the Icelandic government to find buyers for Landsbanki. The HSBC man also revealed that HSBC had talked to 17–20 potential buyers without success, and asked if they were interested. This chance encounter evolved into a serious interest, leading to the aforementioned letter dated June 27, 2002.[22]

With the letter, the Samson group expressed interest in buying "at least" a 33.3 percent share, with an option to buy another 10 percent in the 24 months following the sale. They later modified their intent, increasing the option from 10 percent to 12.5 percent, for a total share of 45.8 percent in the bank.[23]

Prime Minister Oddsson described to the SIC the government's sentiment at the time:[24]

> Yes, I think it was still open to get in a so-called controlling shareholder, preferably a big one. It was considered good to get a big foreign shareholder, and then it was sort of a side benefit of it at the time

to receive foreign currency for the share, not just a small amount. [...] At that stage, I think people had come to realize that, we just have to admit it, that foreign investors had no interest in financial services here.

Selling of Landsbanki

In response to the Samson group letter, the CoP issued a press release on July 10, 2002, asking for bids from domestic and foreign investors for a minimum share of 25 percent in Landsbanki or Bunadarbanki, up to a maximum of 48 percent in Landsbanki and 55 percent in Bunadarbanki, the entire remaining government shares in the banks. A memo from the CoP to the Department of Commerce prior to the press release states that it would be best to sell all the remaining shares of Landsbanki, since the remaining 5 percent, if Samson were to buy 43.3 percent, would "not be worth much to the government."[25]

Five groups of investors, all of them Icelandic, turned in bids following the press release. The CoP selected three of them for further discussions, and met with each of them separately. They were the Samson group, the S-group (first referred to as the Ker group), and Kaldbakur.[26]

On August 28, 2002, the CoP sent the three groups a letter explaining the five factors that would determine who would be selected for negotiations. The factors were (1) ownership arrangement, (2) share size, (3) financing, (4) vision, and (5) buyer consolidation.[27] Apparently, the CoP was no longer requiring knowledge and experience of financial services.

The CoP's advisor, HSBC, compiled the answers from the investors and assigned a score for each factor, a maximum of 20 points per factor, for a maximum total score of 100 points. For some reason, however, the factors scored by HSBC were not identical to those listed in the letter from the CoP. The HSBC factors were (1) knowledge and experience of financial markets, (2) financial standing, (3) financial terms of offer, (4) plans regarding future operations of the bank, and (5) conditions on the part of the buyer.[28] Although not requiring knowledge and experience of providing operating financial services, HSBC was at least requiring knowledge and experience of financial markets.

The government's goal of importing extensive knowledge and experience of operating a financial services company by attracting a foreign investor in Landsbanki had clearly been lowered in priority by the fall of 2002. The government was anxious to sell. It is safe to

Table 5.1 Landsbanki offers: Scores for knowledge and experience of financial markets

Investor	Experience and contacts within international financial markets	Knowledge and experience of domestic financial system	Total points
Samson group	Contacts in international financial markets through previous business. Has international outlook that is likely to support Landsbanki's international plan.	No previous experience of significant ownership in an Icelandic financial institution.	14
S-group	Has indicated that it will use international experience and knowledge from their other companies. Chairman (or CEO?) is a former CEO of a small bank that merged with Landsbanki.	One of the investors is a large shareholder of VIS (the insurance company).	16
Kaldbakur	Did not indicate level of international experience. Indicated plans for an international expansion.	Controlling shareholder in the group has experience from being a controlling shareholder in Islandsbanki (formerly FBA). Chairman (or CEO?) of Kaldbakur has been a member of the board of directors of Islandsbanki and a branch manager of Landsbanki.	14

Source: Special Investigation Commission (SIC), 2008, *Background and Causes of the Collapse of the Icelandic Banks in 2008 and Related Events,* Vol. 1, Chapter 6, p. 247 (Report of the Special Investigation Commission, Reykjavik).

assume that at least some of the investors not only realized that, but also saw an opportunity to take advantage of it.

The S-group scored the highest for the first factor, 16 points (see Table 5.1), while the other two groups scored 14 points each. HSBC provided the following explanation for the score:[29]

> In assessing the investors' knowledge of financial markets, equal weighting has been given to the experience of international financial markets and to knowledge about the local Icelandic markets, the ratio-nale for this being that international expansion is seen as a key growth

area for the bank. Account has been taken, not only of direct experience of acting as a shareholder in financial institutions, but also of the likely ability of the investor to provide a network of useful contacts within the financial markets.

The evaluation did not identify any specific contacts in international markets, nor specific banks with which the investors had done business. Furthermore, the concept of major shareholder, or controlling shareholder, had evolved from referring to somebody with experience of running a bank to someone owning shares in a bank.

The scores for the financial terms of offer ranked the investors differently.

According to the SIC, the S-group alone was told, in a private meeting on August 28, 2002, that they would receive "a plus for foreign currency" (see Table 5.2).[30] Total scores for the Landsbanki offers are listed in Table 5.3.

There is no indication that HSBC used any other information for these evaluations than that provided by the bidders themselves. In other words, the SIC was not able to find any supporting materials from unbiased independent sources.[31]

On September 9, 2002, after going over the evaluations, the CoP selected the Samson group for further discussion and negotiations. One of the key factors in the decision was the fact that Samson would pay in US dollars.[32]

Table 5.2   Landsbanki offers: Evaluation of financial terms of offer

Investor	Share price	Share size	Total points
Samson group	3.00–3.90 Pending due diligence.	33.3% with an option for another 12.5% in the next 24 months.	10–15
S-group	4.10 Pending due diligence and acceptable contract.	25% at minimum, up to the total number of shares owned by the government.	17
Kaldbakur	4.16 Pending due diligence.	30% with an option for 5–10% more over 6 months, and a further option for the government's remaining shares.	18

Source: Special Investigation Commission (SIC), 2008, *Background and Causes of the Collapse of the Icelandic Banks in 2008 and Related Events*, Vol. 1, Chapter 6, p. 248 (Report of the Special Investigation Commission, Reykjavik).

Table 5.3 Total scores for evaluation of Landsbanki offers

Investor	Financial standing	Financial terms of offer	Future plans	Knowledge & experience of financial markets	Buyer's conditions	Total score
Weight	*25*	*20*	*25*	*20*	*10*	
Samson	20	10–15	18	14	8	70–75
S-group	15	17	12	16	6	66
Kaldbakur	13	18	10	14	6	61

Source: Special Investigation Commission (SIC), 2008, *Background and Causes of the Collapse of the Icelandic Banks in 2008 and Related Events*, Vol. 1, Chapter 6, p. 249 (Report of the Special Investigation Commission, Reykjavik).

The following day, a longtime member of the CoP, Steingrimur Ari Arason, the representative for the Minister of Commerce since 1991, resigned. Arason described the handling of the decision to select Samson as the main reason, and claimed that he had never witnessed such unprofessionalism during his 11 years of service for the CoP.[33]

In a report issued by the Icelandic State Auditor's office in October 2002, the auditors concluded that the CoP had modified the evaluation process after receiving bids, and had failed to select the best offer.[34]

During SIC testimony, Arason as well as Minister of Commerce Sverrisdottir described their disappointment on discovering that Skarphedinn Berg Steinarsson, an employee of the CoP, had met with HSBC in London on his own to go over the evaluation model.[35] While Sverrisdottir was frustrated to discover interference with the methods and tools of the government's advisor, she did not pursue it further.[36]

The SIC discovered an email from Edward Williams, the government's contact at HSBC, addressed to Skarphedinn Berg Steinarsson. The email was dated August 29, 2002, shortly before the Samson decision, and included the following explanation from Williams: "By defining the criteria and weighting carefully, it is possible to arrive at the 'right' result in selecting the preferred party, whilst having a semi-scientific justification for the decision that will withstand external critical scrutiny."[37] The selection of Samson was final, and the process moved on to final negotiations.

On December 31, 2002, Samson and the Icelandic government signed a purchase agreement for the sale of 45.8 percent of Landsbanki. With the deal, the Samson group was released from the mandatory takeover rule stipulated by law.[38]

Selling of Bunadarbanki

In October the CoP resumed the sale of Bunadarbanki, with the S-group and Kaldbakur as the two contenders, sending them a modified letter, dated October 23, 2002, explaining the five selection factors.[39]

HSBC completed the evaluation of the bids for Bunadarbanki within two weeks and submitted the results to the CoP on November 4, 2002. Table 5.4 shows the scores for knowledge and experience of the bidders.[40] The CoP quickly selected the S-group for further negotiations. One of the key factors in the decision was the involvement of a reputable international financial institution, Société Générale.[41] The French bank was described as an advisor to the S-group, as well as a possible investor. The S-group's points for knowledge and experience of financial markets therefore reflect the uncertainty of how Société Générale would be involved.

Table 5.5 shows the scores HSBC assigned for financial terms of the offers.

Total scores for the offers for Bunadarbanki are shown in Table 5.6. After receiving a confirmation via HSBC that Société Générale was indeed interested, or at least "potentially interested," as the French

Table 5.4   Bunadarbanki offers: Scores for knowledge and experience of financial markets

Investor	Experience and contacts within international financial markets	Knowledge and experience of domestic financial system	Total points
S-group	Group includes Société Générale or another investor. Has contacts through international experience of investors in the group.	Investor is the largest shareholder of VIS (the insurance company).	14–18
Kaldbakur	International contacts, mainly through a pension fund in north Iceland and the Samherji fishing company. Has been communicating with international investors.	Has operated as deposit institution for cooperatives. Board and members of the group have management and other experience from the financial sector.	15

Source: Special Investigation Commission (SIC), 2008, *Background and Causes of the Collapse of the Icelandic Banks in 2008 and Related Events*, Vol. 1, Chapter 6, p. 250 (Report of the Special Investigation Commission, Reykjavik).

Table 5.5 Bunadarbanki offers: Evaluation of financial terms of offer

Investor	Share price	Share size	Total points
S-group	4.20—4.70 Pending due diligence.	45.8%	19
Kaldbakur	4.10—4.50 Pending due diligence.	45.8%	14

Source: Special Investigation Commission (SIC), 2008, *Background and Causes of the Collapse of the Icelandic Banks in 2008 and Related Events*, Vol. 1, Chapter 6, p. 253 (Report of the Special Investigation Commission, Reykjavik).

Table 5.6 Total scores for evaluation of Bunadarbanki offers

Investor	Financial standing	Financial terms of offer	Future plans	Knowledge & experience of financial markets	Buyer's conditions	Total score
Weight	*30*	*25*	*25*	*20*	*0*	
S-group	17	19	16–20	14–18	0	66–74
Kaldbakur	17	14	18	15	0	64

Source: Special Investigation Commission (SIC), 2008, *Background and Causes of the Collapse of the Icelandic Banks in 2008 and Related Events*, Vol. 1, Chapter 6, p. 254. (Report of the Special Investigation Commission, Reykjavik).

bank contact had put it, the CoP decided to enter into negotiations with the S-group.[42]

When the CoP notified the S-group, it confirmed the importance of an international partner in the deal.[43]

> You have indicated that Société Générale or another international investor will take a stake of 25–30% in your holding company. The Committee would like to emphasise that the participation of Société Générale, or another international financial institution of high repute, as a significant equity investor in the bidder vehicle has been a major factor behind the Committee's decision to initiate negotiations on an exclusive basis with your group. It should therefore be clear that (i) exclusivity will initially only be granted for a limited period of time, sufficient for the bidder to form a more detailed view on valuation, and that (ii) the Committee will be reluctant to extend the right to negotiate on an exclusive basis, if at that point in time, the Committee considers that Société Générale or another international investor are unlikely to take a significant equity holding in the bidder vehicle.

The agreement between the S-group and the Icelandic Government, signed on November 15, included Société Générale "and/or another international financial institution" as one of the investors.[44] It required the S-group to reveal by December 6 the volume of the share that the French bank would invest in Bunadarbanki, or else the negotiations could be terminated.

On December 12, HSBC told the CoP that the participation of Société Générale would be confirmed the next day; but on December 13, the S-group told the CoP that information about an international investor in the group could not be revealed until contract signing. The CoP responded by asking for more information.[45] The HSBC advisor then notified them that, "We do not have absolute comfort, but I think that it is reasonable to proceed on the basis of what SocGen have told me."[46]

The process continued, and on January 6, 2003, the S-group described their negotiations with an international financial institution as being well under way.[47]

On January 9, the advisor from HSBC described the institution as a "good investor" for the Icelandic government, but did not reveal the name of the institution.[48] Bayerische Landesbank was mentioned as an important source of financing at the CoP's meeting on January 10, but no international financial institution was mentioned at the CoP's last meeting, on January 14, 2003.[49]

The purchase agreement for Bunadarbanki was signed on January 16, 2003, finally revealing the international financial institution in the investor group, the German bank Hauck & Aufhäuser Privatbankiers KGaA.[50] In a press release issued by the new owners of Bunadarbanki, Hauck & Aufhäuser (H&A) was described as a privately owned bank with operations in Germany, Switzerland, and Luxembourg, specializing in "fund- and asset-management for institutions and individuals, securities management for funds, and financial management for firms and individuals."[51] The press release also stated that the German bank would provide valuable experience for growing Bunadarbanki beyond the Icelandic market.

The SIC found no evidence that Hauck & Aufhäuser ever provided valuable experience to Bunadarbanki. In fact, their participation in the deal was questioned for several years following the sale. One parliamentarian submitted a formal inquiry to the Minister of Commerce as late as February 26, 2006, and was told that there was no reason to doubt that H&A had been a shareholder. However, during SIC testimony, Sigurjon Arnason, the VP of Operations at Bunadarbanki at the time said: "[H&A] did not in fact have the means to participate [in the deal], despite the fact that Bunadarbanki wasn't particularly big. That's why we always thought it was kind of strange when all this was happening."[52]

After the sale, the Bunadarbanki management thought it would be appropriate to begin some form of cooperation with this new owner, who could supposedly be a great mentor to them. According to Arnason, Bunadarbanki therefore sent one of its managers to Germany to meet with H&A to discuss the possibility of cooperation between the two banks. Much to their surprise, nobody at H&A knew anything about the deal. Furthermore, they had never heard of Bunadarbanki in Iceland.[53]

Financing the Purchase of Landsbanki

As previously mentioned, the Icelandic government was keen on getting some of the payments for the banks in foreign currency, and this was reflected in how they scored the financial terms of the offers.

Samson emphasized that they would make their payments in US dollars. The negotiated price of roughly USD 139 million (USD 139,043,229.92) for their 45.8 percent share would be a welcome addition to the Icelandic Central Bank's currency reserves.[54]

The purchase agreement, signed on December 31, 2002, stipulated that Samson would make three payments, the first two for the 33.3 percent share and the final payment for the remaining 12.5 percent. The first payment of USD 48,081,073.13 would be made within four working days. The second payment of USD 48,272,204.41 would be made on April 30, 2003, and the final payment, in the amount of USD 42,689,294.37, would be made on December 29, 2003.[55]

According to a letter from Samson on September 2, 2002, they would pay 30 percent with their own equity, using part of their profits from the sale of the beer factory Bravo in Russia to Heineken, a sale valued at USD 400 million, and would finance the remaining 70 percent.[56]

On September 6, 2002, Edward Williams of HSBC sent an email to Skarphedinn Berg Steinarsson of the CoP saying:[57]

> On financing, they have had discussions with a bank on a 4 year term loan, with a single bullet repayment at the end of the period. The interest on the loan would be serviced from other assets and not from the dividends of Landsbanki. [...] [Bjorgolfur Thor] claimed that he could finance the transaction 100% out of equity, but does not wish to do so as it lowers the IRR of the investment.

Bjorgolfur Gudmundsson testified before the SIC that Samson had made its payments according to the purchase agreement, specifically with respect to "currency and the ratio of equity to financing."[58]

Samson made the first payment roughly USD 48 million in February 2003, but the SIC was not able to obtain any information regarding the source of those funds.[59]

The source of the second payment, due on April 30, was found in the books of Bunadarbanki (later Kaupthing) as loan number 997. It carried LIBOR interest with a premium of 145 basis points and was a bullet loan with a single payment including interest due on April 29, 2004. Samson later extended the loan for one year, as allowed by the loan agreement, and the loan was paid up on April 29, 2005.[60]

Samson loan number 997, dated April 16, 2003, never went before the Bunadarbanki Credit Committee, but was instead approved between meetings and mentioned in the meeting minutes of the Credit Committee on April 16 as "previously approved larger loans."[61] The loan offer was signed by the Bunadarbanki CEO at the time, Solon Sigurdsson, and the VP of Corporate Banking, Elin Sigfusdottir, and included a statement from the bank saying that it was "ready to extend to the borrower another identical loan as the one described no later than December 29, 2003, to finance the purchase of a 12.5% share in Landsbanki."[62]

Loan number 1427 between Bunadarbanki and Samson, dated January 9, 2004, in the amount of USD 41.8 million, covered Samson's third and final payment for Landsbanki.[63] Elin Sigfusdottir, formerly of Bunadarbanki, had by then become Landsbanki's new VP of Corporate Banking.[64] Samson's second loan was, like the first one, a bullet loan carrying LIBOR interest with a premium of 140 basis points, with a single payment, including interest, due on January 9, 2007.[65]

In October 2008, when Landsbanki collapsed, Samson had paid up their first Bunadarbanki loan (number 997), but still owed Kaupthing (previously Bunadarbanki) over ISK 4 billion, due on December 10, 2008, for their second Bunadarbanki loan (number 1427).[66]

Financing the Purchase of Bunadarbanki

The financing of Bunadarbanki was done in a somewhat similar fashion, except this time it was Landsbanki's turn to do the lending.

The loan agreement, dated March 18, 2003, provided "as much as" ISK 2,995,000,000 (roughly USD 37.5 million at the time) to Egla holding company, the largest member of the S-group, with 71.2 percent of the S-group shares. The no-fee loan was to be paid in a single payment due two years later, on March 18, 2005. Interest was to be paid during the loan term.[67]

Major Ownership Changes

The ownership of Landsbanki remained largely unchanged during the remaining years until its collapse, and its name remained the same. Bunadarbanki merged with Kaupthing and became Kaupthing Bunadarbanki, then KB Banki, and finally Kaupthing—until its collapse—but ownership did not change much. FBA merged with Islandsbanki in 2000, and in 2006 changed its name to Glitnir.[68]

The ownership of Glitnir was marked by conflicts between major owners, and changed substantially in 2007 when investment companies Baugur Group and FL Group gained control through a leveraged buyout.[69, 70]

Chapter 6

Funding the Banks

2003—New Owners Embark upon the Bond Market

As the new owners of the three largest Icelandic banks took over, the funding of the banks consisted of 6.7 percent shareholder's equity, approximately 30.5 percent customer deposits, and 62.7 percent bonds issued to foreign banks based on long-standing business relationships.[1] The funding profile changed after privatization, however, as the banks began issuing bonds in the European Medium Term Note (EMTN) market (see Figure 6.1).

FBA, later named Glitnir, the first of the three banks to be privatized, was also the first one among the three banks to issue bonds in the EMTN market, starting in 1999. Landsbanki, which received a Moody's credit rating in February 1998, didn't enter the EMTN market to any substantial degree until 2003, just after its privatization, when it issued bonds in the amount of 850 million euros, resulting in 60 percent growth in its balance sheet.[2] Bunadarbanki, which received a Moody's credit rating in June 1999, issued its first EMTN bonds in 2002 in the amount of only 250 million euros.

In 2003, however, after Bunadarbanki merged with investment brokerage Kaupthing to become KB Bank, later named Kaupthing, the new bank issued EMTN bonds in the amount of 750 million euros. Total issues of the three banks had then reached 2.6 billion euros, or 25 percent of Iceland's GDP that year.[3]

From 1998 to 2003, the assets of the three banks grew from 4.5 billion euros to 16 billion euros. In the four years that followed, however, from early 2004 until the end of 2007, the banks grew sevenfold. Although part of this growth can be attributed to mergers and acquisitions, the banks still quadrupled again, even excluding acquisitions. This phenomenal growth was financed mostly by bonds issues abroad.[4]

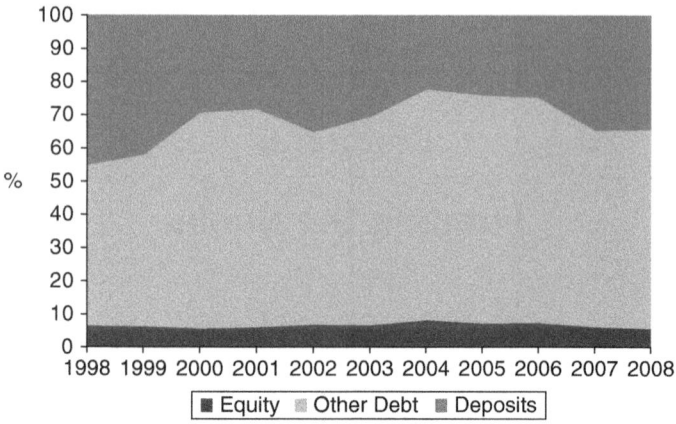

Figure 6.1   Deposits as share of banks' total funding
Source: IceStat, SIC Report, Figure 2, Chapter 7, Volume 2, p. 10.

2004—Sprinting Forward

A marathon runner beginning a race knows that going at the right pace means the difference between a successful run and a complete bust. Any marathon runner could easily sprint forward at the beginning of the race and quickly be at the front of the pack. Fortunately, though, trained runners all know that doing so would not be sustainable. In fact, it would quickly lead to a difficult, if not a failed race.

In 2004, with much liquidity in international financial markets, the three main Icelandic banks all began a financing sprint that would ultimately place them in unsustainable positions. Were the abundant liquidity in the markets not to continue, the substantial growth of their three- and five-year bond issues in 2004 would set the course for difficult refinancing in three to five years' time. For the time being, though, these three systemically important banks, while enjoying the benefit of the low debt levels of the Icelandic Treasury, took advantage of easy funding at favorable rates, and sprinted forward.

Landsbanki issued EMTN bonds in 2004 in the amount of 1.6 billion euros. The average credit default swaps (CDS) premium on Landsbanki's bonds was 20 basis points above LIBOR/EURIBOR for its three-year notes, and 28 basis points for its five-year notes.[5] Glitnir issued bonds in the amount of 2.5 billion euros, with over 2 billion of that in the EMTN market,[6] and Kaupthing issued EMTN bonds in the amount of almost 3 billion euros. The average CDS premium on Kaupthing's three-year notes was around 17 basis points, and 21 basis points on five-year notes. Kaupthing also acquired the Danish bank FIH in 2004, contributing greatly to the tripling of Kaupthing's assets that year.[7] At that point, the Icelandic banks had become international players, and a favorite topic of discussion, both in London and on Wall Street.

By the end of 2004, deposits made up only 22 percent of the funding of the three banks combined, down from 45 percent in 1998.[8]

2005—Outstanding Growth Continues

In 2005, the abundance of liquidity in international financial markets continued and Landsbanki issued EMTN bonds in the amount of 4 billion euros. Its average CDS premium for three-year notes had fallen to 15 basis points, and for 5-year notes to 22 points. Given the favorable funding environment, Landsbanki also managed to increase the average duration of funding. Furthermore, Landsbanki began accepting wholesale deposits in November of 2005, and had collected 300 million euros in such deposits by the end of 2005.[9]

Glitnir issued over 4 billion euros worth of bonds in the EMTN market in 2005, a 100 percent increase from a year earlier. It also acquired BN Bank in Norway and issued another 1 billion euros worth of bonds in the Norwegian bond market, in addition to some 370 million euros worth of bonds in the Australian bond market.[10]

Kaupthing issued more than 6 billion euros worth of bonds in 2005, and the CDS premium dropped to the lowest the bank had ever seen, only 9.5 basis points on average on three-year notes, and 15 basis points on five-year notes.[11]

After a successful year of funding, Icelandic bankers and politicians alike therefore seemed to have plenty of reasons to be optimistic about the future. The banks were enjoying excellent terms of funding, and finding funds easy to obtain. Stock market prices had soared, with the banks leading the market with a 70 percent rise in 2005, compared to only 25 percent for their Nordic counterparts.[12] Although foreign analysts were raising concerns and even worries over the rapid growth of the banks, the Icelandic market was bullish on the outlook for all three Icelandic banks.

2006—Difficulties Arise

On February 14, 2006, David Oddsson, former prime minister of Iceland, but by now the governor of the Central Bank of Iceland, and Sturla Palsson, director of Market Operations, met with representatives from the rating agencies in London and learned of an increasingly negative view toward the Icelandic banks. Governor Oddsson wrote in a memo, "Their main concern is the increased credit, financed mostly by foreign bonds."[13] At a meeting with JP Morgan that same day, Oddsson also learned that there was substantial risk that financial markets would close the door on the Icelandic banks.

A week later, on February 21, 2006, Fitch Ratings issued a negative outlook for the credit rating of the Icelandic National Treasury. Merrill Lynch and Danske Bank, followed with analyst reports also describing a negative outlook for the Icelandic banks.[14]

In its analysis titled, *Icelandic Banks—Not What You Are Thinking*, issued on March 7, 2006, Merrill Lynch warned of a frontloaded funding need, amounting to 1.7 times Iceland's GDP in 2007. Funding cost would therefore be bound to increase, hurting the profit margins of the banks.[15]

The Danske Bank report focused more on the macro picture in their analysis, calling the Icelandic economy the most overheated economy in the OECD, and outlining several alarming trends to support this claim, including a current account deficit approaching 20 percent of GDP.[16]

The Icelandic business community, politicians, and even regulators reacted angrily to the news, and the resulting fanfare became known as the Geysir Crisis (see next chapter), referring to Iceland's largest geyser.

Landsbanki issued bonds in the amount of 2.7 billion euros that year, but its EMTN issues went down to roughly 700 million euros. Instead, Landsbanki entered the USMTN market, issuing USMTN bonds in the amount of 1.5 billion euros in 2006 (Figure 6.2).[17]

Before the Fitch Ratings announcement in February, Landsbanki's three-year notes carried a 15 basis point premium, but later that year, when Landsbanki issued bonds in the USMTN market, the CDS premium on three-year notes had more than quadrupled, to 70 basis points.[18]

Landsbanki also began accepting retail deposits in foreign branches in late 2006, first with its Icesave accounts in the UK, then in Holland over a year later.[19] Icesave accounts were repeatedly listed first on the Internet Bank Accounts page at www.moneysorter.co.uk, resulting in a rapid increase in retail funding for Landsbanki, exceeding 1 billion euros by the end of 2006.[20]

Glitnir issued 2.5 billion euros worth of bonds in the European market in 2006, before it also began issuing bonds in the USMTN market, carrying a CDS premium of 80 basis points.[21]

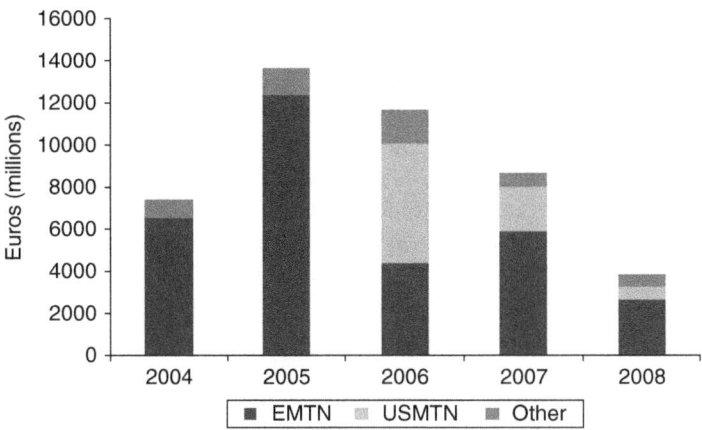

Figure 6.2 Banks' bond issues

Source: Landsbanki Islands hf., Kaupthing bank hf., and Glitnir bank hf., SIC Report, Figure 21, Chapter 7, Volume 2, p. 20.

Kaupthing issued 5.5 billion euros worth of bonds in 2006, but of that, 3.7 billion euros were issued on the USMTN market in October that year.[22] Kaupthing saw its premium on three-year notes rise from 17 basis points in the first half of the year to 75 basis points in the second half. The premium on five-year notes also rose from 20 basis points to 80.[23]

2007—The Wholesale Run

By 2007, the banks found themselves operating in an entirely new environment with respect to funding, and began moving away from bond issues toward deposits. Surprisingly, however, Moody's increased the rating of all three banks to Aaa in late February, declaring their bond issues as risk free as a German Government bond. Analysts from New York to London were quick to point out the absurd rating, and credit analysts from Royal Bank of Scotland published a note titled "Moody's lose the plot completely," stating that, "While defaults in European banking have not exactly been legion in recent years, creating Aaa-rated banks across the board essentially means that there is no risk in investing in financials, that buying a senior Kaupthing bond, for example, is effectively risk-free, the same as Gilts or Bunds," and concluding that, "It is plainly not."[24]

This stellar credit rating proved to be both a blessing and a curse for the already inflated self-esteem of the Icelandic bankers. It was a blessing because American investment bankers were now willing to fund the banks by including them in their Asset-Backed Securities (ABSs). On the other hand, it was a curse because, in addition to clearly being erroneous, the stellar rating brought on negative mass-media coverage about the rapid growth of the balance sheets of the Icelandic banks. It put a spotlight on their intimidating size, which had reached levels never seen before in terms of home-market GDP, already amounting to 7–8 times the GDP of Iceland at year-end 2006. Although many banks in Europe got upgraded that day to Aaa, the Icelandic banks were at the forefront of discussion.

Moody's error originated in an upgrade in their rating model, which now took the "too-big-to-fail" factor literally, deeming all such institutions as systemically important and thus a sure thing to be saved by governments, ignoring the "too-big-to-save" risk.[25]

Unfortunately, that risk also did not seem to concern Icelandic financial regulators at the time. In early March 2007, I wrote an article in Iceland's main business newspaper, *Vidskiptabladid*, concluding that the Central Bank of Iceland would not be able to act as a lender of last resort for foreign depositors of Icelandic banks, due to the sheer size of the banking sector relative to GDP.[26]

Moody's corrected their error in April 2007, bringing the rating of all three Icelandic banks back to Aa3, which, for Landsbanki, was still two notches above where it had been at the beginning of the year.[27]

The improved rating, however, had no significant effect on Landsbanki's bond issues. Landsbanki issued bonds for less than 1 billion euros in 2007, and paid down more than 2 billion euros worth of older bonds.[28] Landsbanki's bond issue of 500 million Euros in May carried 26 basis points above EURIBOR, but by late September CDS premiums were sharply rising, peaking at above 80 basis points for Landsbanki, which enjoyed the lowest CDS premium of the three banks.[29]

At the same time, Landsbanki managed to triple its deposits, from roughly 5 billion euros in mid-2006 to almost 16 billion euros after the middle of 2007.[30] In only nine months, from late 2006 to the middle of 2007, Landsbanki managed to collect deposits in its foreign branches equivalent to almost five times the foreign exchange reserves of the Central Bank of Iceland.[31] So, if there were to be a run on Icesave accounts, the Central Bank of Iceland would be unlikely to be able to act as a lender of last resort, as pointed out in my article in *Vidskiptabladid*.

Glitnir, which was approaching large repayments, having to pay off 2 billion euros worth of older bonds, issued bonds for 4 billion euros in 2007, 2 billion of which was in the EMTN market and 2 billion in the USMTN market.[32] Glitnir's CDS premium peaked at well above 100 basis points in late 2007, when it issued its last large long-term bond.[33] At that time, the bank had become vulnerable, with a front-loaded repayment structure as refinancing became more difficult and expensive.

From early 2005 until late 2006, total deposits at Glitnir had been steady at or above 4 billion euros. In late 2006, however, deposits at Glitnir began increasing, and then jumped substantially in early 2007. They peaked at 8 billion euros by the end of 2007, before starting to fall.[34]

Kaupthing, despite funding difficulties in 2007, issued bonds for roughly 4 billion euros, though it had no issues in the USMTN market. CDS premiums exceeded 100 basis points by year end.[35] Kaupthing's on-line deposits, under the brand Kaupthing Edge, followed a similar trend as Glitnir, remaining steady from just under 6 billion euros in the second half of 2005 and into 2006, before sharply increasing in early 2007.[36]

By the end of 2007, the combined total deposits of the three banks peaked at almost 38 billion euros, before withdrawals began rising.[37] Funding via bond issues had gotten much more difficult, with CDS premiums climbing as much as 240 basis points, as in the case of Kaupthing.[38] As 2008 approached, the banks found themselves severely limited in their funding possibilities, yet with major repayments due in 2008 and 2009.

To counter this situation, the banks increased their collateralized lending from the Central Bank of Iceland and other central banks. Their total collateralized lending from all central banks combined had been steady at around 2 billion euros through all of 2006 and the first half of 2007, but then began rising. By the end of 2007 it was above 5 billion euros, an increase of over 160 percent.[39] By comparison, collateralized lending of all European financial institutions combined increased only about 20 percent that year.[40]

2008—Desperate Measures

Icelanders had just put away their Christmas decoration, in early 2008, when one of the most high-flying investment companies in Iceland went bankrupt. The fall of Gnupur Investment Company sent ripples through Icelandic financial markets, setting the tone for what would follow later in the year. It pushed the cost of funding for the banks even higher, beyond 400 basis points for both Glitnir and Kaupthing, now that the first crack in the system had become visible.[41] As a result, the banks became more creative in finding new funding (discussed in the following chapters).

During the economic boom years of 2003–2007, the Icelandic banks, armed with a stellar credit rating inherited from the virtually debt-free Icelandic state, managed to issue a total of 45 billion euros of bonds, mostly in the EMTN market but also in others, such as the USMTN. One of the key factors in getting easy access to funding was the fact that the banks were ready and willing to pay higher interest rates than other, less developed, emerging market institutions with lower credit ratings.[42]

When the three banks collapsed, their combined outstanding bonds amounted to roughly 35 billion euros.[43]

Chapter 7

The Geyser Crisis

A Missed Opportunity

Every time I think about the Geyser Crisis, the first thing that comes to mind is a missed opportunity—the opportunity for Icelandic politicians and regulators to step on the brakes, apply prudential policies, and avert the full-fledged financial crisis that later ensued.

I had spent considerable energy in 2005 trying to introduce the results of my credit growth research at the International Monetary Fund (IMF) to the Central Bank of Iceland, the Prime Ministry, and the financial supervisory authority, FME. It is probably fair to say that the national mood in Iceland in 2005 had no tolerance for predictions such as those found in the IMF paper. In addition, it would surely have been political suicide for any government official to step up and say: "Listen, we really need to slow down," when the entire nation was enjoying the biggest economic boom in its history.

In early 2006, however, less than a year later, the IMF analysis just might have gotten some attention, thanks to what came to be known as the Geyser Crisis. It would only have required the support of a few brave senior government officials willing to put their political future on the line, and others just might have followed. None did, however, and the crisis, described by the Special Investigation Commission as the point of no return for saving the Icelandic banking system without major losses, passed without intervention.[1]

The Geyser Crisis developed from a few separate events in early 2006. David Oddsson, governor of the Central Bank, and Sturla Palsson, director of Market Operations at the Central Bank, had met with representatives from the rating agencies in London on Valentine's Day, February 14, 2006, where they learned of an increasingly negative view toward the Icelandic banks, as described in the previous chapter.

A week later, Fitch Ratings issued its negative outlook for the credit rating of the Icelandic National Treasury and asserted that officials should begin taking precautions. Then came the Merrill Lynch report on March 7, titled *Icelandic Banks: Not What You Are Thinking,* followed by the research report from Danske Bank two weeks later titled *Iceland: Geyser Crisis.* The Danish report, which focused on the chilling macroeconomic numbers in Iceland at the time, gave the Geyser Crisis its name.[2]

The Danish analysts were sufficiently specific in their analysis for anybody with any knowledge of the matter to take notice. The report stated, "On most measures, the small Icelandic economy is the most overheated in the OECD area. Unemployment stands at 1%, wage growth is above 7%, and inflation is running above 4% despite a strong ISK. The current account deficit is closing in on 20% of GDP."[3]

They predicted that inflation would exceed 10 percent and that the Icelandic currency would depreciate markedly. They also mentioned the debt levels, saying that "on top of the macro boom, there has been a stunning expansion of debt, leverage, and risk-taking that is almost without precedent anywhere in the world. External debt is now nearly 300% of GDP."[4]

The message was clear: "We look at early warning indicators for financial crises and conclude that Iceland looks worse on almost all measures than Thailand did before its crisis in 1997, and only moderately more healthy than Turkey before its 2001 crisis."[5]

Instead of taking the criticism to heart, researching the foundations of the analyst reports, and making necessary changes, the Icelandic business community, politicians, and regulators reacted angrily to the news, putting greater effort into convincing financial markets that the Icelandic banks were in fact on solid footing.

Clues to Credit Problems

The Geyser crisis was a funding crisis, with CDS spreads,[6] signaling the cost of borrowing for banks, jumping 400 percent for the Icelandic banks in just six months, from 18 bps in September 2005 to 100 bps in March 2006, in the case of Kaupthing. As a consequence, the banks suddenly found themselves having funding difficulties in the bond market. The market had started to doubt the quality of the asset side of their rapidly expanding balance sheets, and the market signal was decisive.

Despite the severity of the market signal, however, Icelandic bankers, politicians, and even the financial supervisory authority, FME, didn't take it seriously. Rather, they took it personally, seeing it as hostility toward Iceland's success. In a speech in April 2008, Jonas Fr. Jonsson, director general of the FME, explained his opinion:[7]

> As I mentioned earlier, the so-called CDS spread of the Icelandic banks has grown above any rational level. I am not the only one of that opinion, since the rating agency Moody's said in its report just yesterday that "current CDS spreads unfairly exaggerate Icelandic credit risk." Other credible market analysts, such as CreditSights, have aired similar opinions. In my own opinion, the causes of these wide spreads are psychological, technical, and behavioral in nature. What these CDS spreads mainly reflect is risk aversion, which is general to the international markets; technical flaws in an unorganized, thinly traded market; and a consequence of a less-than-amicable discussion about the banks and the Icelandic economy.

FME didn't seem to understand what the CDS spreads entailed. Already in 2006, Landsbanki and Kaupthing were on the iTraxx-Europe top 25 list of most traded CDSs in Europe. At their collapse, the outstanding CDS contracts on Icelandic banks amounted to a total of USD 70 billion, USD 8 billion net.[8] In comparison, at the collapse of Lehman Brothers, their outstanding contracts totaled USD 72 billion and USD 21 billion net.[9] In light of this, the market for CDSs on the Icelandic banks could hardly be characterized as thinly traded.[10]

Furthermore, a fair amount of naked CDSs[11] had been issued as instruments to short the Icelandic banks, since the outstanding debt contracts at the time were USD 50 billion, or 35 billion euros.[12] This provided yet another signal that financial markets considered the Icelandic banks to be in deep trouble. The markets were placing bets that the house was going to burn, but instead of investigating the house for potential fire hazards, such as faulty wiring, the residents stood outside and criticized the bets.

I often show the graph depicting the changing CDSs to my financial markets students, or to other audiences, gradually revealing the chart and asking them to stop me when they are ready to take action. While students have different views on when to intervene, they never wait for the CDS spreads to reach 1000 basis points, as they were for the Icelandic banks in September 2008 (Figure 7.1).

But then my students ask the inevitable: Why did our politicians and regulators not take action when they saw what was happening? I remind them that we have many skilled geologists in Iceland, who frequently react to seismic data. They give us a warning when it is not safe

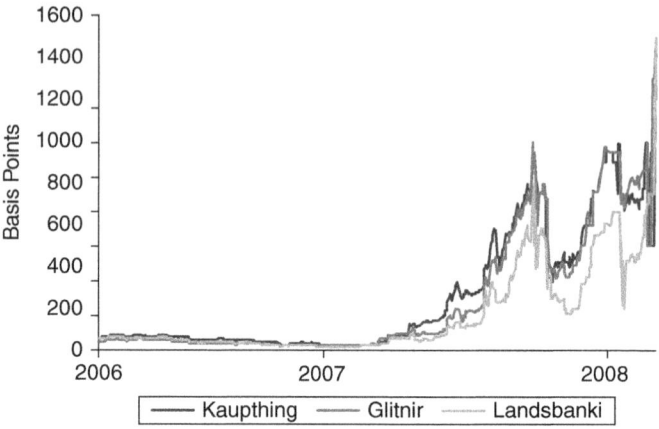

Figure 7.1   CDS spreads of the Icelandic banks 2006–2008

Source: Kaupthing hf., Glitnir bank hf., and Landsbanki Islands hf., SIC Report, Figure 48, Chapter 7, Volume 2, p. 43.

to climb Mt. Hekla, or tell us that a glacial outburst flood (*jökulhlaup*) is expected from underneath one of the glaciers. Sometimes they tell us that we are likely to have an eruption in a particular area very soon. In short, they are experts at reading data; so, given their track record, I am quite certain that Icelandic geologists would not have ignored the strong signals from the financial markets. Rather, they would have commanded Icelandic authorities to react.

But, as students are bound to point out, the financial supervisory authority doesn't employ any geologists.

The Icelandic Response

In an effort to manage the Geyser Crisis, Icelandic bankers colluded on a marketing campaign where the Icelandic Chamber of Commerce (ICC) provided the collusive purpose of providing the collusive mechanism needed for the effort. ICC hired the world-renowned economist Frederick Mishkin, at the time professor of economics at Columbia University, to coauthor a report on financial stability in Icelandic with an Icelandic professor of economics, Tryggvi Thor Herbertsson, who later served as economic advisor to Prime Minister Haarde at the height of the crisis in 2008.[13]

Armed with the so-called Mishkin report, the banks managed to unify the story about their own good standing and to dispute the assessment of the markets regarding their trustworthiness. Elected officials and cabinet ministers also played key roles in reinforcing the message and bringing it to the government level. Prime Minister Haarde and Minister of Commerce Sigurdsson gave speeches on the good standing of the banks at investor conferences such as at NYSE and at the Icelandic-American Chamber of Commerce, thereby helping the bankers drive home their message.[14] This collusive effort successfully managed the eruption in such a way that it blew over just as fast as it blew up—much like the most famous geyser in Iceland (Geysir), after which the crisis was named.

Thanks in part to the Mishkin report, and to the Icelandic banks' successful marketing effort, the banks managed to issue 11 billion euros in bonds during 2006 despite the crisis, crisis (albeit at a higher cost)—of which half was in the United States, which had not previously been open to the Icelandic banks.

Innovations in Funding

In early 2007, during the quiet before the storm in the fall of 2007, financial markets still had an appetite for "high-quality" credit that developed in the fall, financial yields, allowing the Icelandic banks to issue bonds totaling 8.6 billion euros. By fall, however, CDS spreads, ranging from 140 to 300 basis points above LIBOR became unbearable for the banks. By then, wholesale funders had already run on the Icelandic banks by pricing them out of the market, so the banks had to turn elsewhere for funding.

The banks utilized two extreme outlets for refinancing at this point. First of all, they went into the streets to collect deposits from the ill-informed public (Figure 7.2). At their collapse, Landsbanki's Icesave and Kaupthing's Edge online accounts had 12.5 billion euros in total deposits, 7.2 billion and 5.3 billion euros, respectively (Figures 7.3–7.4).[15] The Icelandic State Budget at the time was just 5.5 billion euros, while the Icelandic Central Bank's foreign reserves averaged only ISK 250 billion (about 2.2 billion euros) in 2008.[16]

Landsbanki's deposits were held in its branches in the UK and the Netherlands, while Kaupthing's Edge deposits were held in subsidiaries in Britain, Belgium, Denmark, Finland, Germany, Norway, and Sweden. This distinction between holding deposits in a branch versus in a subsidiary made a world of difference to Iceland when the calamity hit, resulting in the largest foreign dispute that Iceland has had with any nation since the Cod Wars of the 1950s and the 1970s.

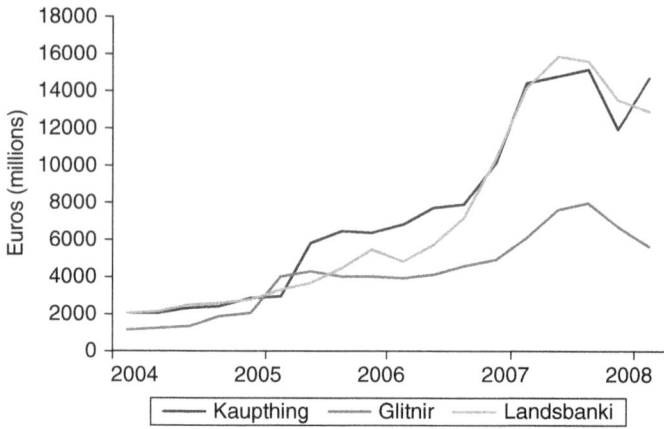

Figure 7.2   Bank deposits on consolidated basis
Source: IceStat, SIC Report, Figure 33, Chapter 7, Volume 2, p. 36.

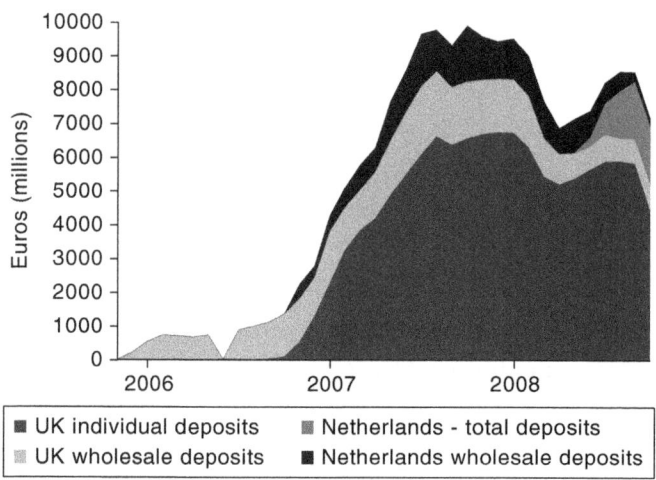

Figure 7.3   Icesave deposits in Landsbanki's branches abroad
Source: Landsbanki Islands hf., SIC Report, Figure 37, Chapter 7, Volume 2, p. 37.

The banks also went to the supremely informed central banks for funding. Before they collapsed, the three Icelandic banks had managed to borrow 9.3 billion euros from central banks in Europe (Figure 7.5). In comparison, to get Iceland out of its financial crisis,

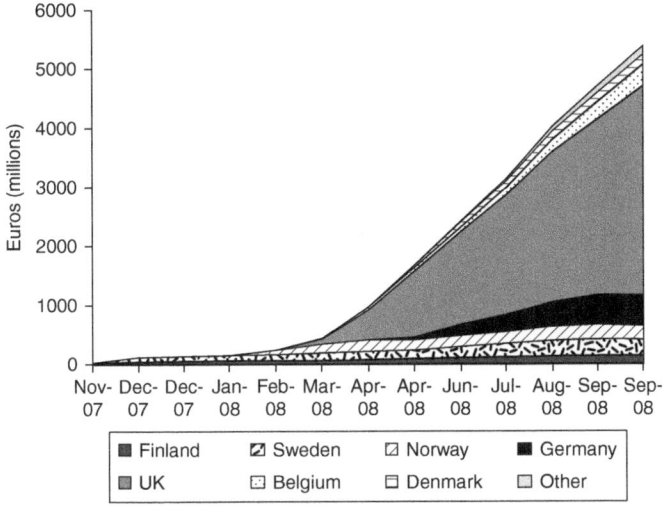

Figure 7.4 Edge deposits in Kaupthing's subsidiaries abroad

As data was missing for Sweden at 12.31.2007, a weighted average between two adjacent points was used.

Source: Kaupthing bank hf., SIC Report, Figure 41, Chapter 7, Volume 2, p .41.

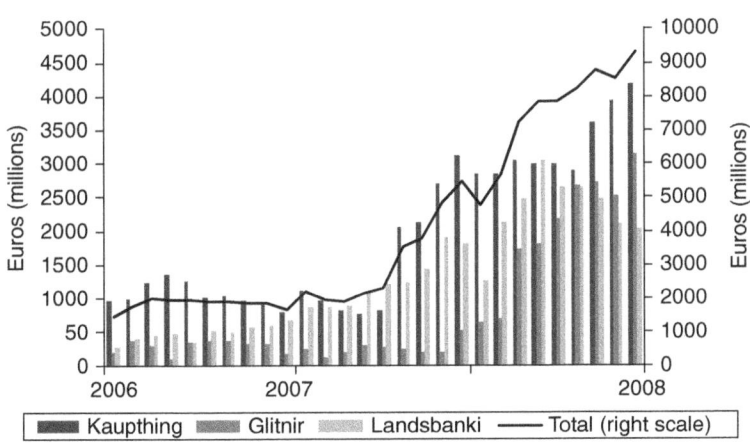

Figure 7.5 Collateralized lending from central banks

Source: Kaupthing Bank hf., Glitnir Bank hf., and Landsbanki Islands hf., SIC Report, Figure 48, Chapter 7, Volume 2, p. 43.

the rescue package that was put together by the IMF and Iceland's neighbors in Scandinavia (including the Faroe Islands) plus Poland only amounted to about 3.4 billion euros (USD 4.6 billion).[17]

Obtaining 9.3 billion euros from well-informed central banks isn't hadn't been easy since Iceland's banks had already been highlighted in the media for growing too fast and for having potentially shaky balance sheets. The Icelandic banks therefore had to come up with new ways of obtaining those funds—brand new ways.

Chapter 8

Love Letters to the Rescue

Liquidity Services of Central Banks

Banks have developed a wide array of methods and tools to manage the risk that is inherent in their business, and to maintain a cushion against changing customer behaviors and needs, as well as the changing conditions in financial markets.

One method they have available to them is to borrow from or lend funds to central banks based on their short-term operating needs, which typically arise from a cash-flow mismatch. That is, since banks usually borrow for short term but lend for long term, they must constantly manage a cash-flow mismatch—a fundamental task of risk management at banks.

Central banks play a key role in these circumstances, such as when deposits suddenly fall faster than anticipated due to withdrawals by large customers needing funds for major investments. Banks must then bridge a short-term liquidity need by obtaining funds from their central bank. The counter at the central bank offers a few choices.

First, there is the so-called discount window, where banks can borrow funds to meet reserve requirements, or lend their excess reserves to the central bank and to other banks that need to meet their reserve requirements. This is usually in the form of overnight borrowing and lending.[1]

Longer-term financing is available for healthy banks for various time periods, such as a week, a month, or even 3 months, given that the banks have securities to pledge as collateral.

Many central banks also offer repurchase agreements, or REPOs, to banks. REPOs offer short-term lending to banks, but with a different substantive effect on their balance sheet. Instead of lending against collateral, and thereby, in effect, expanding the balance sheet of the bank, the central bank purchases eligible assets from the bank, usually state-guaranteed securities. Then, once the liquidity problem of the bank is solved, the bank can buy back these securities from the central bank at a slightly higher price. This transaction leaves the balance sheet of the bank stable; the securities go to the central bank, and cash comes into the bank instead. Once the need has passed, the central bank returns the securities and gets back the cash.

In the case of longer-term refinancing using collateral, however, the balance sheet of the bank expands. That is, the securities used as collateral remain an asset of the bank, but the bank receives the borrowed cash as an asset and adds a matching liability toward the central bank.

Services of the Central Bank of Iceland

The Central Bank of Iceland did not offer repurchase agreements, but only collateralized lending. This was a bit unfortunate since the main problem with the Icelandic banks was their excessive growth.

After the Geyser crisis, the banks maintained some 100 billion ISK in short-term loans from the Central Bank of Iceland, or roughly USD 1.5 billion at the time. Landsbanki was the most dependent on this type of lending until the two rivals, Glitnir and Kaupthing, increased their borrowing through this short-term, fine-tuning lending mechanism of the Central Bank in January 2008, when the banks' collateralized lending doubled in one month (Figure 8.1).

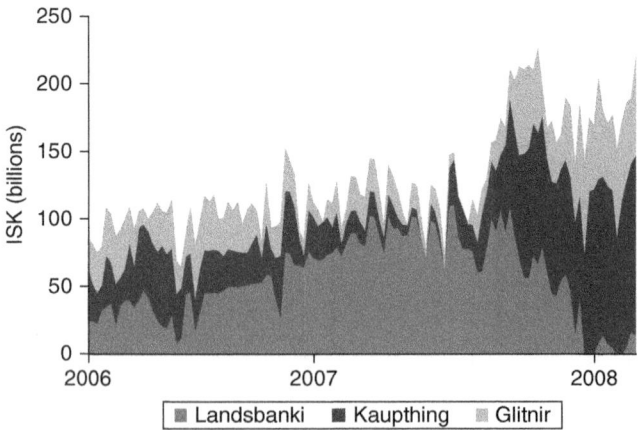

Figure 8.1   Collateralized lending of the Central Bank of Iceland
Source: Central Bank of Iceland, SIC Report, Figure 49, Chapter 7, Volume 2, p. 43.

At first, the banks mainly pledged state-guaranteed assets to the central bank, but when the liquidity squeeze got really serious, they faced a shortage of assets to pledge.

Abusing Liquidity Services

In early 2008, the banks found an ingenious way to essentially take over the monopoly power of the central bank to print money. Instead of using their existing asset portfolio (which was depleted), they issued new unsecured bonds in the domestic market at a favorable rate, then colluded on exchanging these bonds among themselves. Another bank could then use them as collateral against short-term lending from the Central Bank of Iceland.[2] As long as the CBI did not complain, the three banks had a way to extract funds from it without providing any real collateral.

The Central Bank of Iceland soon figured out what was going on. In a Board of Governors meeting in May 2008, Governor Oddsson explained that if the banks were to go bankrupt, these bonds would be essentially just "foam."[3] During Special Investigation Commission (SIC) testimony he also stated that he had explained this fact to the government cabinet. Oddsson, a novelist and former prime minister of Iceland, even claims to have coined the famous term for these bonds, "love letters."[4]

Once the Central Bank of Iceland became aware of the love letters being pledged as collateral, and of their poor quality in case of default, it began trying to stem the growth of these borrowings. In late July or early August, it told the three banks that these loans would have to stop.[5]

But already in the spring of 2008, the three banks had turned to a small cooperative bank, Icebank, the parent bank of the Icelandic savings and loans association, for help in utilizing this money machine. The banks issued new ISK-denominated bonds and handed them over to Icebank, which in turn pledged them as collateral against its own short-term borrowing from the Central Bank of Iceland.[6]

Icebank managed to collect a nice fee in the process by cutting off a small part of the loan from the Central Bank before turning the remainder over to one of the banks. Before they collapsed, Icebank had received 160 billion ISK, or roughly USD 2.2 billion, in the form of short-term loans from the Central Bank of Iceland (Figure 8.2).[7]

Icebank's exposure toward the three big banks, Landsbanki, Glitnir, and Kaupthing, was equivalent to 15 times Icebank's equity.[8] Needless to say, this type of market risk in a depository institution

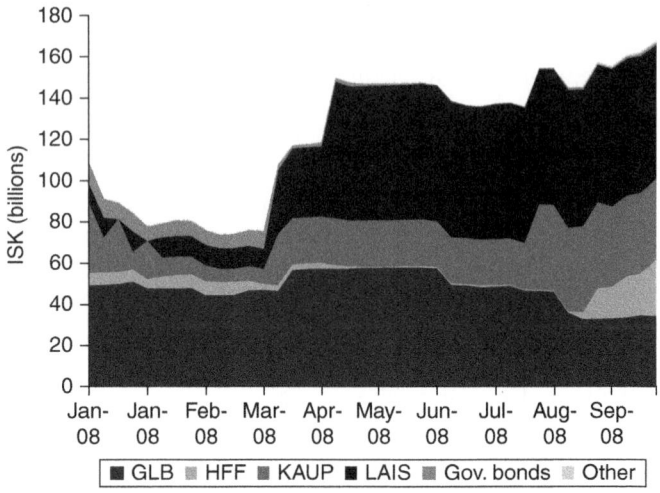

Figure 8.2   Icebank's collateral pledged into the Central Bank of Iceland
Source: Central Bank of Iceland, SIC Report, Figure 54, Chapter 7, Volume 2, p. 45.

would have, say, under any normal circumstances, this set alarm bells ringing at most financial supervisory authorities. The ingenious Icelandic bankers, however, made sure that no one raised a finger.

Apparently aware of the problem, Icebank made efforts to manage the risk, at least on paper. It asked its best customers to sell credit default swaps to Icebank to hedge against their exposure toward the three banks, and at prices far below those quoted in the market.[9]

The CDS with Icebank was structured as follows: The customer either established a new Special Purpose Vehicle (SPV) for this transaction, or used an existing one. The SPV then issued insurance against a default of the bank involved.[10]

One of the customers had an SPV with assets of about 100 million ISK, or about USD 1.6 million, insuring against a potential default by Glitnir bank amounting to 8 billion ISK, or about USD 170 million. Clearly the insurer, the SPV, would not be able to deliver on the insured claim if, as it did, after Glitnir defaulted.[11]

In the Western world, people have a legal obligation to buy fire insurance on their residence. Following Icebank's logic, it would be most economical for a homeowner simply to knock on a neighbor's door and give a candy bar to any child who happens to answer, in return for their signature on an insurance contract thereby insuring the house against fire. The Icebank credit insurance was, of course, bogus, and the insurance and the financial supervisory authority, FME, should have taken drastic measures against Icebank for excessive risk taking.

FME ran a stress test on Icebank in the first quarter of 2008, which the bank failed, right before it doubled its exposure to love letters, taking an additional 80 billion ISK in loans from the Central Bank.[12]

In the stress test implemented by FME, Icebank's capital adequacy ratio fell from 10.4 percent to 7.6 percent under market-risk stress.[13] Had only one of the insurance contracts, amounting to 31 billion ISK, been taken into account during this stress test, the capital adequacy ratio would have measured 6 percent, which is 2 percent below the legal minimum. This should have prompted the authorities to take action against Icebank, which would have made a substantial difference in the events leading up to the bankruptcy of the Central Bank of Iceland.

It wasn't until July 17, 2008, that the Central Bank of Iceland put the brakes on this merry-go-round of collateralized lending to the banks, with a letter sent to all financial institutions in Iceland. The letter said:[14]

> Collateralized lending of the Central Bank of Iceland to financial institutions has increased significantly in recent months. A large portion of these loans has been backed with collateral in the form of unsecured bonds and short-term bills issued by those financial institutions that currently hold an international credit rating, i.e., the three large commercial banks. This development is partly understandable in light of the difficult funding environment both domestically and abroad....The Central Bank needs to safeguard the quality of its loan book, diversification, and counterparty risk towards each financial institution, which now needs to be addressed. It is not natural that a financial institution should be able to manage the short-term lending facility of the Central Bank through issuing bonds and swapping them amongst rivals....From 17th of July no new unsecured bond issues of any domestic financial institution will be accepted as collateral without a due diligence process. The Central Bank will review its rules on eligible collateral to enable financial institutions to use asset backed securities in these transactions.

In his testimony to the SIC, Sturla Palsson, director of Market Operations at the Central Bank of Iceland, stated that short-term liquidity facilities to financial institutions had reached 250 to 300 billion ISK, roughly USD 3.5 to 4.2 billion at the time. When asked whether the CBI hadn't considered trying to lower that exposure, his answer was, "yes, but then I could just as well have closed down their operations."[15]

After the collapse, Icelandic taxpayers had to bail out the Central Bank of Iceland with a 270 billion ISK capital injection (about USD 2.2 billion at the time) due to the losses resulting from the inadequate quality of collateral accepted in the short-term lending facilities from the three big banks, as well as from Icebank.[16] Furthermore, at the end of 2008, the Central Bank of Iceland wrote off an additional 70 billion ISK (about USD 570 million) due to realized losses.[17] Needless to say, the total bill, over USD 2.7 billion just to save the Central Bank, is a hefty price for a nation of just 320,000.

Chapter 9

Playing Tricks on the European Central Bank

Love Letters Reach the ECB

In early 2008, the three banks weren't just experiencing lack of liquidity in Iceland; they also lacked foreign currency, as well as assets to pledge as collateral. Through their subsidiaries in Luxembourg, the banks had access to collateralized lending of the European Central Bank (ECB), the so-called main refinance operations, which are short-term loans, usually for a week.

Imitating what they had heard was common practice among European bankers, and had successfully pulled off in their domestic market against the Central Bank of Iceland, they issued a fresh 500 million euro bond instrument each, essentially new love letters but this time denominated in euros. As before, they swapped the bonds with a rival Icelandic bank and turned to the ECB to pledge these issues, mixed with others, as collateral to get short-term loans from the ECB (Figure 9.1).[1]

No real investor had bought the issues, and the banks certainly hadn't come up with the cash to buy them beforehand from one another. In effect, therefore, they were printing money out of the European Central Bank.[2]

During the Special Investigation Commission (SIC) interrogation, Hreidar Mar Sigurdsson, CEO of Kaupthing, claimed that the three banks had jointly decided on this approach of issuing fresh bond instruments to swap among themselves as collateral into central banks (Figure 9.2). He also stated that they had gotten the idea from Europe where it was common practice among banks to use short-term collateral lending operations of the European Central Bank for funding.[3]

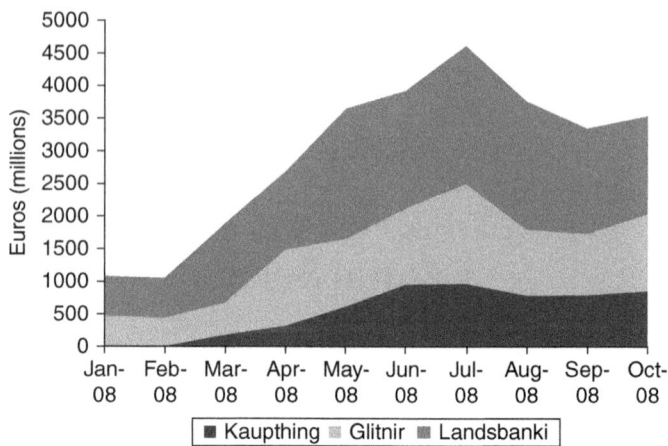

Figure 9.1   Collateralized lending of the ECB to Kaupthing, Glitnir, and Landsbanki

Source: Kaupthing bank hf., Glitnir bank hf. and Landsbanki Islands hf., SIC Report, Figure 57, Chapter 7, Volume 2, p. 46.

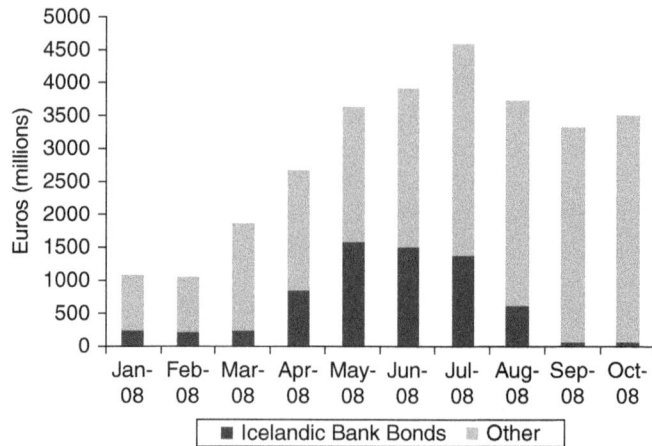

Figure 9.2   Icelandic bank bonds as collateral with the ECB

Source: Kaupthing bank hf., Glitnir bank hf. and Landsbanki Islands hf., SIC Report, Figure 61, Chapter 7, Volume 2, p. 48.

Refinancing Operations at the ECB through the BCL

From the start of the financial crisis in 2007, the ECB held its refinancing operations steady at 400–500 billion euros, except for a one-month spike in long-term refinancing in January 2008.[4] Once Lehman Brothers fell in September 2008, however, the ECB increased its "refinancing operations" sharply, going from 500 billion euros to 900 billion euros in 60 days (Figure 9.3).[5]

Refinancing operations at the Banque Centrale du Luxembourg (BCL) varied a bit more. For the most part, however, they stayed between 30 and 40 billion euros during this period, except for a spike in August 2008 (Figure 9.4).[6]

Refinancing operations for the Icelandic banks for the same period, however, look quite different. Using their Luxembourg subsidiaries, the Icelandic banks increased their refinancing from the ECB through the BCL from a modest 1 billion euros at the beginning of 2008 to 4.6 billion euros just half a year later.[7]

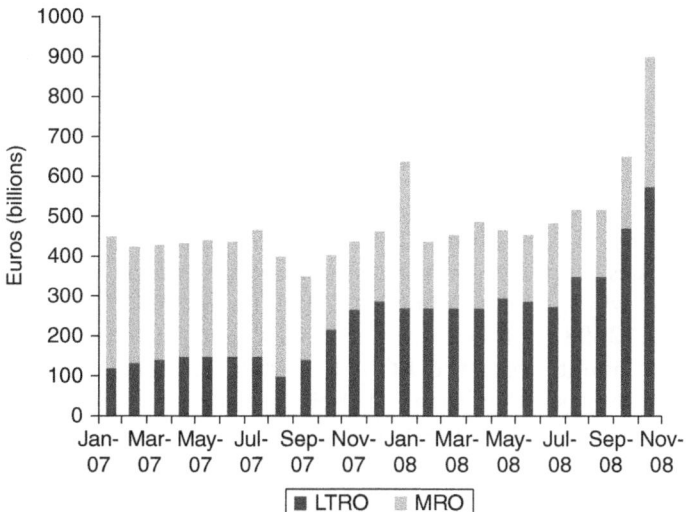

MRO (Main Refinancing Operations): Short term secured loans with one week maturity. LTRO (Long Term Refinancing Operations): Secured loans with maturity of at least 3 months.

Figure 9.3 Collateralized lending of the European Central Bank (ECB)

Source: ECB, h_p://www.ecb.int/mopo/implement/omo/html/ top_historLTROMRO.

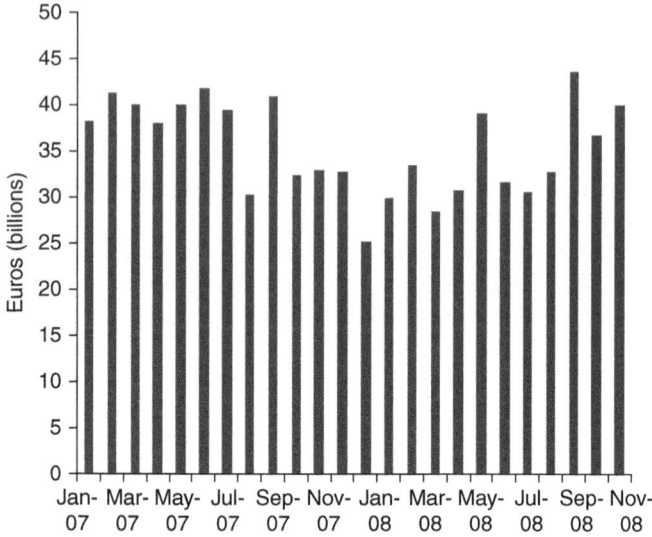

Figure 9.4   Collateralized lending of the Banque Centrale du Luxembourg (BCL)

Source: BCL "Financial statement of the Banque Centrale du Luxembourg", h_p://www.bcl.lu/
en/sta_s_cs/series/01_Mon_Pol_Stat/index.html -document:01_02_Tables.xls,SIC Report,
Figure 56, Chap.

Details of the ECB Love Letters

Bond issues based on the ECB love letters were among the raw data received by the SIC from Glitnir during the investigation.[8] These bond issues reveal the details of the increased borrowing from the ECB and why it started falling in the middle of 2008.

Before 2008, both Glitnir and Landsbanki had borrowed substantial amounts from the ECB, but while, because of the pressing need for cash, Landsbanki had pledged foreign bond issues that were supposed to be kept as assets against the deposit liabilities of its Icesave accounts, Glitnir had almost exclusively pledged securities in Landsbanki.[9]

On March 20 and 27, 2008, Glitnir issued two bonds for 750 million euros in total (500 and 250). Landsbanki borrowed the 500 million euro bond in exchange for cash collateral, and Kaupthing borrowed the 250 million euro bond in exchange for other collateral. By the end of March, Landsbanki's subsidiary in Luxembourg had pledged the 500 million euro bond to the ECB for financing.[10]

On April 2, 2008, Kaupthing issued three bonds totaling 500 million euros. All three also ended up with Landsbanki in Luxembourg, which in turn used them as collateral with the ECB.

Landsbanki also issued a 500 million euro bond on April 2, of which Kaupthing bought 425 million euros, which it used as collateral with the ECB later that month.[11]

While the banks were swapping these love letters, CDS spreads on the banks in the market were between 600 and 950 basis points. The love letters issued by the banks to each other, however, carried the amazingly low interest rates of 275 to 350 basis points above LIBOR.[12]

On April 15, 2008, apparently unaware of the true nature of these transactions, the Central Bank of Iceland, in its dealings with other central banks in Scandinavia, pointed to these favorable terms as an argument to convince their Scandinavian colleagues that the CDS spreads in the market were not depicting the true cost of funding of the Icelandic banks.[13]

It would, of course, have been more appropriate to consider a different bond issue for that purpose. One relevant example could have been the bond that Kaupthing issued through Deutsche Bank a little earlier, on March 10, 2008, for 775 million US dollars, with a premium of 607 basis points, just 65 basis points below the CDS quote that day.[14]

ECB Reacts to the Love Letters

From early February until the end of April, 2008, collateralized lending from the ECB to the Icelandic banks increased by 2.5 billion euros. This, of course, did not go unnoticed at the ECB.[15]

On Friday, April 25, at around 2 p.m., the governor of the European Central Bank, Jean-Claude Trichet, called the governor of the Central Bank of Iceland, David Oddsson. After the call, Oddsson immediately called a meeting at 3 p.m. with FME director Jonas Fr. Jonsson; Sigurjon Arnason, CEO of Landsbanki; Larus Welding, CEO of Glitnir; and Sigurdur Einarsson, Chairman of Kaupthing. Oddsson also brought deputy governor of the Central Bank Ingimundur Fridriksson; Jon Sigurgeirsson, economist from the Central Bank; Sturla Palsson, director of Market Operations at the Central Bank; and Tryggvi Palsson, director of Financial Stability.[16]

According to the meeting minutes, Oddsson informed the group that the purpose of the meeting was to discuss the phone call from ECB governor, Jean-Claude Trichet, who had been quite upset, even somewhat angry on the phone.[17] Trichet had explained that the Icelandic banks had borrowed almost 4 billion euros through the BCL and that some of the bonds pledged as collateral were "abnormal, artificial."[18] Trichet was therefore requesting a meeting on Monday, April 28, with representatives from the Icelandic banks, the Central Bank of Iceland, and the Icelandic financial supervisory authority (FME).

With the bankers as well as the supervisors present at the meeting, Oddsson expressed his concern for the effect a meeting with Trichet would have on upcoming currency swap contracts with the Scandinavian countries. FME director Jonsson commented that although he didn't know the rules of the ECB, he would assume that the banks were operating "within the formal rules of the ECB."[19] Sturla Palsson, director of Market Operations, said that he didn't see "what [was] artificial." The Icelandic bankers then explained their side of the issue.[20]

The chairman of Kaupthing, Sigurdur Einarsson, said that Kaupthing was using the bonds from Glitnir as collateral and added that they were about to pledge a bond from Landsbanki in the amount of 425 million euros. According to data obtained by the SIC, Kaupthing had already pledged the bond to the ECB at the time of the meeting.[21]

Sigurjon Arnason, CEO of Landsbanki, stated that Landsbanki had "higher amounts for sure."[22] The SIC found that Landsbanki had already pledged Glitnir bonds in the amount of 500 million euros and Kaupthing bonds in the amount of 580 million euros through Landsbanki Luxembourg.[23]

Larus Welding, CEO of Glitnir, stated that Glitnir had pledged bonds in the amount of 600 million euros via Luxembourg, including a 100 million euro bond from Kaupthing and a 235 million euro bond from Landsbanki.[24]

During the meeting, Governor Oddsson was interrupted when he received a phone call from Yves Mersch, governor of the BCL. When he returned, he informed the meeting that he had just told his colleague in Luxembourg that there was no crisis.[25]

Yves Mersch was concerned, however, about the amount of loans going to the Icelandic banks. They were already carrying 10 percent of all BCL loans, while constituting only 1.7 percent of the banking system in Luxembourg.[26]

On Monday, April 28, 2008, Sturla Palsson, director of Market Operations at the Central Bank of Iceland, attended the meeting in Luxembourg with representatives from the BCL, representatives from the Icelandic banks, and a representative from the Icelandic financial supervisory authority. According to a memo from Deputy Governor Ingimundur Fridriksson of the Central Bank of Iceland, they reached an agreement as to how much of Icelandic bank bonds could be pledged to the ECB, or 25%.[27]

According to the data obtained by the SIC, the banks exceeded the limit on May 1, 2008, when the love letter bonds reached 43.9 percent of the Icelandic bank bonds pledged as collateral with the ECB through the BCL.[28] From then on, the ratio kept falling, indicating they had found "better" assets to pledge.

BCL Gets Tough

At the end of June, 2008, Governor Oddsson attended a meeting of central bank governors in Basel, Switzerland. During the meeting, he met Yves Mersch in person for the first time. Oddsson described his encounter with Mersch as follows: "I hadn't met him before, but when we were introduced and I had just greeted him with some niceties—beautiful weather here in Basel, or something—then he simply says: 'Your banking system—so-called—is in a lot of trouble.'"[29]

Later that evening, Oddsson tried to get an explanation of the governor's comments. Oddsson finally understood that "he thought that the Icelandic banking system was on the highway to destruction and stood no chance, a conclusion that he drew from how the banks were trying to get money out of the ECB through Luxembourg."[30]

The next day, Governor Oddsson attended a meeting with Governor Mersch and their Scandinavian colleagues. During the meeting, they decided that Yves Mersch would come to Iceland a few days later. Oddsson explained to the SIC: "This was quite remarkable, and widely discussed in this country, among bankers and politicians alike, that things had become very difficult for the Icelandic banks, since they only had access to ISK through the Central Bank of Iceland, but had no access to any euros, and it was confirmed that they had already received up to 5 billion euros [from the ECB] and.... I knew nothing of this."[31]

On July 4, 2008, Yves Mersch attended a meeting at the Central Bank of Iceland, along with Nicolas Weber, the head of short-term facilities at the BCL, and Frank Bisdorff, a representative of the Financial Supervisory Authority in Luxembourg. On behalf of Icelandic authorities were David Oddsson, Ingimundur Fridriksson, Sturla Palsson, all from the Central Bank, and Jonas Fr. Jonsson, director general of the FME.[32]

According to a draft of the minutes of the meeting, Mersch led the discussion on behalf of the guests.[33] He did not try to sugarcoat his message and meaning when he described the BCL's concerns about extensive borrowing on the part of the Icelandic banks, which had grown even more in recent weeks. He also expressed his concern that the Icelandic banks were constantly the highest bidders in the euro system, and said that this had all started in January that same year at a slow pace, but had then grown rapidly during the spring.[34]

Total collateralized lending had now reached 3 billion euros, substantially more than the Central Bank of Iceland's foreign reserves, which caused grave concern at the BCL. He further stated that no formal decision had been taken in April about changes regarding access to short-term facilities since the Icelandic bankers claimed they had an abundance of assets to pledge to replace the love letters.[35]

In April, Mersch had indicated to the banks that it was acceptable to keep 25 percent of total collateral in the form of Icelandic bank bonds, but instead of decreasing the love letter exposure, the banks had increased it even further and borrowed even more.[36]

In addition to the existing collateral, the banks had brought in "structured products, perhaps with half a page of documentation on them, and no details on the underlying assets." Mersch added, "We have no proper information on this at all."[37] He continued to pour anger on the members of the meeting, saying that as of now the banks had received close to 5 billion euros from the ECB, and that Landsbanki was the highest bidder in the entire euro system.

Mersch then listed the borrowing activities of each bank with the BCL and said that this needed to be reversed within three weeks. He then demanded a funding plan from the banks,[38] saying, "I have an increasingly bad feeling there is no funding plan, worse collateral, increased eurosystem funding—I am not sure that this is just a liquidity situation—it may be something different [...] I have talked with our Nordic colleagues and know that this is not a feeling that I alone have—either the banks are not liquid or do not want to restructure."[39]

The Icelandic regulators already had plenty to consider from the meeting, but Mersch continued, saying that at this point in time nobody would accept any type of counterparty risk with the Icelandic banks, and that he would be working on minimizing the damage to BCL. "Our exposure is far beyond the capital of the lender of last resort," he said.[40]

Mersch then demanded that the banks reduce their collateralized borrowing by 25 percent immediately, the following week, or there would be repercussions. He added: "I am concerned that we do not have the presence of a lender of last resort."[41] Oddsson commented that it was important to reach an agreement on this, and Palsson added that it would be helpful if the banks could have more time to adjust. Mersch admitted that it would be difficult for the banks, but they would need to find 3 billion euros in the next six months. Jonas Fr. Jonsson of the FME then asked, "Have the banks breached the rules, or have they breached the spirit of the rules, or does it have to do with magnitude."[42] Mersch replied: "They respect the letter—but not the spirit...it is behavior that signals desperation—are they losing money somewhere?"[43]

Oddsson explained to the SIC that Mersch had been very candid at the meeting with the Icelandic bankers so that they would grasp the severity of the situation.[44] Oddsson also said that, when it was clear that the ECB would shut off its funding to the banks, "in [that] moment I think there was no turning back."[45]

Mersch had sent a letter to the banks before the meeting, dated June 30, outlining his plan that Icelandic bank bonds be brought below 25 percent before July 15, and then phased out as soon as possible.[46] He explained the rationale behind this action, that the Icelandic banks were too connected from a risk management perspective, and added, "In the event of difficulties encountered by any of the involved banks, there would be a significant likelihood that the other banks would be impacted."[47]

By the end of July, all Icelandic bank bonds, the notorious love letters, had been removed from the ECB by the Icelandic banks.[48] The "structured products," however, referred to by Mersch at the July 4 meeting, were still there, along with currency swap contracts between the banks themselves.

Pledging Icelandic Assets into ECB via Backdoor

After the July meeting with Governor Mersch, the Icelandic banks may have followed his instructions and reduced their borrowing from the ECB while also replacing the Icelandic bank bonds as collateral. The replacements, however, were mainly in the form of asset-backed securities that they structured from their loan books—assets, denominated in Icelandic kronas, that would be hard to sell for euros.[49]

At Landsbanki, these structures were formed through special purpose vehicles (SPVs) that received the names Avens and Betula. The securities were constructed under the consultancy of Credit Suisse, according to testimony to the SIC by one of Landsbanki's employees.[50] The variety of assets in a security amounting to 100 billion ISK, roughly USD 1.3 billion at the time, ranged from bonds issued by the Icelandic State Mortgage Fund to a bond issued by Raiffeisen-Boerenleenbank B.A. with maturity between February 2009 and June 2044.[51]

To change the cashflow of the bonds from ISK to euros so that they could pledge them against their euro loan from the ECB, Landsbanki had the SPV engage in a foreign exchange (FX) swap against Landsbanki, the parent company, where FX was supposed to be delivered by Landsbanki to the SPV at a three-month interval until the maturity of the last bond was realized in 2044, or until the loan from the ECB was paid up.[52]

Glitnir created similar SPVs, called Haf and Holt. Approximately one-third of the assets underlying their securities was denominated in ISK. Glitnir's parent company did the same type of FX swap with the SPVs, promising to deliver on the foreign currency at maturity.[53]

These securities, with ISK assets, remained on the books of the ECB as collateral until the Icelandic banks collapsed in October 2008. In May 2010, the Central Bank of Iceland bought these assets from the ECB at a hefty discount.[54]

Part III

Why Did the Bankers Do It?

Chapter 10

The Web of Ownership

Where Did the Money Go?

As early as 2004, market participants noticed the rapid growth of the balance sheets of the Icelandic banks. It was widely acknowledged that the banks were engaged in takeover activities as well as in establishing their branches abroad from the ground up. As it turned out, the year-over-year organic growth of the combined assets of the three banks—excluding all acquisition activities—was phenomenal, ranging from 36 to 66 percent.[1] External growth (reflecting acquisitions) was also intensive, especially in 2004–2005 (Table 10.1).[2]

Over the seven years from 2001 to 2008, the banks grew twentyfold, while bank credit to the private sector in Iceland grew from 100 percent of GDP to 500 percent.[3] Those numbers are so extraordinary that they are hard for even the most experienced economists to grasp.

Imagine what would happen if, in the next two years or so (about 22 months), the US economy were to receive a cash infusion of 15 trillion dollars ($1 \times$ GDP), with the money distributed by leaving a check in each homeowner's mailbox, quite a large check, about $120,000 to $140,000 per household, free to spend with no strings attached. What if this process were repeated two or three times over the next 4–6 years? What would you see happening?

While this scenario provides a rough idea of what happened in Iceland during those years, as far as the magnitude of capital inflows, the money didn't go into every homeowner's mailbox. It went all over Icelandic society and abroad, to individuals, firms, and the public sector. It left valuable assets in some places, and destruction in others.[4] Most importantly, however, the Special Investigation Commission (SIC) discovered that approximately half of the money went into a

Table 10.1   Year-end assets and organic growth (million ISK), sum of the three banks

Year	2003	2004	2005	2006	2007	2008
Total Assets (billion ISK)	1,451	2,946	5,419	8,475	11,354	14,437
Acquisitions (billion ISK)		797	726	0	58	0
Asset Growth Rate (%)		103	83.9	56.4	34.0	27.2
Organic Growth (billion ISK)		713	1949	1988	3052	–219
Organic Growth (%)		51.6	66.1	36.1	36.4	–1.9
Real Organic Growth (%)		43.5	59.5	27.2	28.8	–10.0

Source: SIC Report, Vol. 7. Chapter 21, p. 91, and Flannery, Mark, 2009, *Iceland's Failed Banks: A Post-Mortem*, SIC Report, Vol. 9, (Reykjavik: Special Investigation Commission), Appendix 3.

cobweb of interrelated firms (see the front cover diagram, depicting cross-ownership among large firms in Iceland in 2007), many of which seem to have been set up specifically to disguise true ownership. One of the first tasks of the SIC was therefore to untangle this web of ownership.

Assembling the Loan Books

Given its vast data privileges, and the manageable size of the Icelandic economy, the SIC set up a data warehouse including monthly observations of all loans extended by the parent companies of the three banks during 2004–2008.

Owing to poor data quality at the banks, with background variables and "loan terms" often not included in the banks' databases, the SIC had to rely on paper documents to fill in the gaps. Documentation of loan agreements and collateral was often of poor quality as well. This data deficiency made it difficult to answer some important questions with absolute certainty.[5] Fortunately, however, the SIC was able to use the features of the Icelandic social-security-number system to categorize and describe the loan portfolios of the banks to an great extent, beyond what banks are normally able to do themselves.

The SIC found that, by 2007, 60 percent of the combined loan books of the parent companies of the banks was extended to holding companies in Iceland or to foreign entities.[6] After determining who was behind those foreign entities, the SIC concluded that many of them were also holding companies. Thus the major portion of the loan books of the banks was extended to holding companies. But in addition, many of the foreign entities were not strictly foreign with respect to Iceland, and therefore not entirely independent of ISK risk.

Roughly 50 percent of the loans to customers of Kaupthing were on the books of the parent company, as were 73 percent of the loans to customers of Glitnir, and 83 percent of the loans to customers of Landsbanki, respectively. The remaining percentages were on the books of the numerous numerous subsidiaries abroad.[7]

The SIC didn't have the same data privileges abroad, and thus could not engage in as extensive data analysis of the loan books of the banks' subsidiaries as it did in the case of the parent companies in Iceland. It did, however, receive snapshots of the loan books of all subsidiaries of Kaupthing. And through excellent cooperation with authorities in Luxembourg, the SIC received a regulatory overview of the loan books of the subsidiaries of all three banks there, assembled by KPMG and PriceWaterhouseCoopers, as well as snapshots of the largest exposures in the loan books.[8]

Throughout the expansionary period, bankers and government officials alike claimed that the banks' robust growth was mostly taking place abroad, that is, independent of Iceland-related risk, and therefore that it was pure diversification. This was the main excuse put forth when the banks were scrutinized, and subsequently criticized, by outside analysts. The SIC therefore needed to verify whether the statement was true.

Although the SIC would have needed full access to the loan books of all subsidiaries of the banks to fully verify the facts, the structure of the loan books and data points revealed by cooperative authorities abroad showed that the credit risk of the subsidiaries was, to a large extent, dependent on Iceland's economy.[9]

In a report to the Luxembourg financial surveillance authority (Commission de Surveillance du Secteur Financier), KPMG noted especially that the extensive collateral underlying the Kaupthing loan book in Luxembourg was mostly shares listed in Iceland.[10] A majority of investments funded by the subsidiaries in Luxembourg were located in Iceland; or the collateral was Icelandic; or the borrower was an Icelandic citizen; or the borrower was a legal entity owned by Icelanders. In many cases, the parent company in Iceland guaranteed the loans extended by the banks' subsidiaries to holding companies abroad.[11]

Describing the rapid growth of the Icelandic banks as pure diversification was thus untrue. Not only was more than half of the lending portfolios of the parent companies directly subject to Icelandic risk, but in addition so was a large part of their subsidiaries abroad.[12]

Excessive Leverage and Pyramid Schemes to Circumvent Legal Constraints

Given the small population of Iceland, only 320,000 inhabitants, it was an extraordinary accomplishment to extend credit of more than four times Iceland's GDP, most of it going out over only four years.

The SIC needed to understand how it was possible to extend so much credit into such a small system in such a short period of time. This question is especially interesting in light of the legal constraints, which allowed for only 25 percent of the equity base of each bank to be exposed to related parties.

The answer lies in the cobweb of thousands of interrelated firms, mainly special purpose vehicles (SPVs), which often had little or next to no equity, but sizeable assets and a matching liability in the form of bank credit. The answer also lies in the inability of the legal profession in Iceland—attorneys, regulators, and judges alike—to pierce through the corporate veil, that is, to identify when an SPV was being set up simply and purposefully to disguise ownership and circumvent regulation. This inability, which is by no means limited to Iceland, allowed this cobweb of firms to grow untreated, and ultimately to bring down the Icelandic banking system.

The number of limited liability companies in Iceland grew 50 percent during 2003–2007, from 20,378 to 30,755. Roughly one out of seven limited liability companies did not have a designated owner listed in the enterprise directory, or had "unexplained ownership," as reported in Appendix 2 to the SIC report by Bjarnadottir and Hansen (2010).[13] Moreover, 91 of those companies were in 100 percent ownership of themselves (Figure 10.1).[14] This is clearly in breach of the legal code, since no company can hold, as an asset, more than 10 percent of its shares, that is, shares are by definition a liability of each firm, a debt the company owes its owner.

After extracting the entire enterprise registry in Iceland, Margret Bjarnadottir, PhD in Operational Research, and her coauthor, Gudmundur Hansen, contractors of the SIC, constructed Figure 10.2 with the aid of network analysis. It shows how large firms in Iceland were connected through ownership in one another. Each node in the figure represents a firm with a balance sheet in excess of 500 million

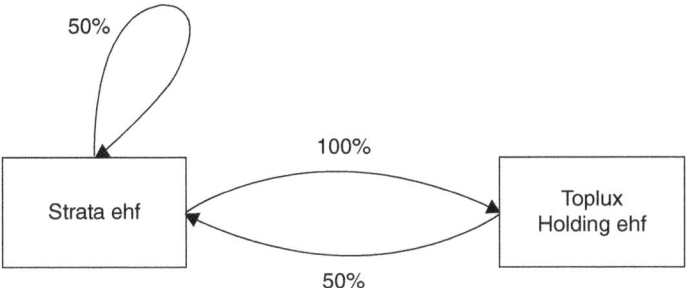

Figure 10.1 Example of cross-ownership structure of Icelandic firms in 2008

Source: Icelandic Enterprise Registry, Bjarnadottir and Hansen, 2010, *Investigation into the Cross Ownership and Bank Credit to Related Parties*. (Report of the Special Investigation Commission (SIC), Vol. 9. Appendix 2, p. 74. [Title in Icelandic: Rannsókn á krosseignartengslum og útlánum bankanna til tengdra aðila] Reykavik: Special Investigation Commission).

ISK (5–6 million USD). At year-end 2007, 1,307 such firms were registered, of which 816 were connected through ownership in one another to some degree. The largest companies—the major nodes identified in the figure—were Glitnir, Landsbanki, Kaupthing, Exista Investment Company, and Straumur Investment Bank.[15]

It is quite difficult to identify distinct business groups only by looking at Figure 10.2, but Figure 10.3 shows the result when a 10 percent minimum ownership filter has been applied, leaving 453 cross-owned firms.

One of the discoveries of Bjarnadottir and Hansen was the existence of business entities in circular ownership, where firm A owned firm B, which owned firm C, which owned firm A. Thus no identified individual was behind the ownership of these firms. A prime example reported by the SIC is depicted in Figure 10.1, where Strata ehf. (owns Toplux Holding ehf. (equivalent to English LLC or American Inc.)), which in turn owns 50 percent in Strata ehf., while Strata ehf. owns 50 percent in itself.[16] In many cases—utilizing qualitative information from loan applications or minutes of meetings of banks' credit committees—the SIC managed to fill in the gaps in the registration of the Icelandic Enterprise Registry.

Icelandic law left much room for interpretation as to what could be considered as "related parties," hence the definitions used by the banks varied substantially.[17] While Glitnir and Landsbanki considered the grocery store chain Hagkaup to be a related party to business tycoon Jon Asgeir Johannesson—who, through his ownership in the holding company Baugur Group, was one of the main shareholders of Hagkaup—Kaupthing did not consider Hagkaup to be a

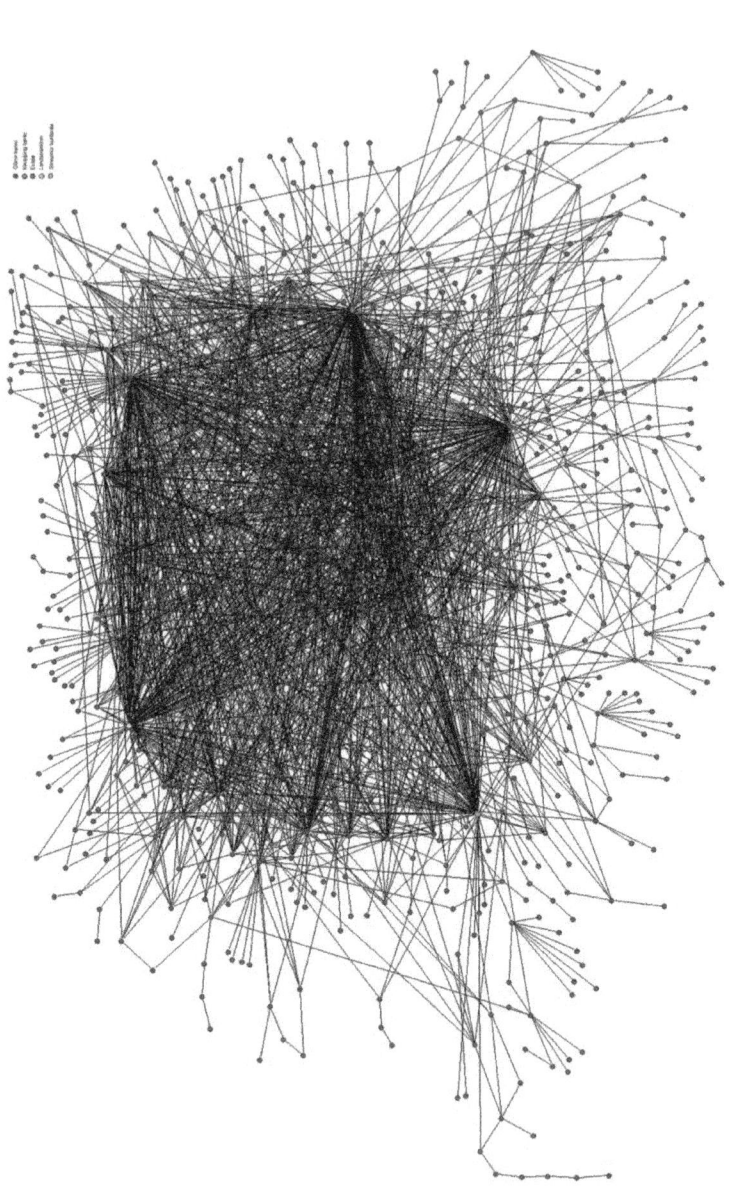

Figure 10.2 Cross-ownership structure of 1,307 firms in Iceland with balance sheet larger than USD 6 million (500 million ISK) in 2008

Note: Major nodes are, clockwise from 11'oclock, Landsbanki, Glitnir, Kaupthing, Exista Investment Firm, and Straumur Investment Bank.

Source: Bjarnadottir and Hansen, 2010, *Investigation into the Cross Ownership and Bank Credit to Related Parties*. (Report of the Special Investigation Commission (SIC), Vol. 9. Appendix 2, Figure 6. [Title in Icelandic: Rannsókn á krosseignartengslum og útlánum bankanna til tengdra aðila] Reykjavik: Special Investigation Commission).

Figure 10.3 Cross-ownership structure of 453 firms in Iceland with balance sheet larger than USD 6 million (500 million ISK) in 2008

Note: Filtered for ownership larger than 10%.

Source: Bjarnadóttir and Hansen, 2010, *Investigation into the Cross Ownership and Bank Credit to Related Parties.* (Report of the Special Investigation Commission (SIC), Vol. 9. Appendix 2, Figure 7. [Title in Icelandic: Rannsókn á krosseignartengslum og útlánum bankanna til tengdra aðila] Reykjavík: Special Investigation Commission).

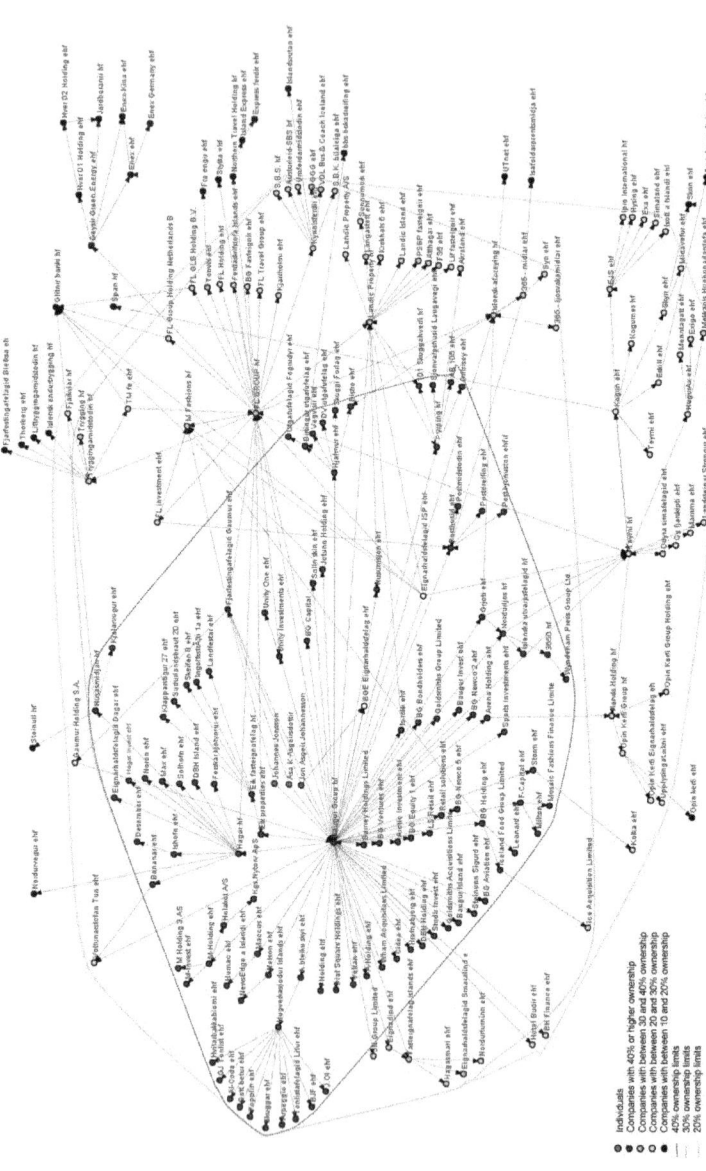

Figure 10.4 Cross-ownership structure of Baugur Group and related parties (184 firms)

Source: Bjarnadottir and Hansen, 2010, *Investigation into the Cross Ownership and Bank Credit to Related Parties.* (Report of the Special Investigation Commission (SIC), Vol. 9, Appendix 2, Figure 23. [Title in Icelandic: Rannsókn á krosseignartengslum og útlánum bankanna til tengdra aðila] Reykjavík: Special Investigation Commission).

related party to Johannesson.[18] Such legal ambiguities may provide lawyers much appreciated legal running room, but they are a supervisor's nightmare.

According to a standard rule of thumb assigned by the SIC team to identify related parties,[19] Johannesson's Baugur Group and related parties included 184 firms, the largest business group identified. Even with a 20 percent ownership filter applied, Johaannesson—the largest shareholder in Baugur Group—had 75 firms related to him Figure 10.4. Finnur Ingolfsson, a former Minister of Commerce, had the sixth largest group with 48 firms related to him.[20]

Those who have the connections and opportunities to exploit legal ambiguities may have great incentive to do so, given the expected benefits one can extract, as this story shows. On the other hand, a supervisor—who should have incentive to uphold the law—may not have the adequate resources to do so, given the opponent.

The dynamic nature of ownership and equity bases doesn't make the task of the supervisor any easier; a firm could be in compliance with the law on a credit ceiling of 25 percent of equity-base extended to related parties on Wednesday, but in breach of it on Friday. The supervisory authority thus needs daily updates to its data.

The Largest Borrowers

Having identified the business groups that best matched the legal term "related parties," the SIC merged the loan book dataset with the business groups. Using monthly loan data, the SIC could then identify when the related parties were in breach of the law of 25 percent maximum exposure.[21]

Perhaps not surprisingly, a common lending pattern appeared, supporting the famous hypothesis of William C. Black that "the best way to rob a bank is to own one." The largest borrowers from the Icelandic banks were their largest owners.[22]

Chapter 11

Tunneling Money through Related-Party Lending

What Did They Do with the Money?

Every bank has a certain level of moral hazard. When banks take on big risks, shareholders and employees, who are incentivized through cash bonuses, benefit from the if the results are positive. If market circumstances are unfavorable—even if fraudulent behavior has been practiced within the bank—the shareholder only bears part of the loss. The rest of the loss from the risk taking is borne by creditors, bondholders, uninsured deposit holders. In the case of systemically important institutions it is the public that picks up the tab. This is commonly referred to as privatization of gains and socialization of losses.[1]

Creditors and the state only bear costs if the loss of the bank is so much that the public doesn't cover it. If the bank's equity is very low relative to total assets, socialization of losses becomes more likely, especially if investments and lending practices are marked by excessive risk.[2] Admati and Hellwig's argument is thus sound, that banks—especially those that are systemically important—should be required to use a funding mix that includes much more equity than is currently common, typically only a capital adequacy ratio of 8–10 percent, or even less.[3]

To assess banks' risk-taking, one must look at individual large exposures and assess their nature and how much downside risk could be realized by the bank due to those exposures. In addition, one must assess whether any particular loss would affect other assets in the loan portfolio.

Measuring correlation in rates of return of an asset portfolio is absolutely key in successful risk assessment, particularly correlation or probability of simultaneous losses on several assets.

Diversification, both on the lending side and on the funding side, is key to the healthy operation of a bank.[4] The fall of large banks has often been attributed to some sort of concentration of credit risk.

In a 1993 report, the US Federal Reserve identified three types of concentration of credit risk. First is an unusually high lending to an individual borrower, or related parties. Second is a large amount of credit risk that exists due to a large amount of credit extended against the same collateral, or same type of collateral, with identical features or quality. Third is sector concentration: a large amount of credit extended to the same type of borrowers, such as those who operate in the same sector, or those exposed to a common risk factor.[5]

The Special Investigation Commission (SIC) found that this 1993 description of the risks of concentration of credit also described the loan portfolios of the three Icelandic banks in the run-up to their demise 15 years later.[6]

As noted above, as the SIC untangled the ownership cobweb, it found that the biggest borrowers of the banks were often their own owners. In addition, the largest sector receiving credit from the banks was holding companies with similar collateral. These holding companies were also systemically exposed to the economic well-being of one and the same small island nation. This pattern varied a bit in levels among the three banks, but it was essentially the same pattern that appeared in all of them.

This pattern of behavior by the bank owners is akin to the legal embezzlement experienced in the Czech Republic after the privatization of state enterprises in the 1990s, which became known to the Czechs as "tunneling."[7] A formal description of this phenomenon was laid out in the widely cited paper "Tunneling," by Simon Johnson, Rafael La Porta, Florencio Lopez-de-Silanes, and Andrei Shleifer, published in the *American Economic Review* in 2000.[8]

Gutting Glitnir

Baugur Group and related parties were by far the biggest customers of all three Icelandic banks in the run-up to the collapse. By the end of 2007, they had borrowed 5.7 billion euros, or more than half of the combined equity base of the three banks—53 percent to be exact (Figure 11.1). This single conglomerate accounted for 11 percent of all loans extended by the parent companies of the three banks, not including loans from subsidiaries abroad.[9]

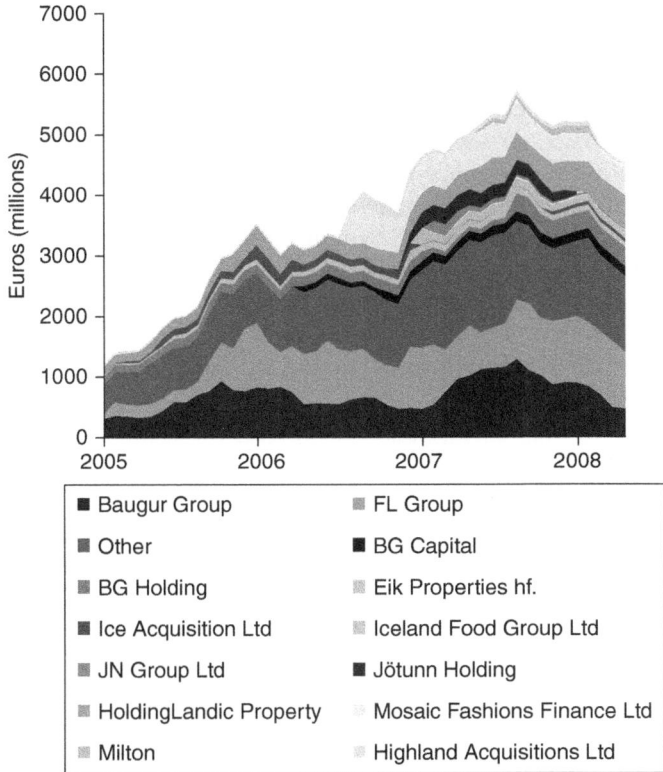

Figure 11.1 Total lending by the three banks to Baugur Group and related parties
Source: Kaupthing bank hf., Glitnir bank hf., and Landsbanki Islands hf., SIC Report, Figure 51, Chapter 8, Volume 2, p. 137.

In June 2007, after a power struggle that had started in, and several attempts to become controlling shareholder in one bank or another, Baugur Group (through ownership in FL Group) gained a controlling share in Glitnir. In the following three months, Gitnir's exposure to the Baugur Group and related parties went from 30 percent of its equity base to almost 90 percent (Figure 11.2).

According to the SIC's calculations (described above), as early as 2005, and continuously until the collapse of the banks, Baugur Group was in breach of legal provisions on large exposures of Glitnir (Figure 11.2), Kaupthing (Figure 11.3), and Landsbanki (Figure 11.4).[10]

From mid-2008, there is a large apparent decline in Gitnir's credit to Baugur and related parties (Figure 11.2), but this resulted from debt restructuring, not from loans being paid off. Baugur's most valuable asset, Hagar—which operates the largest grocery stores in Iceland, Bonus and Hagkaup—was moved from the balance sheet of Baugur to a special purpose vehicle called 1998 ehf. After the restructuring, 1998 ehf, and, therefore, Hagar, with Bonus and Hagkaup, were, technically, no longer a part of the Baugur Group and related parties, but instead became a subsidiary of Gaumur holding company, Baugur's parent company. This restructuring secured Kaupthing's access to solid collateral (Bonus and Hagkaup) for its bank's lending to Baugur, but at the expense of other creditors of Baugur, such as Glitnir.

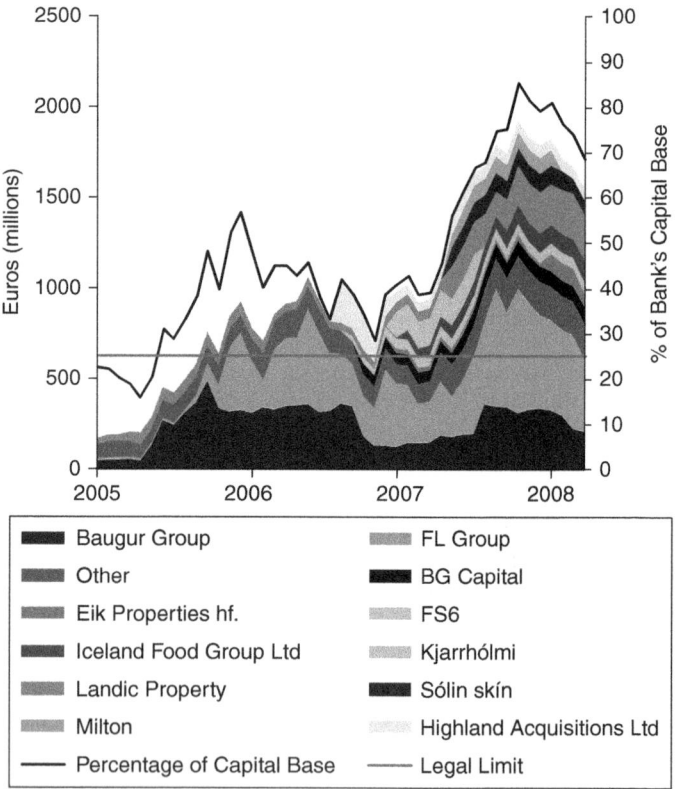

Figure 11.2   Total lending by Glitnir to Baugur Group and related parties
Source: Glitnir bank hf., SIC Report, Figure 52, Chapter 8, Volume 2, p. 137.

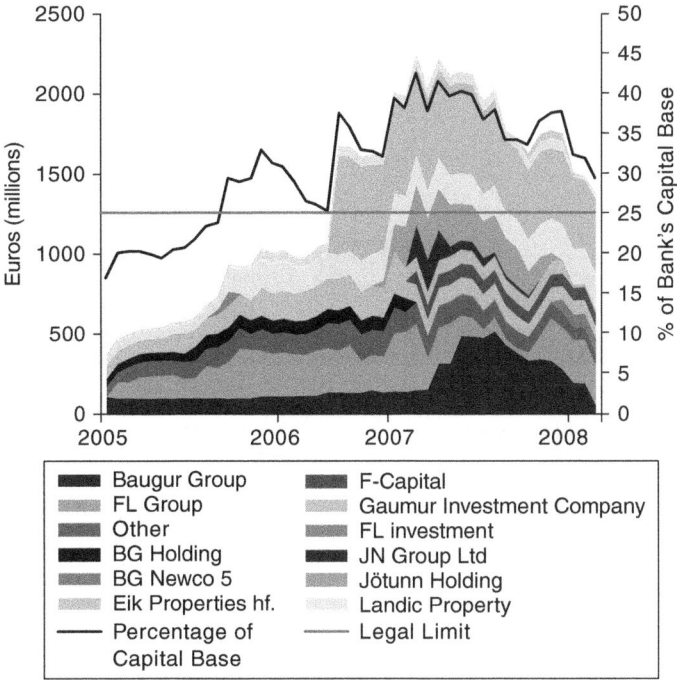

Figure 11.3 Total lending by Kaupthing to Baugur Group and related parties
Source: Kaupthing bank hf., SIC Report, Figure 53, Chapter 8, Volume 2, p. 137.

Incidentally, Fons ehf—Baugur's business partner in, among other things, controlling Glitnir from June 2007 onwards—had received little or no credit from Glitnir prior to that. In just the next three months, however, Fons received about 500 million euros in credit, 23 percent of Glitnir's equity base (Figure 11.5).

The story of Hagar's transfer from Baugur's balance sheet to its parent company Gaumur's via 1998 ehf. shows the kinds of challenge facing supervisors in trying to monitor large exposures of banks and keep track of whom the money is actually lent to. Who is the ultimate beneficiary, who are related parties? If bankers are to be able to maintain the health of loan portfolios, and if supervisors, through proper law enforcement of financiers, are to prevent contagion in the system if things go wrong, they all need to know how lending is connected and correlated among borrowers. The law, therefore, needs to be more explicit regarding definitions of related parties.

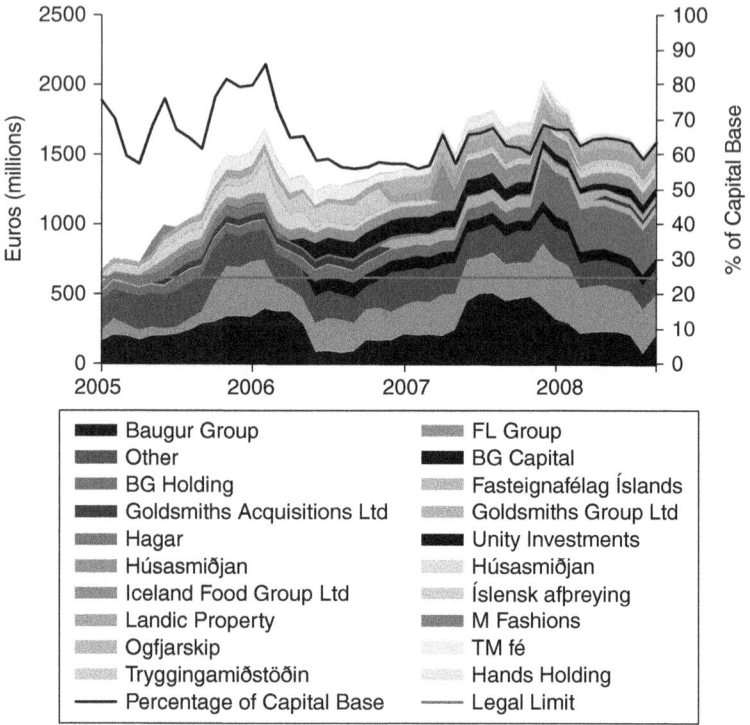

Figure 11.4 Total lending by Landsbanki to Baugur Group ehf. and related parties
Source: Landsbanki Islands hf., SIC Report, Figure 54, Chapter 8, Volume 2, p. 138.

The SIC mapped out the portfolio exposure of all three banks to each of the business groups it had identified at various ownership thresholds.[11] Figure 11.6 presents the loan exposure of each of the three banks to Baugur and related parties as defined at ownership thresholds from 5 to 55 percent. If an ownership threshold of 40 percent were used for determining related parties—instead of the 20 percent rule of thumb established by the SIC—each bank's exposure to the group was still in breach of the law on large exposure limits in at year-end 2007. However, a 40 percent ownership threshold is clearly too high since the law imposes mandatory takeover of listed firms by a shareholder who owns 40 percent of shares or more.[12]

Loaded with borrowed money from the three Icelandic banks, Baugur Group engaged in leveraged buys and buyouts of Britain's most famous retail companies, including the House of Fraser, Goldsmiths, Hamley's, Debenhams, Wittard of Chelsea, Karen Millen, and French

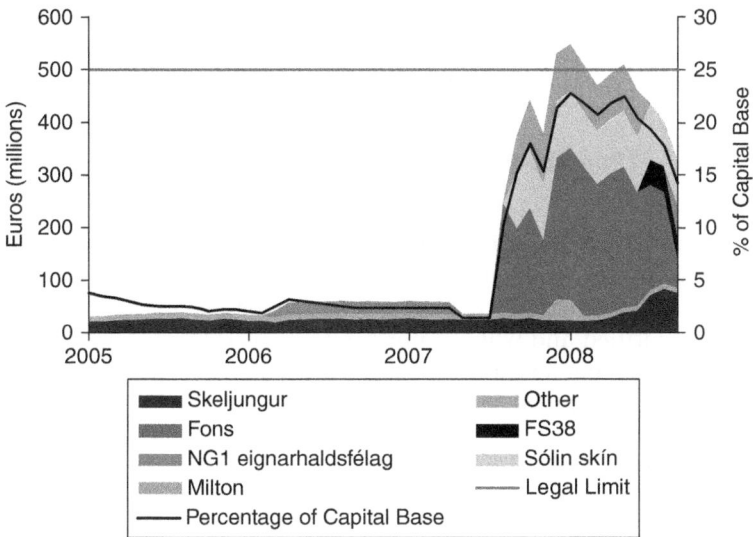

Figure 11.5 Total lending by Glitnir to Fons and related parties
Source: Glitnir bank hf., SIC Report, Figure 90, Chapter 8, Volume 2, p. 151.

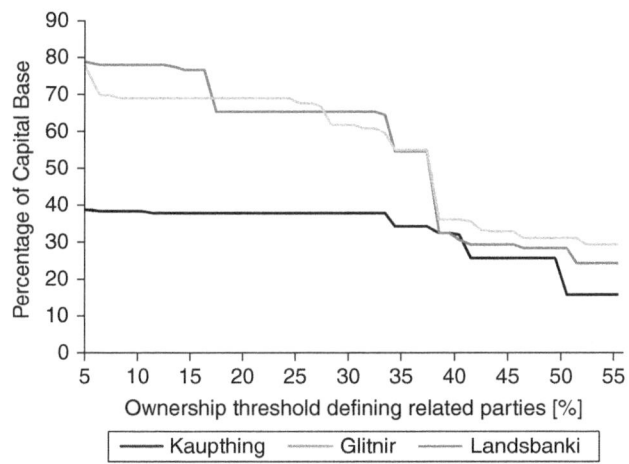

Figure 11.6 Total lending of the three banks to Baugur and related parties at year-end 2007 as percentage of capital base using ownership thresholds from 5–55%
Source: Director of Internal Revenue (RSK), Kaupthing bank hf., Glitnir bank hf., and Landsbanki hf., SIC Report, Figure 30, Appendix 2, Volume 9, p. 53.

Connection, to name a few. Baugur also took a stake in the most famous retail stores in Denmark, including Illum-Bolighus and Magasin du Nord.[13]

"Pseudo-person Abroad"—The Largest Dividend Recipient

The Icelandic Tax Authority gathers information on individual shareholders who receive dividends each year. According to tax records, dividends are sometimes paid out to individuals living abroad who are not identified and who do not pay taxes in Iceland. For the sake of record keeping, tax authorities record payments to such recipients under an assigned identification number with the designation "pseudo-person abroad" (Icelandic: gervimaður útlönd).

According to Icelandic tax records, pseudo-person abroad was the fifth largest dividend recipient from Iceland in 2007, seventh in 2008. The combined dividend payments received by pseudo-persons abroad amounted to 2 billion ISK (200 USD million) each year. In 2006, FL Group alone paid pseudo-persons abroad a total of 6 billion ISK (about 90 USD million) out of a total of 6.3 billion ISK in dividends paid out; in 2007, 7 billion ISK of 14.9 billion ISK.[14]

In 2007, Baugur Group was the single largest recipient of dividends receiving 10 billion ISK (USD 150 million) from its subsidiaries. On the other hand, its subsidiary, FL Group, was the largest payer, paying out 14 billion ISK (ISD 210 million) in dividends to its owners (including Baugur Group). Another subsidiary of Baugur Group, Baugur Holding ehf, paid 90 USD million (6.2 billion ISK) in dividends that year.[15] The largest individual shareholder of Baugur,[16] Jon Asgeir Johannesson was not among the largest dividend recipients, but his wife Ingibjorg Palmadottir, received about 9 USD million (600 million ISK) in dividend payments. According to tax records, Palmadottir was the third largest individual dividend recipient that year.[17]

Kaupthing and Landsbanki Looted?

Father and son, Bjorgolfur Gudmundsson and Bjorgolfur Thor Bjorgolfsson, along with their partner, Magnus Thorsteinsson, bought a 45.8 percent share in Landsbanki for USD 139 million during the privatization phase in 2003. During the next five years—before the bank collapsed—they received combined credit from Landsbanki's parent company of over 60 percent of the equity base of the bank, or about USD 1.7 billion (1.2 billion euros),[18] plus USD 450 million (320 million euros) from a Landsbanki subsidiary in Luxembourg.[19] During 2003–2008 they also received 4.3 billion ISK (USD 270 million) in dividends.[20, 21]

Neither the bank itself nor the SIC, according to the method used, considered the father and son to be "related parties." Hence, lending to the father was in consistent breach of the 25 percent exposure limit (Figure 11.7), while lending to the son just barely touched the red zone on September 30, 2008 (Figure 11.8), a week before the fall of the bank. The father later suffered bankruptcy, while the son avoided it by striking a deal with his creditors to restructure his debt.

While they were the controlling shareholders of Landsbanki, the father and son acquired many companies while being the controlling shareholders of Landsbanki, including the generic drug producer, Actavis; the largest newspaper in Iceland, *Morgunbladid*; the Bulgarian Telecommunications Company, BTC; and the shipping company, Eimskip, to name a few.[22]

From 2005 until the collapse of Kaupthing, the largest owner of Kaupthing, Exista, and related parties borrowed 25 to 30 percent

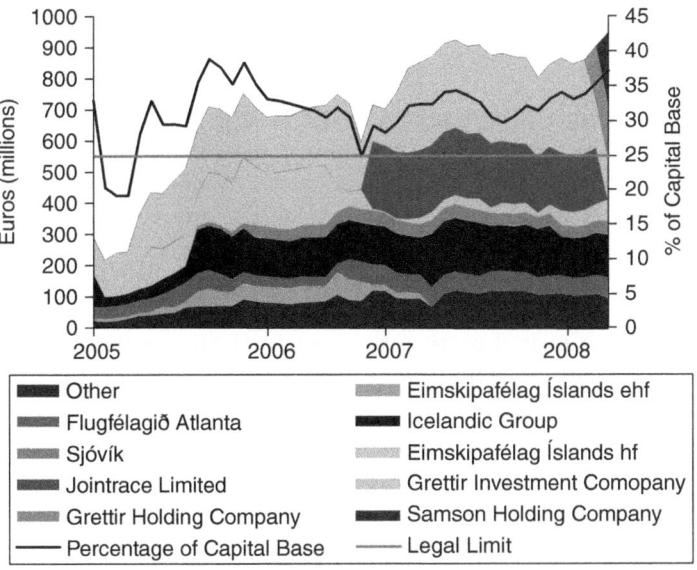

Figure 11.7   Total lending by Landsbanki to Bjorgolfur Gudmundsson related parties
Source: Landsbanki Islands hf., SIC Report, Figure 69, Chapter 8, Volume 2, p. 146.

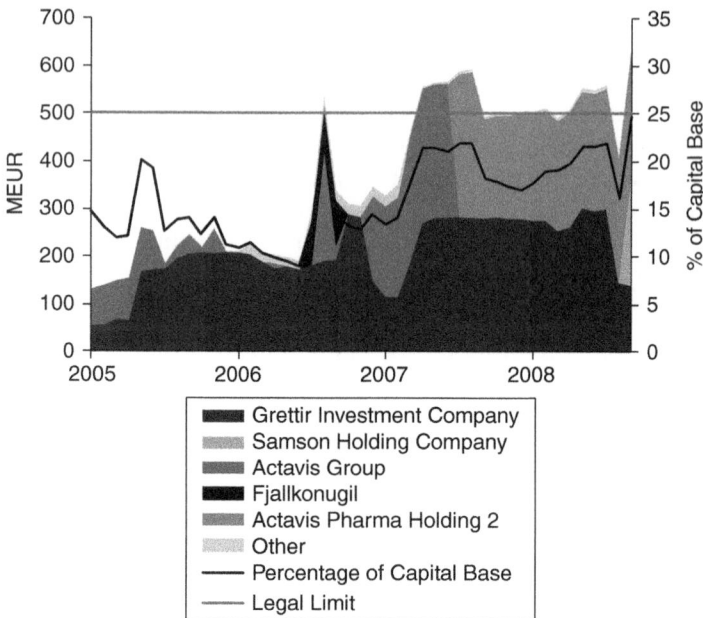

Figure 11.8   Total lending by Landsbanki to Bjorgolfur Thor Bjorgolfsson related parties

Source: Landsbanki Islands hf., SIC Report, Figure 64, Chapter 8, Volume 2, p. 145.

and 30 percent of the bank's Capital base (Figure 11.9). The second largest owner, Olafur Olafsson, through his shareholding in Kjalar and related parties, borrowed only a modest 18 percent of the bank's capital base (Figure 11.10). Olafur However, he had good credit with Glitnir, from which his firm, Kjalar, and related parties borrowed 350 million Euros or about 35 percent of the bank's capital base.[23]

Along with related parties, the Iranian/British real estate mogul Robert Tchenguiz—who was also on Exista's board of directors—was among the biggest clients of Kaupthing.[24] According to the SIC, Kaupthing's credit to Tchenguiz and related parties passed the legal limit of 25 percent of the bank's equity base in early 2008, reaching 2 billion euros before the bank collapsed (Figure 11.11). Including Kaupthing's Luxembourg lending to the Tchenguiz group, it's exposure reached 45 percent of the bank's capital base.

Much of the lending to Tchenguiz was to meet margin calls from financial services firms such as Dawnay Day; the American investment

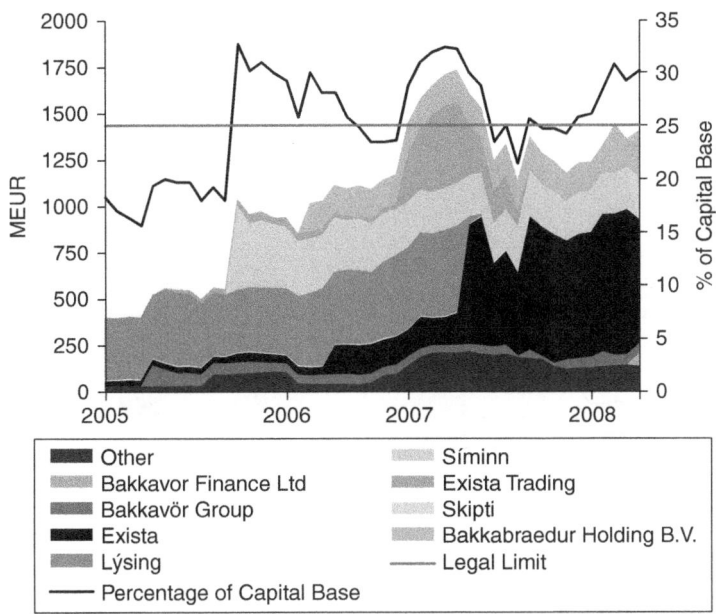

Figure 11.9 Total lending by Kaupthing to Exista and related parties
Source: Kaupthing bank hf., SIC Report, Figure 58, Chapter 8, Volume 2, p. 143.

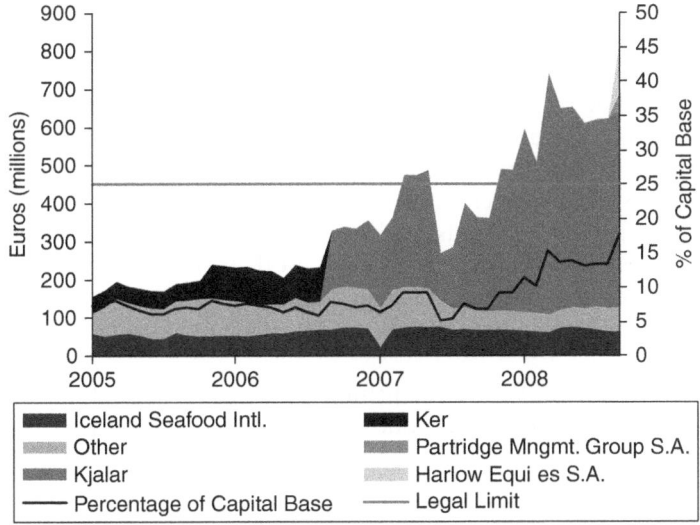

Figure 11.10 Total lending by Kaupthing to Olafur Olafsson related parties
Source: Kaupthing bank hf., SIC Report, Figure 87, Chapter 8, Volume 2, p. 150.

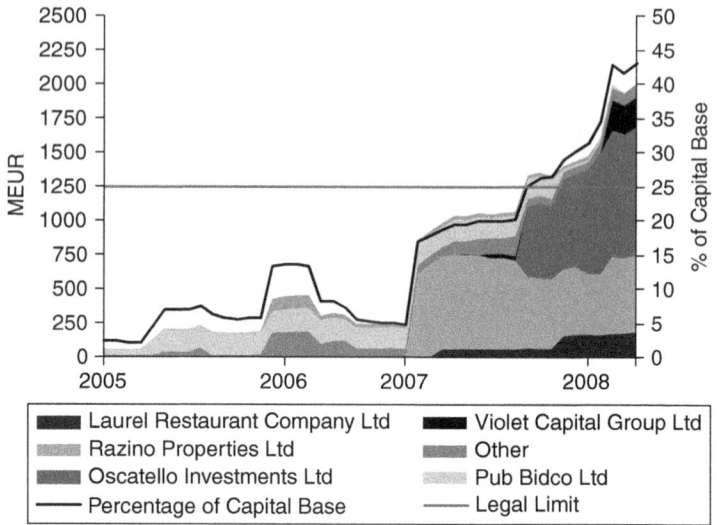

Figure 11.11   Total lending by Kaupthing to Robert Tchenquiz related parties
Source: Kaupthing bank hf., SIC Report, Figure 60, Chapter 8, Volume 2, p. 143.

bank, Morgan Stanley; and Kaupthing's subsidiary, Kaupthing, Singer, & Friedlander, which were all securing their position because of the the ever-decreasing value of collateral.[25]

Kaupthing's credit to Tchenguiz and related parties was largely in the form of overdraft, which stood at 600 million pounds (roughly 750 million euros and USD 1.2 billion at the time), when the bank collapsed.[26,27] Tchenguiz and related parties received these unsecured loans at just 2.75 percent above LIBOR when, according to credit default swap (CDS) spreads at the time, Kaupthing itself was experiencing terms of 4.2 percent above LIBOR.[28] This was contrary to practice with overdrafts, which generally carry high interest since there is no collateral, and no scheduled payments until the overdraft matures.

In February 2009, the Kaupthing estate sued the holding company Oscatello Investments, one of Tchenguiz's related parties, for the unpaid overdrafts. A year later, the company was liquidated, according to the *London Gazette*.[29]

For comparison, just the 2 billion euros (USD 2.8 billion) that Tchenguiz borrowed from Kaupthing in Iceland was not too far from the USD 3.2 billion net expenses incurred by the US Federal Reserve System to carry out its responsibilities in 2010.[30] In Icelandic terms, USD 2.8 billion would cover Iceland's entire law enforcement operation for over 16 years.[31]

Loan-Portfolio Quality Eroded

Analyzing the supply side of credit gives policy-makers and market speculators information on trends regarding how banks allocate credit to different sectors. This public information, mainly collected and distributed by central banks, gives a sense of the flow of funds, which sectors credit is being allocated to, and at what pace.

Central banks' monetary bulletins and scholarly articles thus can document adequately document the supply side of credit booms.[32] Given the level of confidentiality on bank credit, however, the demand side of credit remains less known. Scholars cannot get hold of detailed bank data, and therefore haven't been able to map out the demand side of credit booms in any detail.

Professor John Geanakoplos of Yale University has written on what he calls "leverage cycles" since 1997.[33] He points out something completely overlooked by standard economics textbooks. Credit is determined not only by interest rates, but also by the type of collateral the borrower can come up with to borrow against. Furthermore, the amount of credit extended is determined by the lender's appetite for risk and how much of the value of the collateral is leveraged.[34] Geanakoplos and others[35] have made the point that, as collateral requirements get looser, asset prices increase. Geanakoplos emphasizes that central banks should therefore manage leverage as they manage interest rates (discussed more in the next chapter).

It is somewhat surprising that, all this time, the scholarly community in economics has overlooked this factor while describing the general equilibrium of the economy. Some 400 years ago, although he wasn't studying monetary policy, Shakespeare recognized the importance of this point in the *Merchant of Venice*. No one remembers at what rate Shylock offered his loan to Antonio, but everyone remembers that he demanded a pound of Antonio's flesh as collateral, to be taken from wherever Shylock wanted.

This is yet another unique aspect of the SIC report. For the first time in modern financial history, the demand side of a credit boom has been meticulously documented and reported in detail. Policy-makers, central bankers and bank supervisors, on the other hand, had all the data privileges needed to assess the level of leverage and asset quality. Even the limited data provided to the public gave the ample reason for escalating oversight as loans to foreign entities doubled in just one year (Figures 11.12 and 11.13), increasing portfolio risk due to winner's curse. As entrant banks embark on a new market where competition is already high, the clients the new bank gains are likely to have been declined by incumbent banks, hence not trustworthy.[36]

Concurrently, the share of loan portfolios allocated to Icelandic operational firms took a sharp downturn, as investment banking activities rose. The banks entered the mortgage market with a force in 2004, lending up to 100 percent of the market value of houses. Such lending can only be categorized as very risky.

In April 2005, the Central Bank of Iceland began gathering information on the increasing amount of credit being allocated to Icelandic holding companies. Holding companies are particularly vulnerable since they have the sole purpose of owning shares in other firms. Lending to a holding company is therefore just like lending its operational firm a subordinated loan. If a firm owned by a holding company experiences operational difficulty, the creditors of the operational firm are first to be served out of the assets of the bankrupt firm. The shareholder, that is, the holding company, is a residual claimant, making the lender to the holding company also a residual

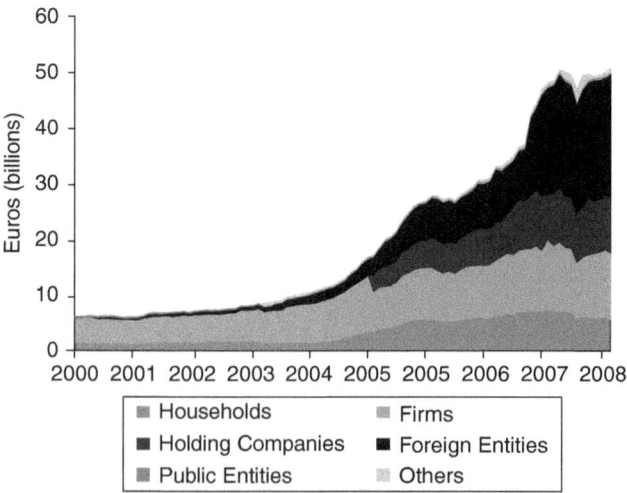

Figure 11.12 Lending by the three banks, by type of borrower

Source: Central Bank of Iceland, SIC Report, Figure 15, Chapter 8, Volume 2, p. 96.

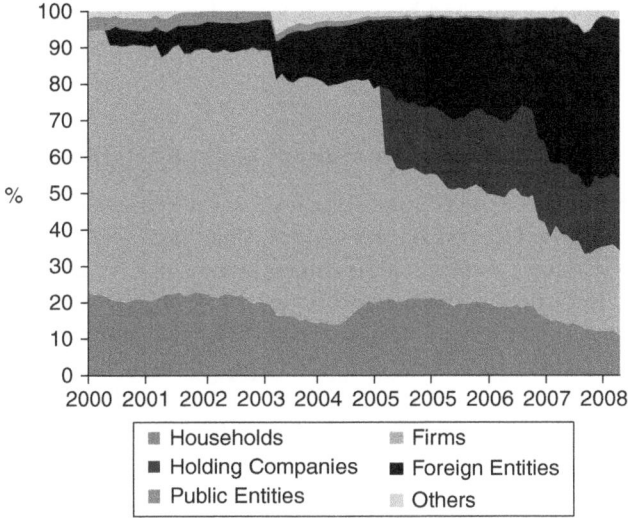

Figure 11.13 Percentage of total lending of the three banks' parent companies, by type of borrower

Source: Central Bank of Iceland, SIC Report, Figure 16, Chapter 8, Volume 2, p. 96.

claimant. Increased credit to holding companies—and to foreign entities, and for 100 home mortgages—should have robbed supervisors of their sleep.

As loans to foreign entities doubled after 2004, credit to holding companies and foreign entities became the largest portion of the banks' loan portfolios, almost 65%.

The SIC requested detailed information of the banks' loan portfolios, such as interest-rate terms, payment schedules, and in what currency the loans were extended. Two banks, Glitnir and Kaupthing, could not electronically deliver information on detailed lending terms of the quality requested, particularly on payment schedules of loans. Consequently, the SIC had to extrapolate payment schedules of the loan books of Glitnir and Kaupthing based on the data received from Landsbanki, which was the only bank that had adequate information systems and databases that could deliver information with the level of accuracy needed.[37]

Once the SIC had assembled loan portfolio data of all three banks, it was apparent that enormous risk had been building up in the Icelandic financial system during the four years leading up to the collapse, in terms of both refinancing and foreign exchange risk.

The majority of loans had been extended in foreign currency, and the largest part of each of the portfolios consisted of bullet (zero-coupon) loans.

Flowing in the Direction of Least Resistance

In an attempt to curb inflation, credit growth, and general economic overheating, the Central Bank of Iceland had kept ISK interest rates above 13 percent from late 2006 through the whole of 2007. In May 2008 it raised them further, to 15.5 percent. Consequently there was an incentive for lending in foreign currency. By the time the banks collapsed, 56 percent of Glitnir's total loan portfolio had been extended in foreign currency, as had been 68 percent of Landsbanki's and 72 percent of Kaupthing's.[38] Overall, even 24.7 percent of domestic loans to individuals had been extended in foreign currency, including 21.6 percent at Landsbanki and 17 percent at Kaupthing.[39, 40]

This foreign exchange imbalance of the banks, and the vast foreign exchange risk of individuals with no foreign currency revenues, were either ignored by the Central Bank. Even more surprisingly, those who were supposed to safeguard financial stability and the interests of the public made no demand for higher equity ratios to hedge against the increasing systemic risk (discussed in Chapter 16).

A Rolling Loan Never Incurs a Loss

In simple terms, a good banker would categorize borrowers as follows. First are borrowers who are able to pay off their loans with interest during the lifetime of the loan. Second are borrowers who are able to pay interest on the loan during the lifetime of the loan and can pay the principal back at maturity. But, according to SIC estimates, 50 percent of the borrowers of the three banks were in a third category, those who neither paid off their loan nor *any* interest during the lifetime of the loan. As alluded to above, According to the SIC estimate, 52–54 percent of the loan portfolios of the three banks was in the form of bullet (zero-coupon) loans.[41] At Landsbanki, up to 88 percent of the loans extended to holding companies were bullet loans (Figure 11.14).

With roughly half of the loan portfolios in the form of zero coupons, it was no wonder that the delinquent payments measured by the FME were at a historic low in the run-up to the crisis, between 0.03 percent and 0.33 percent of the total loan portfolio of the banks in January 2006, only up to 0.3–0.7 percent in October 2008.[42]

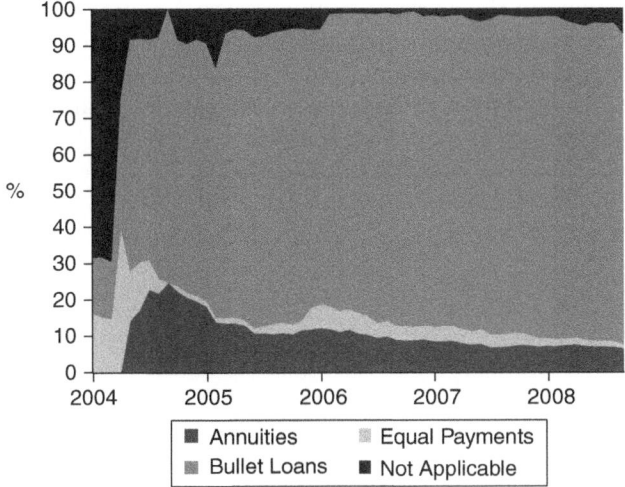

Figure 11.14 Percentage of total lending by Landsbanki's parent company to Icelandic holding companies, by installment arrangement

Source: Landsbanki Islands hf., SIC Report, Figure 31, Chapter 8, Volume 2, p. 101.

In its public reporting, the FME only collected information on delinquent payments in the system, that is, the sum of all payments that were 90 days overdue, not the traditional and more informative nonperforming loans (NPLs), that is, the size of the loan on which payments have not been made for over 90 days. NPL is a very important barometer of the health of loan portfolios, and is generally issued by regulators as public information. The SIC calculated the NPL level at 0.5–5.5 percent in January 2006, rising to almost 10 percent in August 2007, and as 1.5–5.5 percent at the collapse.

Still, these numbers are rather small, compared to the result (collapse). The banks had so much of their portfolios in zero coupons that they had no way to know whether borrowers were still willing and able to pay off their loans, since the loans did not yield any cashflows.

For this reason, and others, many regulators also report NPLs in more conservative terms; namely, if the borrower does not make a payment on one loan, but stays current on all others, the regulator reports all the borrower's loans as nonperforming, to better reflect the overall health of the portfolio. But even if the FME had followed this more prudent practice in reporting NPLs, it would not have given an accurate picture because of the amount of zero-coupon loans. Or as a popular saying in the world of banking goes: A rolling stone gathers no moss; a rolling loan incurs no loss. That is, zero coupons, when rolled over, give no indication of loss.

Now that the SIC had managed to describe the main features of the loan portfolios of the banks, the next task was to figure out what type of collateral the bankers accepted against all this lending.

Chapter 12

Market Manipulation and Falsification of Equity

Collateral Analysis

At any given time, the value of a loan is determined by the interest rate it carries, current interest rates in the market, and the probability of the loan being repaid. Loan value also reflects the expected value recovered in the case of a default, which in turn is determined by the value of the collateral, and how expensive it would be to realize cash from the pledged asset.[1] To properly assess the quality of a loan book, it is therefore necessary to analyze the quality of all collateral.

The Special Investigation Commission (SIC) requested data from the banks needed to analyze the quality of their collateral but, as it turned out, the banks were unable to deliver this information. They simply didn't have the proper systems in place for storing data on collateral, or for analyzing it. Partly this was because of the rapid growth of their loan portfolios, but collateral complexity and other problems also contributed.

Sometimes, even for a single loan, several assets are used as collateral. At other times, a single asset may be used as collateral for several loans. These one-to-many and many-to-one relationships were not properly tracked by the banks.[2] In addition, the SIC found instances where a negative pledge was issued against the same asset more than once! A negative pledge is a collateral agreement stipulating that the creditor has the sole right to claim the entire asset in case of default. These and other problems made it practically impossible for the SIC to carry out collateral analysis.

However, loan portfolio analysis revealed that a large amount of credit was extended to holding companies to fund stock purchases. The SIC therefore decided to focus its analysis on this type of loan, in particular the collateral behind them. It obtained monthly data from both Kaupthing and Glitnir going back to the middle of 2006, and quarterly data from Landsbanki from the end of 2005.[3]

Listed Stocks Pledged into the Banking System

The collateral analysis revealed a bleak picture. At the peak of the economic boom, in the summer of 2007, the market value of stocks pledged to the banks as collateral amounted to roughly 1.2 trillion ISK (about USD 12 billion), more than 100 percent of Iceland's GDP (Figures 12.1, 12.2, 12.3).[4]

In the cases of some of the better-known companies in Iceland, a majority of shares were pledged as collateral. For instance, over 75 percent of all outstanding shares of FL Group's closed-end investment fund were pledged into the banking system, and around 70 percent of another investment fund, Exista, which was simultaneously the largest owner of Kaupthing (Figure 12.4).[5] In fact, throughout 2007 and until the banks collapsed, 40 to 45 percent of the total outstanding shares of Kaupthing were pledged to Kaupthing itself (Figure 12.5). Furthermore, around half of the total outstanding shares of the three banks were pledged into the banks themselves. See Figure 12.4.

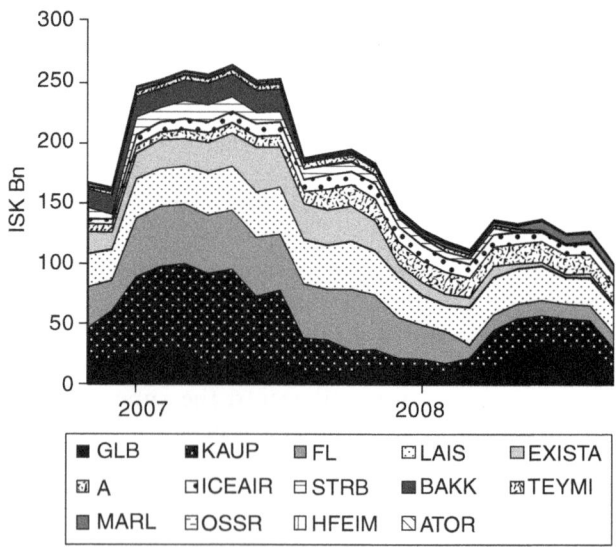

Figure 12.1   Total value of blue chip stocks pledged to Glitnir as collateral
Source: Glitnir bank hf., SIC Report, Figure 38, Chapter 8, Volume 2, p. 104.

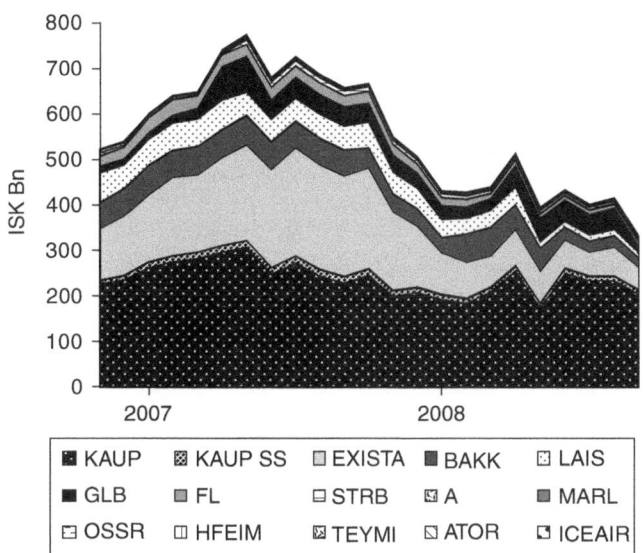

Figure 12.2   Total value of blue chip stocks pledged to Kaupthing as collateral
Source: Kaupthing bank hf., SIC Report, Figure 39, Chapter 8, Volume 2, p. 104.

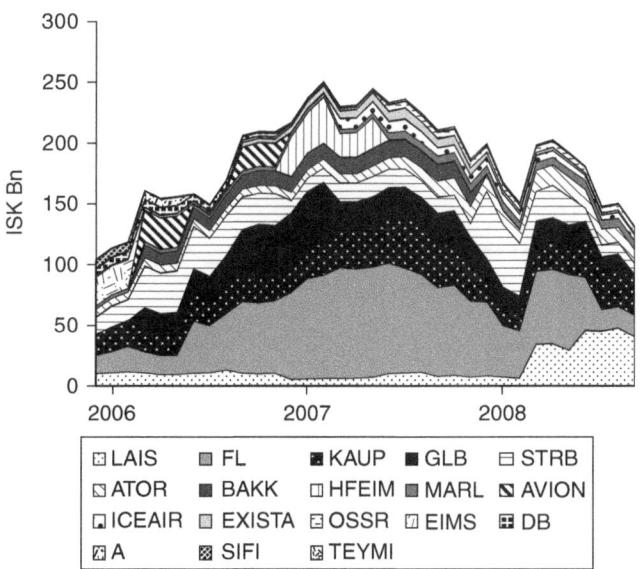

Figure 12.3   Total value of blue chip stocks pledged to Landsbanki as collateral
Source: Landsbanki Islands hf., SIC Report, Figure 40, Chapter 8, Volume 2, p. 104.

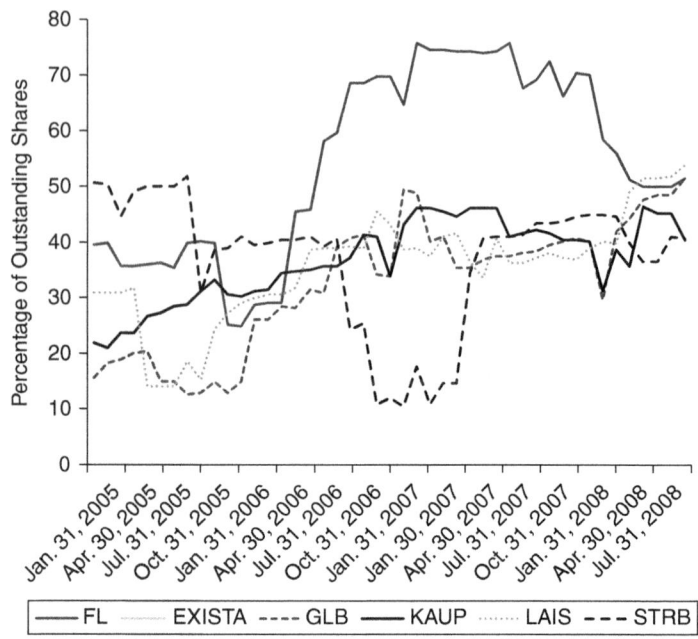

Figure 12.4 Percentage of outstanding shares of banks and holding companies pledged as collateral to listed banks

Source: Kaupthing bank hf., SIC Report, Figure 46, Chapter 8, Volume 2, p. 108.

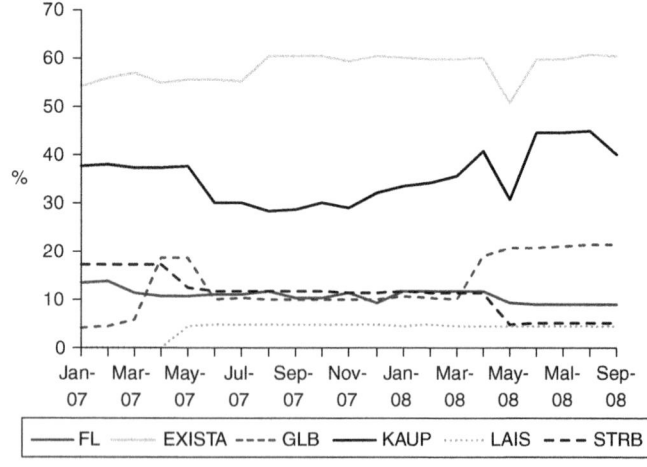

Figure 12.5 Percentage of outstanding company shares pledged as collateral to Kaupthing

Source: Kaupthing bank hf., SIC Report, Figure 46, Chapter 8, Volume 2, p. 106.

In a situation like this, the banks had become desperately dependent upon their own stock prices. If the stock price fell, the banks would have to call on the margins, asking the borrowers to further secure their borrowing by bringing new collateral to the table, or else they would have to sell shares to pay off the debt. Of course, they didn't do that, as that could have started a downward spiral, bringing down the house of cards that the bankers had built.

According to Icelandic corporate law,[6] a corporation may hold up to 10 percent of its own shares for a short time. When the banks accepted shares in themselves as collateral on a large scale, they must have known that such assets were such assets were troublesome collateral to hold, aside from being illegal beyond the 10%. Having accepted your own shares as collateral against a loan, the only time the borrower is in default is at the same time when your own shares are going down in value or the company can not deliver on dividends which are potentially intended to service the debt. At that time the bank will need to take over the collateral and liquidate it to pay up the loan. Under such circumstances management is under the temptation to manipulate the market and hold the shares rather than sell them. In the case of bankruptcy of the bank itself, such collateral are worthless leaving creditors empty handed, since the equity cushion wasn't there all along. Prudent accountants would therefore deduct all own-share holdings from the capital base. This was not the case with the Icelandic banks, yet they were audited in accordance with International Financial Reporting Standards (IFRS), which require such deduction from the capital base.[7]

Maintaining the Market Price

Having discovered the vast collateralization of listed shares, the next obvious question the SIC needed to answer was, how did the bankers behave in the stock market?

First the SIC looked at Kaupthing's buying and selling of its own shares in the market from 2004 to 2008 (Figure 12.6). The bars above the zero line represent Kaupthing shares that Kaupthing bought as a percentage of total buying of Kaupthing shares that month by all market participants in the stock exchange. The bars below the zero similarly represent shares that Kaupthing sold. In both cases, purchases or sales may have been initiated by Kaupthing or by others.

The first thing that jumps out from the picture is that the bars above and below zero are not symmetric. From early on, Kaupthing bank bought more shares in itself on the stock exchange than it sold.

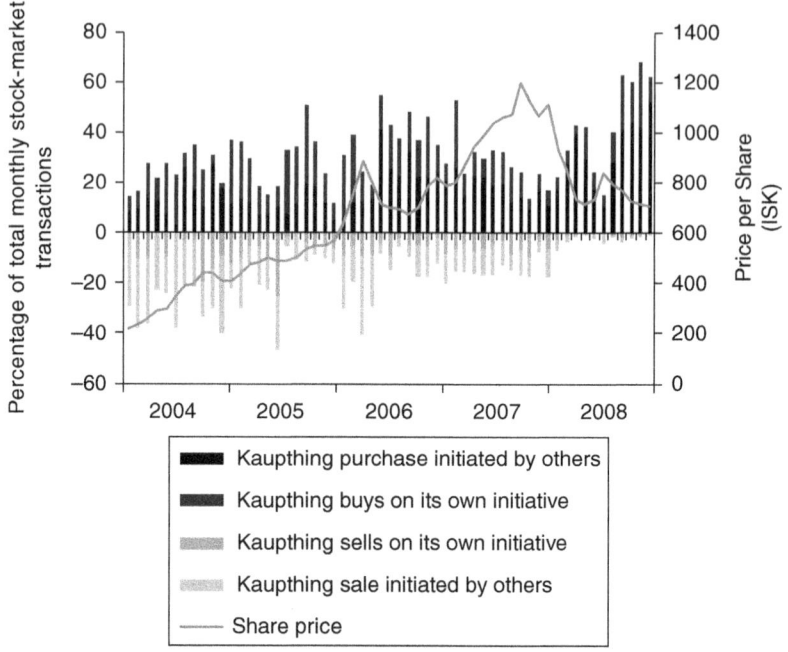

Figure 12.6 Kaupthing's buying and selling of its own shares as percentage of all its stock exchange turnover, by initiator, with share price (right scale)

Source: Iceland Stock Exchange (ICEX), Kaupthing bank hf. and Iceland Securities Depository (ISD), SIC Report, Figure 8, Chapter 12, Volume 4, p. 24.

Furthermore, in some months it bought up to **68** percent of the traded volume.

In the year of the collapse, 2008, Kaupthing hardly sold any shares in itself on the exchange. So what did they do with these shares? To answer that, the SIC had to compare the bank's proprietary trading in its own stocks on the stock exchange with its over-the-counter trading. Then the picture gets clearer.

Figure 12.7 shows Kaupthing's net trade each month, of its own shares on the stock exchange and over-the-counter, with a positive number if the bank bought more of than it sold. From January 2004 until the bank collapsed in late 2008, Kaupthing net-sold eight of its own shares over the counter for each one it sold on the stock exchange.[8] Conversely, it net-bought four times more shares on the stock exchange compared with over-the-counter.

One way to assess whether abnormal trading occurred in the case of Kaupthing's trading in its own shares is to draw the same picture

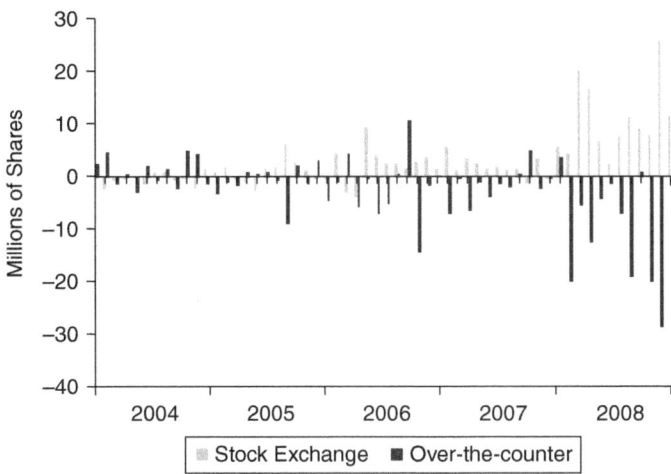

Figure 12.7 Kaupthing's monthly trading in its own shares, stock exchange and over-the-counter transactions

Source: Iceland Stock Exchange (ICEX) and Kaupthing bank hf., SIC Report, Figure 13, Chapter 12, Volume 4, p. 26.

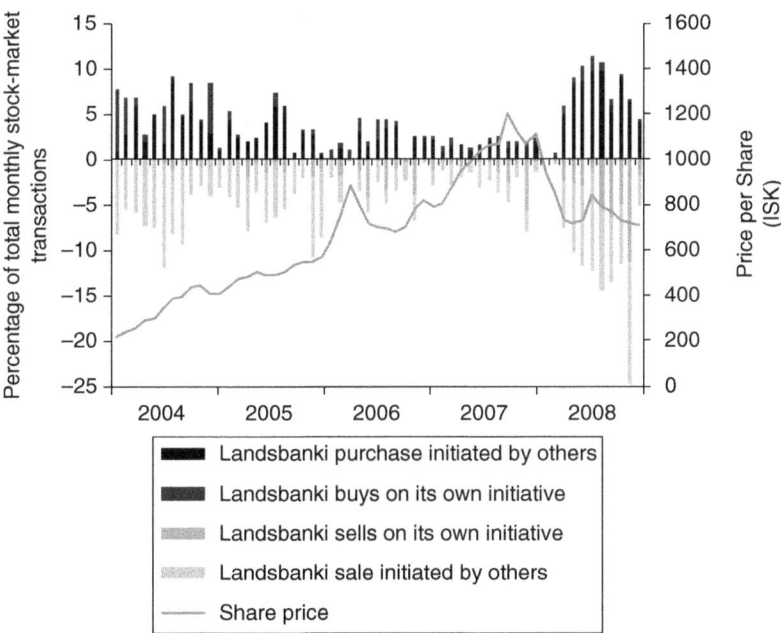

Figure 12.8 Landsbanki's buying and selling of Kaupthing shares as percentage of all Kaupthing's stock exchange turnover, by initiator, with share price (right scale)

Source: Iceland Stock Exchange (ICEX) and Landsbanki Islands hf., SIC Report, Figure 14, Chapter 12, Volume 4, p. 33.

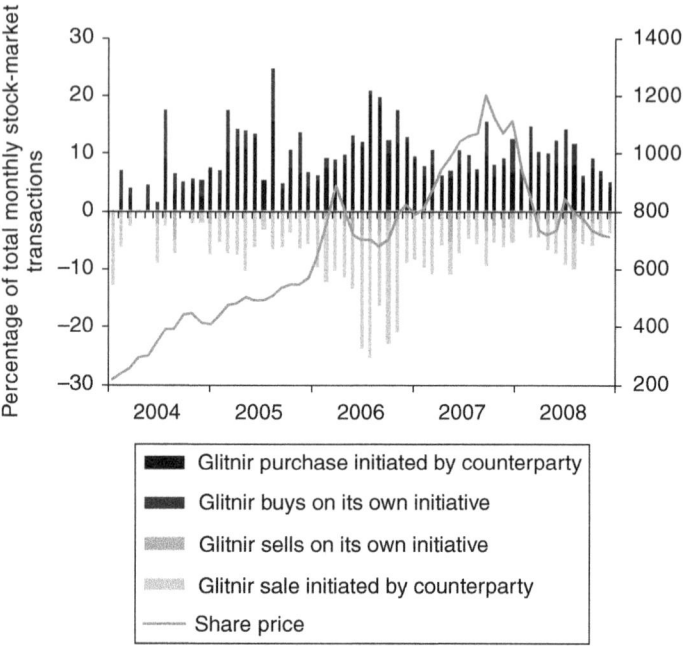

Figure 12.9   Glitnir's buying and selling of Kaupthing shares as percentage of all Kaupthing's stock exchange turnover, by initiator, with share price (right scale)

Source: Iceland Stock Exchange (ICEX) and Glitnir bank hf., SIC Report, Figure 16, Chapter 12, Volume 4, p. 34.

of trading by rival banks in Kaupthing shares. As Figures 12.8 and 12.9 show, the pattern of trades is different when it is Landsbanki and Glitnir who were buying and selling shares in Kaupthing. The pattern is much closer to symmetric around the zero line, meaning that the rival banks were more like simple market-makers in the shares of Kaupthing, buying at a price slightly lower than they sold. According to the SIC estimate, on the other hand, Kaupthing bought 237 billion ISK worth of shares in itself on the stock exchange from 2004 to 2008, but sold only 97 billion ISK worth of shares on the exchange.[9]

Thanks to the excellent data privileges granted the SIC by the Icelandic Parliament, the SIC could generate Figure 12.10, which so vividly shows the formation and collapse of an asset bubble. The figure shows the relationship between increased leverage and asset prices in the Icelandic stock market from 2004 to 2008, illustrating the point of Prof. Geanakoplos (Chapter 11) on the importance

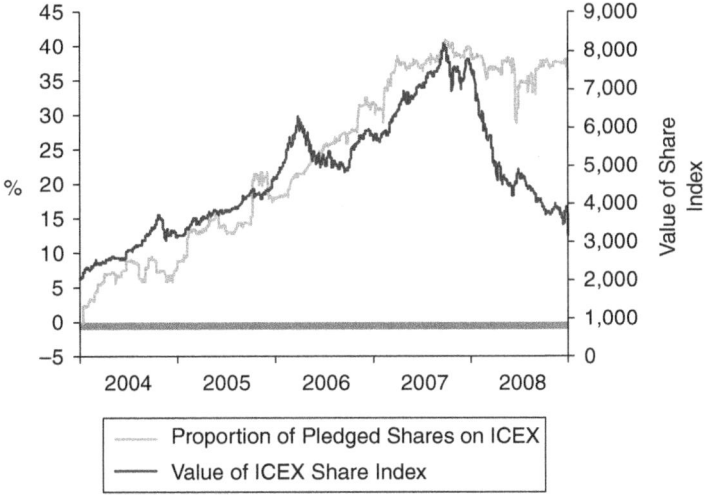

Figure 12.10 Percentage of Icelandic listed shares pledged as bank collateral after 2004, with stock-market price index (right scale)

Source: Iceland Stock Exchange (ICEX), SIC Report, Figure 4, Chapter 12, Volume 4, p. 16.

of central banks monitoring the level of leverage as well as interest rates.

At least from 2004 onwards, as the listed shares of the Icelandic stock market were leveraged further by being used as collateral for stock purchases, reaching 40 percent of all listed shares being pledged to the banks at the peak—prices in the stock market rose. When the banking system stopped accepting more listed shares as collateral, prices in the market dropped like a rock. The SIC did not have data on how many listed shares had been pledged as collateral prior to 2004, so the level of leverage in the figure is underestimated.

Of course, listed shares may be used as collateral against loans to buy unlisted shares. In addition, when buying shares on margin, buyers need to come up with some equity of their own, so leverage was not the only factor contributing to the witnessed rise in market prices.

After publication of the SIC's report, one of its more outspoken critics—among those under investigation—was the former chairman of Kaupthing, Sigurdur Einarsson, who publically claimed that the SIC had this analysis all wrong.[10]

According to the Einarsson, Kaupthing was merely responding to large-scale demand for its shares building dark pools to trade to favored customers who wanted to become large shareholders, buying over-the-counter while accepting the market price set by the exchange.

In March 2013, the Icelandic Special Prosecutor issued indictments for fraud against Einarsson—as well as the former CEO of Kaupthing, Hreidar Mar Sigurdsson, and seven other Kaupthing employees—alleging they manipulated the market price of Kaupthing by selling its shares to special purpose vehicles owned by favored customers of the bank, who in turn bought the shares with funds borrowed from the bank, in the amount of the shares purchased, or even exceeding that amount. As this is written, the jury is still out on whether the former Kaupthing bankers will be found guilty of massive market manipulation.[11]

Loans to favored customers were allegedly provided without any credit analysis of the borrower prior to lending, which was not only in breach of the bank's credit rules, but also in breach of Iceland's general penal code.

The alleged fraud covered by the indictments relates to the buying of shares in Kaupthing in excess of sale in the amount of 93 billion ISK, or just under USD 1.3 billion at the time, and issuing credit without sufficient collateral exceeding 60 billion ISK, or roughly USD 845 million at the time.[12]

Kaupthing's proprietary weren't the only ones engaged with "asymmetric trading" in their shares on the stock exchange. Glitnir and Landsbanki both behaved similarly.

From 2004 to 2008, Glitnir's proprietary trading was involved in 29 percent of all trades on the stock exchange with Glitnir's shares on the buying side, in only 1.65 percent on the selling side (Figure 12.11).[13] During this period, Glitnir had bought on the exchange 52 percent of total outstanding shares more than it had sold. Glitnir thus bought more than half of its own outstanding shares but it did not hold those shares, as one might think based only on its trading behavior in the stock exchange. The bank systematically bought its own shares on the stock exchange and negotiated the sale of those same shares outside of the exchange, selling them over the counter (Figure 12.12).

Although Glitnir engaged in this behavior since late 2004, there was a major change in the middle of 2007, when the stock price started to fall and Glitnir substantially increased buying of its own shares. Although Glitnir considered itself to be a market-maker in its own shares, which is not illegal in Iceland, it did not behave as such. The bank spent 136 billion ISK buying its own shares on the stock exchange, while selling for only 4.4 billion ISK.[14]

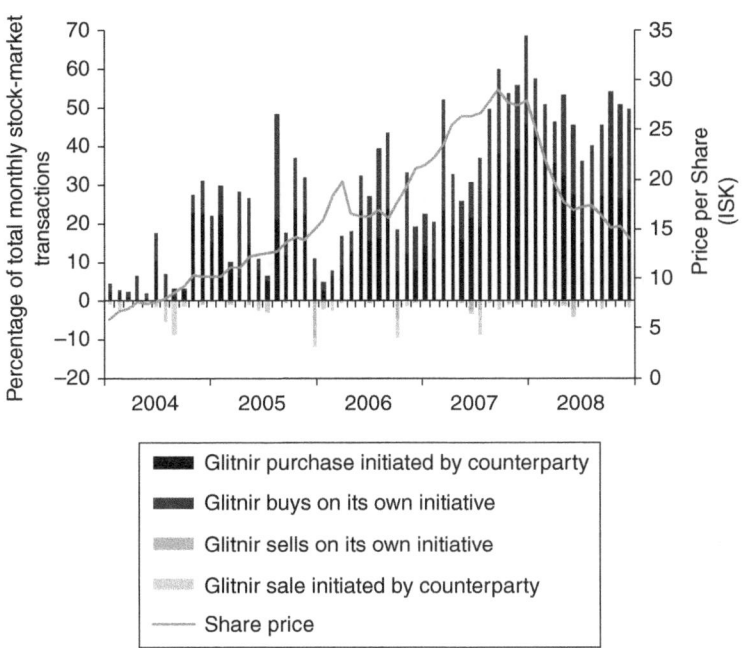

Figure 12.11 Glitnir's buying and selling of its own shares as percentage of all its stock exchange turnover, by initiator, with share price (right scale)

Source: Iceland Stock Exchange (ICEX), Glitnir bank hf., and Iceland Securities Depository (ISD), SIC Report, Figure 16, Chapter 12, Volume 4, p. 36.

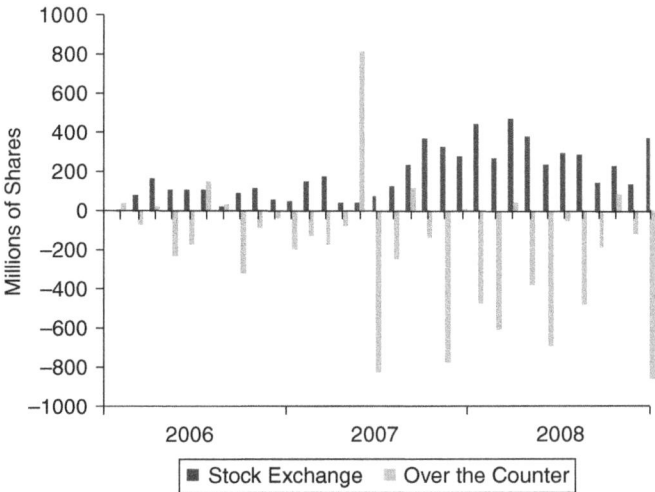

Figure 12.12 Glitnir's monthly net trading in its own shares, stock exchange and over-the-counter transactions

Source: Glitnir bank hf., SIC Report, Figure 23, Chapter 12, Volume 4, p. 37.

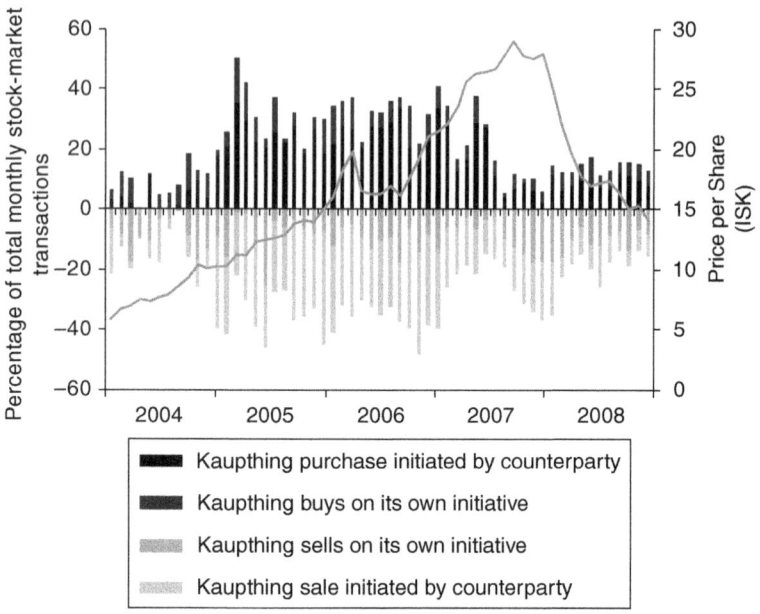

Figure 12.13   Kaupthing's buying and selling of Glitnir shares as percentage of all Glitnir's stock exchange turnover, by initiator, with share price (right scale)

Source: Iceland Stock Exchange (ICEX), Kaupthing bank hf., and Iceland Securities Depository (ISD), SIC Report, Figure 24, Chapter 12, Volume 4, p. 46.

Kaupthing was a market-maker in Glitnir's shares (Figure 12.13). The pattern is much closer to symmetric around the zero line, meaning that Kaupthing was acting more like a simple market-maker in Glitnir's shares—buying at a price slightly lower than they sold— just as we saw that Glitnir and Landsbanki had done in Kaupthing's shares.

The same pattern emerged for Landsbanki as for Kaupthing and Glitnir, regarding trading in its own shares on the stock exchange (Figure 12.14). From 2004 to 2006, the bank bought in total 79 billion ISK of its own shares on the stock exchange, while it sold only 13 billion ISK.[15] This manipulative behavior was not consistent, however. During the Geysir Crisis, Landsbanki's proprietary traders retreated from the market. From mid-year 2006 to mid-year 2007, on average, they were only on the buying side 4 percent of the time, compared to 12 percent in 2005 and 35 percent of the time in 2008 (Figure 12.15).

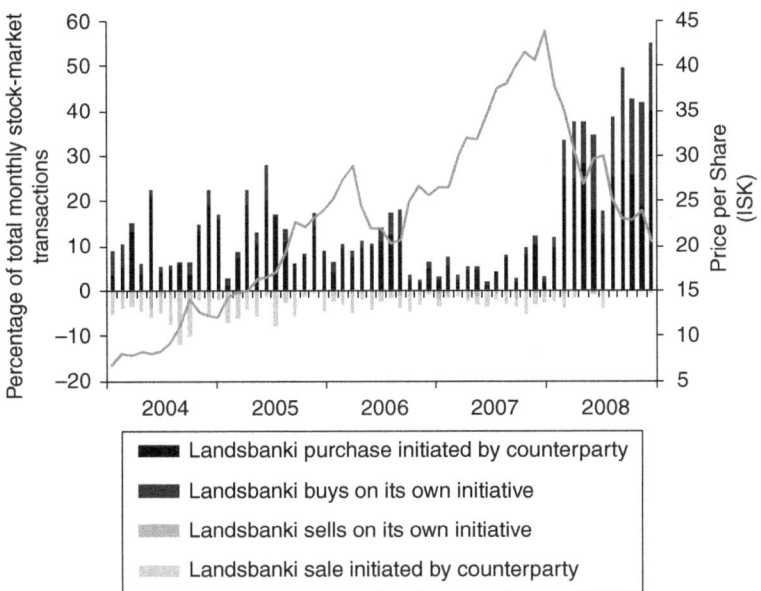

Figure 12.14 Landsbanki's buying and selling of its own shares as percentage of all its stock exchange turnover, by initiator, with share price (right scale)

Source: Iceland Stock Exchange (ICEX), Landsbanki Islands hf. and Iceland Securities Depository (ISD), SIC Report, Figure 30, Chapter 12, Volume 4, p. 48.

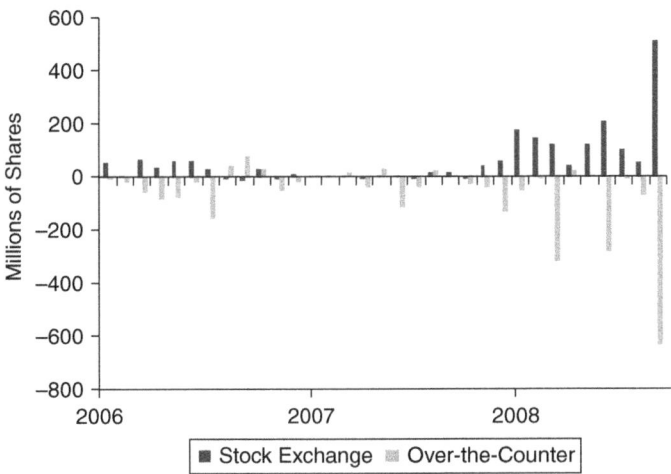

Figure 12.15 Landsbanki's monthly net trading in its own shares, stock exchange and over-the-counter transactions

Source: Landsbanki Islands hf., SIC Report, Figure 33, Chapter 12, Volume 4, p. 49

Betting for Life and Falsifying Equity

The largest Icelandic investment companies, which were the main owners of the banks, had not only borrowed from their own banks, but they had also been doing business with foreign banks, and borrowed from them as well. Several of those loans were secured by pledging the shares of the Icelandic banks. As share prices fell after the summer of 2007, the quality of the collateral of the Icelandic investment companies declined. The foreign banks made margin calls, or closed credit lines, and Glitnir, Kaupthing, and Landsbanki all reacted, in January and February 2008, by taking over the financing of their owners so that loans to the foreign banks could be paid off. The Icelandic banks therefore lent out large sums at the same time that they were suffering from a considerable shortage of liquid assets.[16] Why would they do that?

The performance of the banks had become too intertwined with the performance of the investment companies that owned them, so the only way they could see to move forward was to make a life-or-death bet and lend money for these margin calls.

The banks took over the financing of foreign loans in order to prevent the selling of their own shares, which had been posted as collateral, in an effort to maintain the value of those shares and prevent negative publicity.[17] To a large extent, the banks thus accepted their own shares as collateral for loans. By this time, own-shares held by the banks in their treasury or as collateral amounted to over a quarter of their reported capital base.

This is what the SIC called "debt repatriation." Most of the risk related to the Icelandic banks had now reached the shores of Iceland, ignoring all the depositors in Britain and the Netherlands. By the beginning of 2008, foreign lenders to the Icelandic investment companies had largely started netting-out Icelandic risk.[18]

As stated earlier, Icelandic law on limited liability companies, as well as prudent accounting rules, the banks were obliged to deduct their own-shares held as collateral from their capital base, as such collateral could not be liquidated in the case of the bank's bankruptcy.[19] As noted earlier, no such deduction had been made by any of the three banks. It is therefore evident that the capital levels of the Icelandic banks in the run up to their collapse were grossly misreported. In addition, the three banks engaged heavily in funding the shares of their rivals: Kaupthing funded large owners of Glitnir, and so on. About 33 percent of outstanding shares of the three banks were either funded by themselves (24%) or their rivals (9%).[20] In light of this extensive cross-funding of the three banks, it is evident that if one of them were to fall

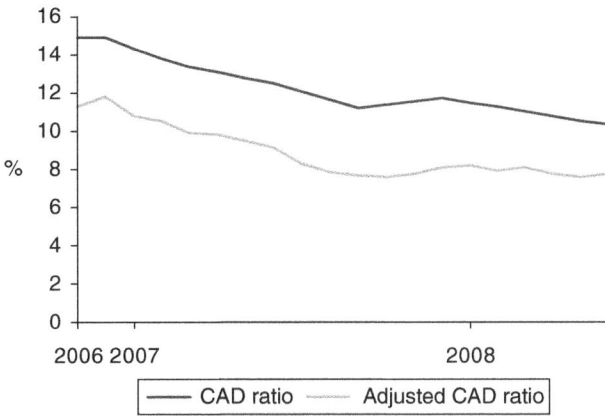

Figure 12.16 Landsbanki's capital adequacy (CAD) ratio, adjusted to exclude own-shares

Source: Landsbanki Islands hf., SIC Report, Figure 9, Chapter 9, Volume 3, p. 20

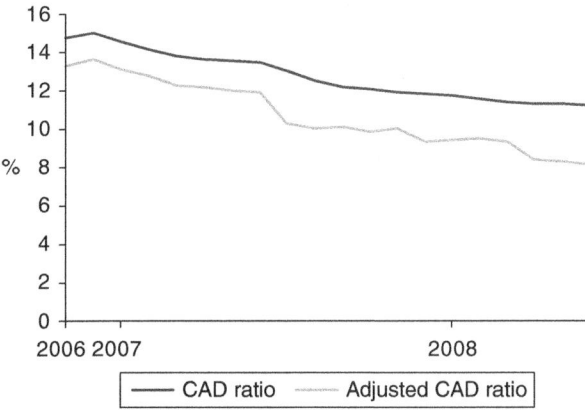

Figure 12.17 Kaupthing's capital adequacy (CAD) ratio, adjusted to exclude own-shares

Source: Kaupthing bank hf., SIC Report, Figure 6, Chapter 9, Volume 3, p. 19.

fall, all the others would go along with it, or at least face severe difficulties staying afloat. The probability of saving the system under such circumstances would have depended on the strength of the Central Bank as lender of last resort.

After deducting treasury stocks and collateral in own-shares from the equity base of the banks—as required by prudent accounting

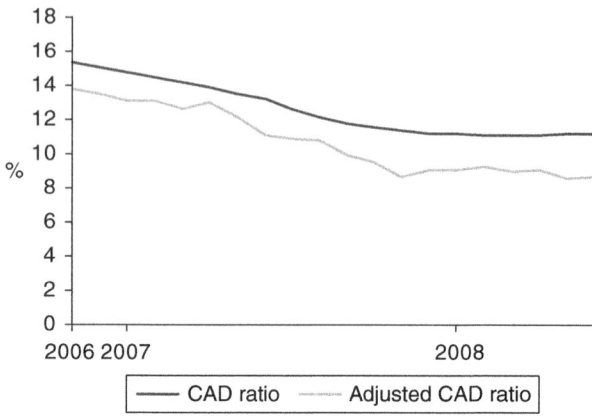

Figure 12.18   Glitnir's capital adequacy (CAD) ratio, adjusted to exclude own-shares

Source: Glitnir bank hf., SIC Report, Figure 3, Chapter 9, Volume 3, p. 18.

rules as well as Icelandic law—in the spirit of Icelandic legislation, the SIC estimated that, already in August 2007, Landsbanki's capital adequacy (CAD) ratio—at 7.86 percent—did not meet the minimum legal requirement (Figure 12.16).[21] The CAD ratio was stated to be 11.7 percent in the bank's annual report for 2007.[22] Misreporting of Kaupthing's and Glitnir's equity can be seen in Figures 12.17 and 12.18.

Capital ratios of banks are of utmost importance to investors when deciding to grant credit to financial institutions. Given the low capital requirements in the run-up to the collapse in 2008, for every dollar of its equity the financial institution could borrow and subsequently lend 12 dollars without violating the minimum capital adequacy requirement (8 percent). Higher reported capital levels are therefore instrumental for banks' balance sheet growth. It is hard to predict the fate of the Icelandic banks had they reported their equity levels truthfully. It is, however, easy to envision that their growth would have been substantially slower.

The managers of the banks were very much aware of this issue, judging from the means they used to falsify their the equity bases. Employees of the banks were instrumental in falsifying equity levels, as described in the next chapter.

Chapter 13

Wages of Failure*

Questioning Motivation

People sometimes ask me whether it is possible that the Icelandic bankers, given the rate at which they drove their banks into the ground, always expected that as the eventual outcome.

It is hard to imagine that anybody could ever be motivated like that. However, it is also hard to imagine that they did not foresee the risk in expanding the Icelandic banking sector twenty-fold in seven years. We, then, are left with the question, given the risk, why did they behave as they did?

Ever since Adam Smith, economists have been pointing out that those who manage corporations are often not vigilant in protecting the interests of those who own them.

In an important paper from 1976, Jensen and Meckling defined the concept of agency cost in a systematic manner. Agency cost includes costs created as a result of hidden action by managers or by hidden information, influence costs, and the costs of implementing institutional structures to deal with them. Despite agency cost, Jensen and Meckling showed that, because of coordination costs among multiple owners, both firms and society as a whole are better off releasing owners from managerial duties and handing them over to professionals who may own no part of the company. Since then economists have spent much time figuring out how best to reduce agency cost and reduce moral hazard when control is separated from ownership. This, according to economic theory, can be done by tying the interests of the two together through instruments such as stocks, stock options, and long-term incentive plans, to name a few.

Building on this "principal-agent theory," U.C.-Berkeley law professor Eric Talley and I in 2005 formalized a theory on interactions among three major incentivizing tools: corporate governance, incentive pay, and the threat of litigation. The other major incentivizing tool is market discipline, exerted through stock markets, product markets, and labor markets.

Through empirical analysis we discovered that if the shareholder decides to spend the company's resources on incentivizing the manager through incentive pay, the likelihood rises of the firm being sued by shareholders for false reporting. When managers have targets to aim for, but fail to meet them, they have an incentive to misreport business results in order to acquire the bonus. Peng and Roell also found a similarly increased probability of litigation as reported in a 2008 paper *Review of Finance*.[1]

Judging from the comprehensive bonus schemes implemented in the failed Icelandic banks, their controlling shareholders were fully aware of the power of incentive pay. However, assuming they intended for the banking system to survive, they grossly underestimated the negative impact that such incentive schemes could have.

Ironically, if tunneling money to themselves was their aim all along, the controlling shareholders didn't need to incentivize the bank managers with bonuses to secure their loyalty and obedience. Judging from research in social psychology, humans are obedient and will follow orders at least two-thirds of the time if they trust the line of command.[2]

Glitnir Started Out with Good Intentions

For decades before privatization, while under state ownership, many Icelandic bankers enjoyed 13 months' compensation for 12 months' work, as they received double salary in December each year without without regard to performance. Bonuses were first introduced in Icelandic banks at FBA, the Icelandic Investment Bank, by its young and charismatic CEO, Bjarni Armannsson, a computer scientist fresh out of MBA studies at IMD business school in Switzerland. Armannsson was only 29 years old when he was promoted to the position of CEO at FBA in 1997.[3]

The plan was called the EVA-Bonus Scheme, for Economic Value Added. EVA is net earnings after taxes, interest, and allocated returns on equity. This bonus plan was later adopted by Glitnir, after its merger with FBA, to incentivize the CEO and his management team.[4]

It had all the important elements of a good incentive plan. Staff shared profits with shareholders after compensating them for their having paid for shareholders' opportunity costs. One month's salary was allocated as a bonus for maintaining last year's economic value added, plus a fraction of monthly salary for every unit of improvement in economic value added.

Two-thirds of the total bonus was paid out each year, while one-third was put in a bonus bank to maintain long-term incentives. The system would also punish for poor performance via a claw-back if the bank made losses. The bonus bank could even accumulate a negative balance, so that future profits could make up for past poor performance.[5] It was almost as if Jensen and Meckling themselves had designed the bonus scheme.[6]

Escalation and Rent Extraction Undermine the Glitnir's Incentive Pay System

Only three years into the well-constructed EVA plan, Bjarni Armannsson, now the CEO of Glitnir, started to amend the system by asking the Board of Directors for discretionary pension and bonus payments for himself on top of those allocated by the system.[7] Armannsson also bargained for an amendment to his compensation in December 2003 when the chairman of Glitnir approved an additional 2003 bonus of one month's salary, approximately 1.2 million ISK.

A new board was elected in March 2004, and the former vice chairman of the Board, Einar Sveinsson, became chairman. Now Armannsson bargained for a raise in his base monthly salary, by half, to 1.8 million ISK. In addition, he got a discretionary bonus payment of 10 million ISK, plus an additional 10 million ISK contribution to his pension would be made to the CEO's pension fund for 2003 performance, to be paid in that month.[8]

The next year, 2005, discretionary bonus to the CEO was doubled from the previous year, to 20 million ISK, approximately 11 months' salary at the current rate. Another lump-sum pension contribution of 10 million ISK was also paid out for 2004 in the same ad hoc manner. For comparison, shareholders received just 19.83 percent return on equity in 2003, and 22.75 percent in 2004, as reported by the bank.[9]

After a change of ownership, a new board was elected, and a new chairman appointed, in the spring of 2006. This time around, an extensive overhaul was made to the bank's bonus system and the CEO's compensation agreement. The CEO's monthly base salary was raised by two-thirds, from 1.8 to 3 million ISK. The EVA bonus plan was discarded. All bonuses would now be allocated in line with the bank's return on equity. No bonus was to be paid out if return on equity was less than 15 percent. Above that, for each additional percentage point of return on equity, one-fifteenth of annual salary would be paid out as bonus.

The whole bonus was to be paid out immediately, with no provision for claw-backs. In addition to the 20 million ISK bonus already allocated to Bjarni Armannsson for 2005 according to the old bonus plan, yet another discretionary bonus was paid to his pension plan, a one-time payment of 18 million ISK. In addition, for the first half of 2006, the board granted the CEO a bonus of 43.2 million.[10] Half-year return-on-equity had been 41.8 percent.[11]

Another overhaul was made to the system in May 2007 when there emerged a new controlling shareholder, Jon Asgeir Johannesson, through his ownership in FL Group and Baugur Group.[12] The tenure of Bjarni Armannsson was at an end.

Armannsson didn't leave empty-handed, however. In an agreement stipulating his departure, the bank agreed that he would receive his fixed monthly salary for 18 months after he stepped down as CEO.[13] For his service to the company, he was also to receive, on January 15, 2008, 270 million ISK (roughly USD 4 million at the time, 90 times his monthly base salary). An additional bonus of 50 million ISK was to be paid out for the bank's performance during the first 5 months of 2007. The agreement further stipulated that Armannsson would have no claim on the bank for any further bonus pay that he might have earned through the bank's bonus plan.

It is hard to see, however, why Armannsson would have a reason to make a claim on the bank that exceeded 50 million ISK in bonus for five months' work at the bank.[14] For a bonus claim of this size, the return on equity would have needed to be 65 percent that year—a pretty steep return for a systemically important bank with decades of operational history.

Despite his more-than-reasonable compensation package, Bjarni Armannsson did not do nearly as well as his successor. Larus Welding, another young banker, was recruited to be Glitnir's new CEO with a signing bonus of 300 million ISK (USD 5 million at the time), plus another 300 million ISK lump-sum payment at the end of February 2008 for still being on the job 9 months after he started. Larus Welding also received a more generous monthly salary, 5.5 million ISK (equivalent to annual salary of USD 1.1 million at the time), in addition to performance-based bonus.[15]

Payments of discretionary bonuses, in addition to the bonus plan already in place, bear witness to the poor state of contractual enforcement and the poor quality of corporate governance at the bank.

The aforementioned salary information did not include Bjarni Armannsson's stock options, his exercising of those options, loan agreements for stock purchases, or other credit facilities Armannsson enjoyed while serving as CEO of Glitnir. Outstanding credit lines to Armannsson's investment companies (SPVs), with collateral being shares in the bank, amounted to 4.2 billion ISK when he stepped down as CEO, and they grew to 5.6 billion before the bank collapsed.[16]

The frequent and radical amendments to the employment agreement of the CEO at Glitnir, followed by election of a new chairman of the Board of Directors, serve as a useful lesson to directors and shareholders alike: Frequent turnover on the board creates room for a CEO to extract rents, especially if contractual enforcement is placed solely upon directors and not institutionalized further, such as through a compliance officer.

Increases in the CEO's pay may have been part of result of a general escalation of CEO pay among the three banks, as predicted by Paul Oyer in 2004. Oyer pointed out that firms may compensate their employees with various kinds of incentive pay, such as stocks, options, and cash retainers, even though their only intention is to deter the employee from taking a job elsewhere.[17] It is not unreasonable to assume that Glitnir's board chairman the Board of Directors felt he had no option but to keep the CEO happy by giving in to his demands regarding pay, in order to retain him. However, that does not excuse the lack of contractual enforcement, and lack of disclosure to shareholders.

Staff Used as Vehicle to Falsify Equity

In 2000, when Landsbanki was still under state ownership, it introduced a stock-option program to the bank's compensation plan. Unlike the usual practice of issuing new equity instruments when the call options, instead of stock options vested,[18] Landsbanki decided to imitate the practice set up by Bunadarbanki, and inappropriately "hedge" the call options through off-shore trusts; off-balance sheet special purpose vehicles. The trust, in turn, owned the limited liability companies LB Holding Ltd., Marcus Capital Ltd., and Proteus Global Holding S.A. Ltd. Landsbanki established at least three such off-shore trusts from 2000 to 2006.[19] The registered beneficial owner of one of the trusts was the Red Cross.[20]

At least 13.2 percent of total outstanding shares of Landsbanki were purchased on the market or even new shares were issued and bought by the off-shore companies—using funds borrowed from the

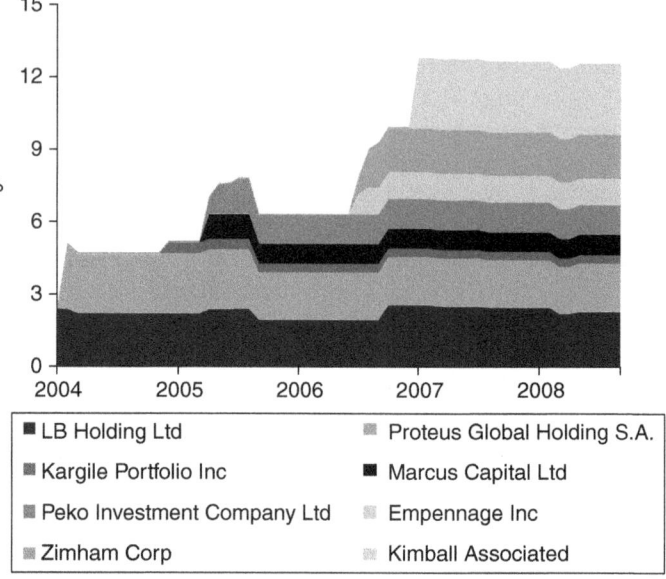

Figure 13.1   Percent of Landsbanki's outstanding shares owned by limited liability companies owned by off-shore trusts

Source: Landsbanki Islands hf., SIC Report, Figure 44, Chapter 10, Volume 3, p. 68.

bank—through borrowed funds from the bank and placed in at least eight off-shore limited liability companies (Figure 13.1). In fact, the off-shore companies, if combined, formed the second largest shareholder in Landsbanki.[21]

While these off-shore entities were ostensibly independent, they were in fact under the control of Landsbanki's management. Before the annual general meeting in 2007, the CEO of Landsbanki, Sigurjon Arnason, approached the in-house counsel, Kristjan Gunnar Valdimarsson, and asked him to collect proxies from all boards of the off-shore entities, located in Luxembourg, Panama, and the British Virgin Islands, in order to use their votes to support the bank's remuneration policy at the annual general meeting.[22]

Landsbanki hedged employee stock options as follows. After issuing stock options to employees, the bank lent money to one of the off-shore companies, which essentially had no equity. The off-shore firm then used the borrowed funds to buy shares in Landsbanki in the stock market "or newly issued stocks." In return, Landsbanki made a forward contract obligating the bank to buy those shares back from the off-shore company as the options vested.[23] Evidently, when the off-shore company went into the market to buy shares in Landsbanki, for billions at a time, the price of the stock rose, and the options were immediately "in the money" (i.e., likely to be exercised).

Besides ignoring the obvious room for market manipulation it put in the hands of Landsbanki's management—by allowing them to time the extensive purchase of the bank's own shares in the market—this hedging of options might seem to have been a good idea for the bank. The cost of the forward contracts allegedly covered the cost of funding from Landsbanki as long as the shares continued to rise, and only under those circumstances would employees exercise their options.

It seems to have been a common understanding at Landsbanki that the bank would need to go into the market to buy the shares and deliver them to the employees as the options were exercised. With the alleged hedging, then, the bank avoided any cost related to issuing the options. It could retrieve the borrowed funds, as well as its own shares bought at the strike price instead at the elevated market price that would stimulate exercising of the options.

On the other hand, if the share price fell, no staff member would exercise the options, and the bank would not exercise the forward contract. Landsbanki would then avoid buying its own shares at an elevated price compared with the market, although, by definition of a forward contract, it was obliged to do so.

Contractual enforcement was nonexistent, since Landsbanki sat at both sides of the table and was therefore making deals with itself. Had the stock price fallen substantially, or worse still, in the case of bankruptcy of Landsbanki, the off-shore companies could not possibly deliver on the borrowed amounts, and were doomed to default at least in some way. In this scenario, the hedging of the options therefore turned into a bad idea for the creditors of Landsbanki.

Working with Accomplishes

The off-shore companies' purchases of Landsbanki's shares were funded by Landsbanki up until 2006, when Landsbanki's rival banks took over the funding role.[24] At the collapse of the banks, the off-shore companies owed 21.5 billion ISK to the other banks (approximately USD 300 million).[25]

Kaupthing and Glitnir had only been ready to lend money to the off-shore companies if Landsbanki issued a banker's guarantee for the companies. Only the small investment bank Straumur, mainly owned by Bjorgolfur Thor Bjorgolfsson—who was also a controlling shareholder in Landsbanki—did not request such a guarantee. To return the favor, Landsbanki funded Straumur's off-shore companies, which had the same role, buying shares in Straumur to deliver on employee stock options.[26]

By issuing banker's guarantees, Landsbanki had essentially issued put options to the off-shore companies. Armed with a banker's guarantee, the off-shore companies would always be able to pay off their loans irrespective of the value of the collateral—which also happened to consist of shares in Landsbanki—as long as Landsbanki itself didn't go bankrupt. This is a main point in finance. What happens, and where does the risk lie, in the case of a default or bankruptcy?

Shareholders are required to invest in equity in order to protect creditors from losses, so that, in the case of a failure, if assets don't cover the debt of a company, the shareholders' equity serves as a cushion for creditors to tap into. That is also the reason why the equity ratio is the primary parameter in lending decisions, as well as an indication of when legal actions can be taken against a financial firm by the financial supervisor to protect the interest of the public. The equity ratio of banks is in fact so important that we stipulate the minimum in the law. If the equity claimed on the books isn't there, all creditors and other stakeholders have been deceived.

To help us ascertain that the equity really exists, we have accountants and accounting standards, such as the International Financial Reporting Standards (IFRS) and the International Accounting Standards (IAS).

IAS 32 is quite clear about any put options of a firm that have the effect that the firm itself is responsible for securing the residual claimant, that is, the equity holder who will be compensated if the equity falls in price or becomes worthless. All put options issued against a firm's equity must therefore be deducted from the firm's equity for the simple reason that it is, in effect, a promise of the firm to reimburse the equity holder for the stake that they provided the firm, if the price declines. Hence a put option is a liability that wipes out equity previously granted. Other creditors can no longer rely on that equity if the firm fails.[27]

It is the conclusion of the SIC that Landsbanki never deducted those off-shore loans, or banker's guarantees, from its equity.[28] Investors and rating agencies were led to believe that international investment companies were among the largest shareholders of Landsbanki, as Empennage, for example, was listed as the 11th largest shareholder in Landsbanki in Moody's analysis of the company's profile in June 2007.[29] In fact, 13.2 percent of all outstanding shares of Landsbanki, those bought with funds borrowed from Landsbanki, never left the books of the bank and should have been deducted from its equity.[30]

The reason for placing the stocks in so many firms was simply to circumvent the legal responsibility of disclosure toward the market as well toward as the surveillance authorities.[31] Managerial ties between the entities were obvious. In addition to the proxy voting in 2007, the forward contract, and the banker's guarantee, Kimball Associates, one of the off-shore companies, borrowed shares in Landsbanki from Proteus Holding to pledge as collateral against a loan from Straumur, to lower the loan-to-value of the deal.[32] The eight companies were obviously related parties to Landsbanki, and should have been included in the bank's consolidated accounts.

Reasons for Off-Shore Holdings

Why did the bankers go to all the trouble of hedging options via off-shore companies? The SIC did not reach a conclusion about that, but a possible explanation lies in the protection it gave to the controlling stake of Samson Holding in Landsbanki.

When Bjorgolfur Gudmundsson and Bjorgolfur Thor Bjorgolfsson initially invested in Landsbanki, during the privatization phase, their holding company, Samson Holding, received an exemption from the mandatory takeover rule and was allowed to buy a 45.8 percent stake in the bank in order to secure their control of the bank.[33] Had options been issued in the regular manner, the Samson stake would have been diluted. Chances are that Samson Holding would then have fallen under the mandatory takeover rule, so to secure control of the bank they would have had to bid for the entire bank. By putting options for 13.2 percent of the bank off-blance-sheet under management control, their controlling stake was preserved.

But it could also have been the second reason may have been that the bankers simply didn't know any better. This was the practice that was in place when they took over the bank from the government, and since the auditors didn't raise serious objections, they simply assumed the government would uphold its own laws in this respect.

A third possible reason is malfeasance, in that the bank's controlling shareholder, as well as the bank's management, might have intentionally falsified equity in order to secure cheap lending based on favorable equity ratios, and thus boost the bank's returns.

Whatever the intent, the inappropriate hedging of employee stock options did in fact increase the equity ratio, lower the bank's cost of funding, and boost the bank's profits.

The annual reports of Landsbanki during this period included no descriptions of these off-shore companies, as they were off-balance-sheet items. Further evidence to support the notion that the stock options were intended to inflate equity is the fact that options weren't always granted to employees as a result of bargaining over pay. One of the junior-level staff members described his experience when asked by the SIC how it came about that he received a stock option in the bank. He said, "I got to know about the option through a phone call from the HR chief, when he asked me to come down to his office one day. When I arrived I saw a stack of contracts on his desk which Sigurjon Arnason [the CEO of Landsbanki] had signed. […] and I was told that I had been granted an option in the bank."[34]

When options vested in December 2007, Landsbanki employees were not allowed to exercise them.[35] The CEO reported to the SIC that the bank's liquidity was not such that it could lend to the employees for purchasing the stocks as they exercised their options. When asked why the employees weren't allowed to simply net them out and retrieve the profits in the market, the CEO replied that it would not have looked good if the bank's employees, one after another, had sold shares of the bank in the market at that time. When the SIC report was issued in April 2010, many of those employees still had not received the contractual benefit stipulated by their options.[36]

The SIC found no evidence that the bank used the hedging instrument to deliver on the 217 million share options that were in fact exercised during this period, out of the 1.48 billion issued.[37]

Meanwhile at Kaupthing

The same misreporting of equity occurred at the other banks.[38] Kaupthing, however, abandoned its option program after employees requested a more cost-effective means to the same thing—loans to purchase shares in the bank. That way, employees avoided income tax, and instead paid only capital gains tax on the equity part of their pay. Kaupthing increased its shareholder equity by 32 percent from 2005 to 2006[39] while granting its employees loans of around 15 billion ISK (approx. USD 227 million) during 2006 for stock purchases in the bank.[40]

Initially, Kaupthing decided that employees should not bear any downside risk on these shares, so it issued put options in parallel with granting the loans.[41] In light of IAS 32 (discussed above), however, Kaupthing's accountant pointed out that those put options needed to be deducted from the equity base. Kaupthing's ingenious management team then found a way around that.

Kaupthing called in the put options, but since they were accepting only the pledged shares as collateral, they asked for a modest

10 percent personal guarantee against the loan in case the price of the shares were to decline.[42]

When the former chairman of Kaupthing, Sigurdur Einarsson, was asked by the SIC what was different about, on the one hand, granting a loan without a personal guarantee and only accepting pledged shares as collateral, and, on the other hand, issuing a put option, he replied: "I guess there is very little difference."[43]

Glitnir issued loans to employees either through SPVs in 100 percent ownership of its employees, who therefore were free of any type of downside risk, or with a rather exotic put option. Neither was deducted from equity. They amounted to 17 percent of the bank's equity when it collapsed.[44]

Managerial Misreporting

Theory predicts that one of the consequences faced by shareholders requiring counter-measures if they decide to install bonus plans, is the incentive to misreport earnings in order to meet the bonus targets.[45]

Managers may rationalize their actions with the idea that difficult times are only temporary, so making a few adjustments to keep earnings numbers steady will do no harm, since things will rationalize.

The SIC came across a few such cases of managerial misreporting. One of them involved reporting on profits and the loss of a total return swap (TRS). Although the misreporting did not have a large effect on bonus pay in this this case, it shows how difficult it is for banks to measure the performance upon which bonus pay is based. It also shows how easy it is for management to manipulate performance reporting, especially in the case of banks.

The Icelandic banks got involved in TRS deals with several foreign banks in 2007 and 2008. Landsbanki engaged in a TRS with Barclays and others in the amount of 90 billion ISK (USD 1.2 billion at the time) and received funding from Barclays to lend to another firm, which did not have a credit rating. Based on Landsbanki's assessment of the creditworthiness of the other firm, Landsbanki was willing to bear all the credit risk related to the firm. Barclays, on the other hand, demanded cash collateral from Landsbanki. In addition, if the firm defaulted, or if the loan declined in value, it was Landsbanki that had to pay for maintaining the margin against Barclays.[46]

In January 2008, the underlying TRS assets started to deteriorate in value. During the first quarter in 2008 the loss on the deal became 6 billion ISK, a third of the reported profit. Barclays started to call on the margin, and Landsbanki had to hand over much-needed euros. As a result, its management started looking for a way to contain the loss. The IAS accounting standard came to their rescue, since it allowed them to count both the asset side and the funding side of such combined contracts, through the income statement at "fair value." That way the loss could be offset by the discount that Landsbanki received on the funding of these loans, compared with what was on offer in the market at the time. How much loss was incurred on these deals was now only left to the judgment of fair value.[47]

The accounting standard demands that any significant impact of such fair value should be reported in the financial statements, as well as how that fair value was determined. The TRS was funded at the favorable rate of 45–75 basis points above LIBOR, since both cash collateral and a bankers' guarantee backed the funding. Looking toward a favorable benchmark—the higher, the better—management decided on a quote that they had been offered, but didn't accept, at 350 basis points.[48] So by counting the difference between funding at 350 or 45–75, the loss was for the most part wiped out.

None of this was mentioned in the interim financial statements for 2008, yet it accounted for 20 percent of Landsbanki's semi-annual profit. As mentioned earlier, this type of fair-value assessment leaves a lot of room for judgment, especially when markets are in crisis, as was the case with Landsbanki at the time.

Right before closing the semi-annual results, Landsbanki did refinance one of the TRSs with JPMorgan, and paid 100 bps.[49] Had that benchmark been used in the fair value, the loss on the asset side would only have been offset by 0.5 billion instead of the 5.6 billion reported in the semi-annual results.[50]

Pay without Performance

Right after privatization, the wage distributions in Glitnir and Landsbanki were comparatively narrow. The 10 percent highest earners divided among themselves roughly 30 percent of total salary payments of the banks, whereas the highest 10 percent cohort at Kaupthing received 45 percent. This wide wage-distribution at Kaupthing was consistent throughout the period under investigation, from 2004 to 2008, as the 10 percent highest earners received 45–51 percent of total compensation paid by the bank.[51]

Landsbanki and Glitnir managed to catch up with Kaupthing as time passed, although the exercising of options largely explains the increase in 2007.[52]

By 2007, Landsbanki's 10 percent highest earners received 53 percent of its salary payments, while Glitnir's 10 percent highest earners received 43 percent.[53]

The increase in total salary of top 10 percent earners in 2008 was largely explained by bonuses for half-year results. That year, middle management at Glitnir and Kaupthing received the largest bonus payouts of all the years under investigation, although performance that year was the worst in those years (even apart from the total failure of the banks later that same year).[54]

The following email, sent on July 9, 2008, from Sigurdur Einarsson, chairman of Kaupthing, to Magnus Gudmundsson, managing director of Kaupthing Luxembourg, may shed some light on the sentiment at the time:[55]

> Hi, Magnus, We never decided on your bonus for last year. I propose 1 million Euros. What do you say. Rgds. Se.

Sigurdur Einarsson received an answer from Magnus Gudmundsson the same day:

> Thanks More than enough ☺.

Table 13.1 Icelandic banks' CEO compensation by year and bank, 2004–2008, USD thousands (nominal)

	Bank	2004	2005	2006	2007	2008	Total
Sigurjon Arnason	Landsbanki	600	1,797	3,130	3,661	4,462	13,651
Halldor J. Kristjánsson	Landsbanki	482	4,185	2,065	1,654	1,679	10,064
Bjarni Armannsson	Glitnir	1,142	2,189	3,305	8,919	140	15,696
Larus Welding	Glitnir	-	-	-	6,057	450	6,507
Hreidar Mar Sigurdsson	Kaupthing	2,023	4,941	11,803	12,687	5,765	37,220
		-	-	-	-	-	83,138
Median CEO pay among all Icelandic corporations		97	151	162	187	165	762

Source: Special Investigation Commission (SIC), 2008, *Background and Causes of the Collapse of the Icelandic Banks in 2008 and Related Events,* Vol. 3, Chapter 10. (Report of the Special Investigation Commission (SIC). Reykjavik: Special Investigation Commission).

Table 13.2   Icelandic banks' CEO's dividend payments from the banks, by year, 2004–2008, USD thousands (nominal)

	2004	2005	2006	2007	2008	Total
Bjarni Armannsson	472	497	1,273	3	-	2,245
Halldor J. Kristjansson	26	172	155	169	-	522
Hreidar Mar Sigurdsson	143	446	1,089	1,949	-	3,627
Sigurdur Einarsson, Chairman	179	596	1,279	2,244	-	4,298
Total	820	1,711	3,797	4,364	-	10,692

Source: Special Investigation Commission (SIC), 2008, *Background and Causes of the Collapse of the Icelandic Banks in 2008 and Related Events*, Vol. 3, Chapter 10, p. 91. SIC staff estimations. (Report of the Special Investigation Commission (SIC). Reykjavik: Special Investigation Commission).

Total Take-Home Pay of CEOs

The three Icelandic banks gave their CEOs USD 83 million in compensation from 2004 through 2008[56] (Table 13.1). Hreidar Mar Sigurdsson, CEO of Kaupthing, received by far the most in compensation, USD 37 million in salary, bonus, and profits from exercised options during these years. In addition, the SIC estimated that he received around USD 3.6 million in dividend payments from shares in the bank he hadn't paid for (Table 13.2).

For comparison, the median CEO among all Icelandic corporations received USD 760 thousand in total compensation for the same period.

After the collapse of the three banks, as public anger grew regarding the compensation of bank CEOs, Bjarni Armannsson, former CEO of Glitnir, reimbursed the bankrupt estate an amount equivalent to the golden parachute he had received when he stepped down as the down as CEO in 2007, roughly USD 5.6 million at the time.[57]

Part IV

Why Didn't Anybody
Stop the Bankers?

Chapter 14

Funded by the Ill-Informed

After the wholesale run on the Icelandic banks during the Geysir crisis in 2007, they needed to find alternative means of funding. Landsbanki, better prepared for this drought on the wholesale market, had already in early 2007 started to pay down its bond issues with wholesale deposits.[1]

In October 2006, Landsbanki had launched a very successful retail deposit campaign under the brand name Icesave.[2] In an attempt to copy the success of Landsbanki's Icesave accounts, Kaupthing and Glitnir also aimed at getting much-needed funds from those who have the least means to assess the risk associated with them.

Kaupthing set up online accounts under the brand name Kaupthing Edge, offering superior deposit rates for depositors in Finland, Sweden, Norway, Germany, and Austria, but none in the Netherlands, starting in November 2007. Kaupthing's subsidiaries, one after another, also opened online accounts, from February to July 2008, in the UK, Denmark, Luxembourg, the Isle of Man, and Switzerland. Glitnir followed suit with their Save&Save accounts in June 2008.[3]

In just over a year, from mid-2006 to 2007, Landsbanki managed to triple its deposits, from roughly 5 billion euros to almost 16 billion.[4] Landsbanki's position in the "best-buy" tables was instrumental for that success. The CEO of Landsbanki, Sigurjon Arnason, described the bank's objective as being ranked "constantly good, not necessarily best, but constantly good," saying that it wasn't necessary to be at the top, just to be listed in those tables.[5]

But while the well-executed Icesave campaign brought in much-needed foreign currency for Landsbanki, those deposits were actually very sensitive to Landsbanki's position in the Best-buy tables.

Extrapolating from a rather crude regression analysis performed by the SIC, if Icesave managed to offer the best deposit rates, according to the Best-buy tables, the accounts would yield a significant net inflow of funds. However, if they dropped to fifth place, they would yield almost as significant an outflow. The Icesave funding was thus not only very costly, but, more importantly, it was volatile.[6]

Small changes were made to Landsbanki's lending strategy, now that the bank was funded mainly by deposits. During 2007 the bank allocated 30 percent of deposits into a reserve fund, holding only government bonds and other liquid assets to meet short-term fluctuations in the accounts. However, this fund was quickly utilized as collateral in order to get cash via repurchase agreements (REPOs) with the European Central Bank, so it could therefore no longer be used as a buffer for the accounts.[7]

When asked how Landsbanki had planned to meet fluctuations in the accounts, since the foreign exchange reserves of the Central Bank of Iceland were only a fraction of the Icesave deposits, the CEO told the SIC that he considered the bank to have access to euros through the aid of the European Central Bank, as well as access to other currencies through the swap market.[8]

Just as rapid credit growth is inherently risky, so too is rapid deposit collection. That risk was addressed neither by Landsbanki's management nor by their financial supervisors until the beginning of 2008, then only at the initiative of the British regulator, FSA.[9] A subtle but later very important distinction lay in whether the banks collected deposits through foreign branches or foreign subsidiaries. The main reason why Landsbanki decided against establishing a subsidiary in Britain to host the Icesave accounts was stringent British regulation on large exposures and lending between a parent company and its subsidiary. In such a structure, the Icesave deposits could not have been up-streamed to Iceland at the whim of Landsbanki's management.[10] In addition, as stipulated in European directives, a subsidiary of a foreign bank was under the supervision of the host country, while a branch was still under the financial supervision of its home country, apart from liquidity requirements, which were supervised by the host country.[11]

At the outset, Landsbanki had received an exemption from liquidity supervision of the FSA, so it was still up to the parent company of Landsbanki, under the supervision of the Central Bank of Iceland, to monitor the liquidity of the bank's branch in the UK.[12] This exemption was revoked on May 29, 2008, as the British regulator became concerned about the financial sustainability of the Landsbanki branch and the Icesave accounts.[13]

To put Landsbanki's foreign deposit collection efforts into perspective, in only 9 months, from late 2006 to the middle of 2007, Landsbanki managed to collect deposits in its foreign branches equivalent to almost five-fold the foreign exchange reserves of the Central Bank of Iceland.[14] In other words, as I pointed out in an article in the Icelandic business newspaper *Vidskiptabladid* in March 2007, if there were to be a run on the Icesave accounts, the Central Bank of Iceland would have been unable to act as lender of last resort because it simply wouldn't have the currency to do so. Unfortunately, this is precisely what happened.

Run on Icesave Brings down Landsbanki

Shaken by the first bank run in the UK in 150 years, British supervisors and media began looking for other vulnerabilities in their system after the failure of Northern Rock in the fall 2007. They came to see the ever-increasing online deposits in the branches and subsidiaries of the Icelandic banks as a potential risk.

In early February 2008, financial analysts and the British media began to warn against the vulnerabilities of the Icelandic banks and the Icelandic economy. Despite the rosy picture painted by the Icelandic banks' annual reports, *The Daily Telegraph* reported:

> Results published by the key players in Iceland's financial sector last week helped alleviate fears that the country is on the cusp of a Northern Rock-style bank-funding crisis. But analysts reckon that, thanks to a series of cross-shareholdings across the Icelandic economy, it would not take much for the whole country's financial system to go into meltdown.[15]

On February 10, *The Sunday Times* reported, "British savers have billions in Icelandic accounts, but its banking system is looking shaky."[16] On February 14, the media correctly pointed out the contagion building up in the Icelandic system when *Reuters* reported, "Like many Icelandic companies, FL owned big stakes in other local blue chips. Such cross ownership has been cited as a chief vulnerability in the Icelandic system, because it means that when one company's shares are hit, others are as well."[17]

Such remarks bear witness to the aptitude of the international market in analyzing Iceland's vulnerabilities. Foreign observers' focus was not only on the funding crisis that the banks were experiencing, but also on a homegrown weakness, the high level of cross-ownership, correlation and the low quality of lending portfolios, casting doubt on the banks' solvency.

At the same time, the FSA started to push hard for restructuring of Landsbanki, to move its online deposits from its branch into Heritable Bank, its subsidiary, which was under UK jurisdiction for financial supervision and under UK deposit insurance.[18]

To move deposits into UK jurisdiction, however, assets would need to follow, and the liabilities amounted to half of Iceland's GDP.[19] Furthermore, moving deposits from one bank to another could not be done without the consent of the depositor, unless under *force-majeure* circumstances or special legislation from Parliament.[20]

Landsbanki, on its own initiative, had two legal briefs prepared, by two well-known law firms in London, on the administrative power of the FSA to force the moving of Icesave accounts into its subsidiary, and how such a move could be implemented.[21] The FSA and the legal briefs were both clear that such a move could under no circumstances happen overnight, nor over a fortnight, for that matter, but rather over three to four months.[22]

From February 10 to April 22, when media attention became still more intense, the online savings accounts experienced a run, as UK savers withdrew 20 percent of the accounts. Figure 14.1 shows the buildup of deposits and the run in early 2008.

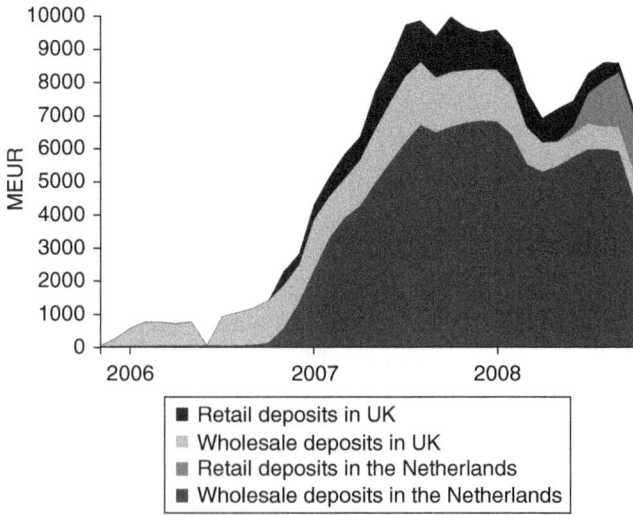

Figure 14.1 Deposits to Landsbanki's branches in the UK (wholesale and retail) and the Netherlands

Source: Landsbanki Islands ehf., SIC Report, Figure 37, Chapter 7, Volume 2, p. 37.

On March 30, the CEO and the deputy CEO of Landsbanki requested a meeting with the Board of Governors of the Central Bank of Iceland to report on their bleeding online deposit accounts. The CEOs told the governors that the underfunded Icelandic Deposit Insurance Fund was now the main point of criticism in the British media, exacerbating the run on Icesave accounts.[23]

Sigurjon Arnason, CEO of Landsbanki, told the governors that there were two ticking time bombs threatening the existence of the bank: Icesave and the wholesale deposits. The Central Bank of Iceland minutes from this meeting also record Arnason explaining, "The probability that the Icelandic banks will be able to withstand this is very, very low."[24]

On April 1, after the alarming meeting with Landsbanki's CEOs, the governors of the Central Bank of Iceland requested a meeting with the two leaders of the cabinet, Prime Minister Geir Haarde and Minister of Foreign Affairs Ingibjorg Solrun Gisladottir.[25]

The Minister of Foreign Affairs described the meeting in a memo: "David Oddsson, leading the discussion on behalf of the Board of Governors, started by reporting that 193 million pounds had poured out of Icesave accounts over the weekend and until this day. Said that Landsbanki had 6 days left." She also quoted the governor as saying that the FSA was requesting that the Icesave accounts be moved over to a British subsidiary, "probably due to rules on deposit insurance."[26]

The SIC found no evidence that the cabinet ministers, or the Icelandic administration as a whole, took any action as a result of this alarming news, even though the immediacy of the threat—involving assets of foreigners, in a foreign country, and caused by the poor standing of an Icelandic company—was clearly stated in meeting minutes and memos. In case of Landsbanki's bankruptcy, foreign deposit holders would have a compensation claim of the size of Iceland's GDP against the Icelandic Insurance Fund, which had less than 2 percent of that amount at its disposal.[27]

Furthermore, the SIC—despite its comprehensive data warehouse, including all emails sent to and from ministers' email accounts—found no evidence that the Ministry of Foreign Affairs took any action to prepare for such an event, establishing diplomatic relations to discuss possible scenarios, or even gathering information on the severity of the situation and its possible consequences for foreign or domestic interests.[28]

After the fall of Landsbanki, the dispute over compensation to the Icesave depositors turned into the largest foreign dispute that Iceland has had since the Cod Wars in the 1950s and 1970s. On January 28, 2013—over four years later—the Icesave dispute culminated in an EFTA court ruling in favor of Iceland—but not before great damage was done to Iceland's reputation both at home and abroad.[29]

Withdrawals from Icesave accounts ceased in April, and the fall of Landsbanki was avoided for the time being. The Icelandic administration therefore got a bit more time to prepare before the calamity finally hit, when Landsbanki was run upon again in September 2008.

Despite FSA's repeated efforts throughout 2008, and until the collapse of Landsbanki, to engage the Icelandic authorities to successfully push the management of Landsbanki to move the Icesave liabilities under UK jurisdiction, Landsbanki management did not budge the entire year. The reason was simply that the bank did not have enough assets to move alongside those liabilities so that its subsidiary, Heritable Bank, could meet the criteria to be a sustainable deposit holder according to UK requirements.[30] In addition, it is quite likely that the contractual covenants of bonds issued by Landsbanki would have been triggered by such a move, requiring the bank to refinance large amounts of its bond issues. Interest rates offered to Landsbanki at the time, reflected in credit default swap (CDS) quotes, were too high for the bank to operate without a loss, had it gone into the market for refinancing under those circumstances.

On October 3, 2008, after the fall of Lehman as well as Glitnir—with a run on the Icesave deposit accounts, which were denominated in a foreign currency, in the amount of five times the Central Bank of Iceland's foreign reserves, and with a margin call from the ECB due to declining collateral values—Landsbanki could not meet the liquidity requirements of the FSA.[31] Having decided to give Kaupthing a loan of last resort on October 6, the Central Bank of Iceland had no means to do the same for Landsbanki. Thus, Landsbanki could not be saved.

To protect the interests of UK depositors, the UK regulator ordered the Financial Services Compensation Scheme (FSCS) to put in place arrangements to allow the approximately 300,000 UK depositors to be compensated.[32]

At the same time—in order to get a chance to reclaim some of the deposited money—the FSA ordered the closing of Landsbanki's UK branch and the freezing of all Landsbanki's assets, plus all commercial assets of the Government of Iceland in the UK.[33]

The FSA used the authority bestowed upon it under *force majeure* legislation set up in the aftermath of the 9/11 attacks, infamously known in Iceland ever after as the British terrorist law.[34]

Implementation of the freezing order had unpleasant side effects for many if not all Icelandic citizens. In addition to freezing assets of Landsbanki itself, and of the Icelandic government, it also froze assets related to Iceland in general, to the extent that even many Icelandic students abroad could not receive money for rent or food through traditional international wire transfers.[35]

Kaupthing Suffers the Same Fate

Even after the CBI loan of last resort mentioned above—owing to covenants of debt instruments that Kaupthing had issued on the EMTN market—Kaupthing's fate lay in the hands of its subsidiaries. According to the covenants, if any of Kaupthing's subsidiaries failed, that would trigger an immediate payback of the covered debt.[36]

Unlike in the case of Icesave, the UK's Financial Supervisory Authority was the authorized regulator of Kaupthing's UK subsidiary Kaupthing Singer & Friedlander, because deposit collection of a foreign bank in its subsidiary abroad is under the supervision of the host country.

At 1:30 p.m. on October 8—when Kaupthing Singer & Friedlander could not meet the liquidity requirements of its regulator in the UK—the UK treasury, under the authority of the Banking (Special Provisions) Act of 2008, revoked KSF's license to receive deposits, and put the operation into receivership.[37] Kaupthing Edge accounts had experienced a run, and KSF could not raise the 300 million pounds demanded by the regulator on October 3 to keep the operations going, let alone the additional 1.3 billion pounds needed to fulfill its liquidity requirements.[38] In light of the ongoing financial crisis—and the foreseeable panic that would be triggered among UK depositors if 170,000 Kaupthing Edge depositors had to wait for compensation from the British Deposit Insurance Fund, the Treasury deemed that the requirements for such a drastic administrative measure had been fulfilled.[39] The law clearly states that such actions could only be taken to safeguard the stability of the UK financial system.

On July 10, 2009, the High Court of Justice, Queens Bench Division—ruling in a case brought by Kaupthing's Resolution Committee against Her Majesty's Treasury for unlawful administrative enforcement—agreed with the Treasury that the legal requirements had been met.[40]

FSA's efforts in safeguarding financial stability against vaulnerabilities in KSF's operations started on February 4, 2008, after Kaupthing Edge had begun offering on-demand deposits as well as term deposits.

The UK regulator (FSA) demanded that the new online deposits undergo stringent liquidity requirements, in particular, that 95 percent of all deposits be safeguarded in liquid assets that could easily be converted into cash within 24 hours. In March 2008, Kaupthing Singer & Friedlander asked for an exemption from this requirement.[41]

In the spirit of "*Kaupthinking*,"[42] while the exemption request was still under review by the FSA, KSF made a "liquidity swap" with its parent company. KSF extended a rolling overnight loan to the parent company in the amount of 1.1 billion pounds. In exchange, the parent company lent the subsidiary, KSF, the same amount, but on a rolling three-month basis. In the event of a run, whether or not these funds could be made available would have been up to the parent company and its ability to pay.[43]

When the British regulator denied KSF the exemption from the 95 percent liquidity rule, the rolling overnight instrument fulfilled the requirement for liquid funds, since it was, apparently, only for one night! But meanwhile the parent company had lent the funds to the subsidiary as a three-month loan. Now the subsidiary could do whatever it wanted with the money, including lending it back to the parent company.[44] That's how Kaupthing management outwitted the British regulator, as commended by in-house propaganda.

It was only much later, in the middle of the run on the Iceland-related online accounts, on September 29,[45] that the FSA realized that these "liquid" funds were not available, and that Kaupthing was thus in breach of the 95 percent liquidity rule. Moreover, KSF had paid 500 million pounds worth of margin calls for the parent company, in addition to the 1.1 billion in the liquidity swap, adding further to the already serious breach of regulation.[46] The FSA began insisting that KSF comply and raise at least 300 million pounds to cover the bleeding online accounts. Furthermore, Kaupthing was to move the full 1.6 billion pounds over to KSF before Monday, October 6, or face the consequences.[47]

As noted above, on Monday, October 6, the Central Bank of Iceland decided to give Kaupthing a loan of last resort, of 380 million pounds (500 million euros at the time) to cover the bleeding Kaupthing Edge accounts. The following day, Hector Sants, Director General of the FSA, again asked Hreidar Mar Sigurdsson, CEO of Kaupthing, when the 300 million pound requirement would be met.[48]

The loan of last resort, 380 million pounds, was however, never paid into the subsidiary. In fact it never reached the shores of the UK.

On October 8, 2008, after having waited for a reaction from KSF management for ten days, the UK regulator took over the Kaupthing

Edge accounts and put the entire KSF operation into receivership, as described earlier. Because of covenants in debt contracts requiring immediate reimbursement of funds in the event of the failure of the subsidiary, the Board of Kaupthing had no option but to resign and request that the Icelandic regulator, FME, take over the power as shareholder, putting the entire group into the control of a resolution committee.[49]

When the three banks collapsed, their combined outstanding bonds amounted to roughly 35 billion euros.[50]

With the three largest banks in receivership and not knowing the true causes of the collapse, Icelanders now found themselves terrified and betrayed by a once-friendly neighbor, as the financial abyss stared them in the face.

Chapter 15

A Debt-Free State; Isolated and without Credit

The Curse of a Credit Rating Relationship

In early 2003, the three Icelandic banks had inherited a good credit rating from the virtually debt-free Icelandic state (4.4 percent of GDP net debt), which allowed their borrowing to go into high gear.[1] By early 2008, however, the Icelandic state was inheriting the bad credit ratings of the banks.[2] In just three months, the credit default swap (CDS) rate on Icelandic sovereign debt climbed twenty-fold, from 11 basis points in November 2007 to above 200 in February 2008 (Figure 15.1).

It was only when prompted by the Moody's report on Iceland's government, issued on January 28, 2008,[3] that the Central Bank of Iceland began its search for ways to increase its foreign currency reserves. Reserves had been relatively stable, apart from a level-change in January 2007, when they jumped to about 120 percent of the country's quarterly imports (Figure 15.2).[4]

Given the daunting size of the banking sector, at 10 times Iceland's GDP, interested investors were hard to find. The Central Bank first turned for assistance to its corresponding institutions nearby, its fellow central banks in Scandinavia as well as the Bank of England.[5]

Desperately Seeking Swaps

On March 3, 2008, the governor of the Central Bank, David Oddsson, and the deputy governor, Ingimundur Fridriksson, had a meeting with the governor of the Bank of England, Mervyn King, and his deputy, John Gieve. According to the minutes of the meeting, the

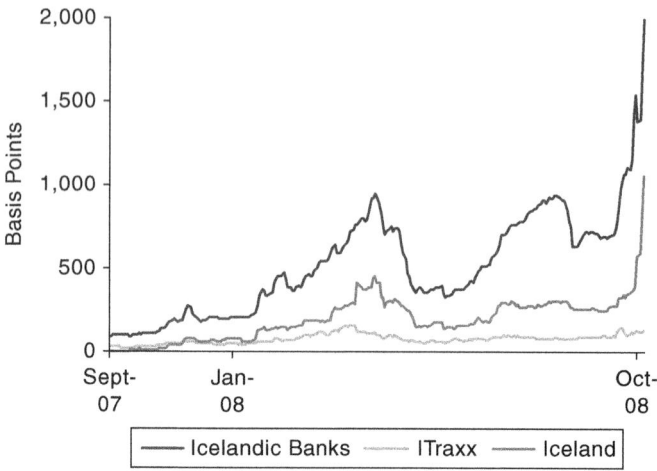

Figure 15.1   CDS spreads on five-year Icelandic sovereign debt and bank debt, plus the ITraxx financial index

Source: Landsbanki Islands ehf., SIC Report, Figure 10, Chapter 4, Volume 1, p. 74.

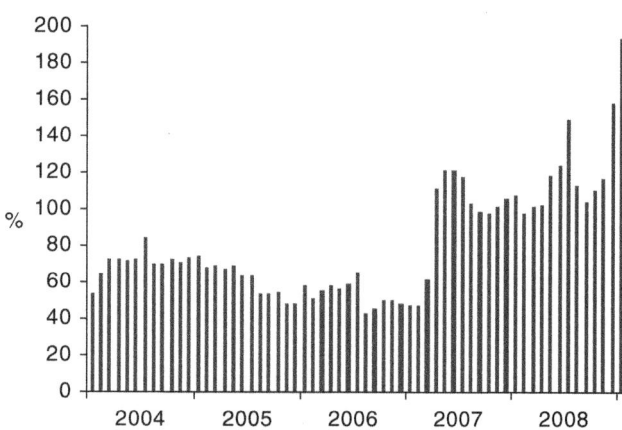

Figure 15.2   Ratio of foreign reserves to quarterly imports

Source: Central Bank of Iceland, SIC Report, Figure 66, Chapter 4, Volume 1, p. 167.

three Icelandic banks were the main topic of discussion, but a formal correspondence between the two central banks was also discussed.[6]

On March 17, the Central Bank of Iceland put forth a formal request, in an email from Deputy Governor Fridriksson which stated: "Further to our conversation in London, and in light of what major central banks have recently agreed among themselves, we would like to ask you whether the Bank of England might consider entering into a bilateral currency swap arrangement with the Central Bank of Iceland."[7] Before the day was through, the Icelandic krona had fallen by 6 percent against the British pound, the largest drop since the Geysir crisis in 2006.[8]

In response to the request from Iceland, Paul Tucker, executive director for markets at the Bank of England, requested a teleconference with Fridriksson. During the teleconference, Tucker asked how much money the Central Bank of Iceland was requesting, and what the bank intended to do with that money.[9]

Fridriksson replied that no particular plans had been outlined by the Central Bank of Iceland, but that the amount requested would probably be between one and two billion pounds (150–300 billion ISK at the time).[10] Tucker replied that he would need to discuss the matter with Governor King.[11]

On March 21, late at night, the Central Bank of Iceland received an email from Tucker, in which he described the initial response of the governor of the Bank of England. King was open to the idea, but felt it needed to be discussed further. Tucker also asked whether the European Central Bank shouldn't be consulted on the same matter, and even the Bank of International Settlements (BIS).[12]

Fridriksson then reiterated the request, with further explanation of the bank's plans regarding the currency swap agreement.[13]

> Further to our earlier conversation, what we are interested in is committed access to an amount of the order of 1 to 2 billion Pounds Sterling for a period of at least several months, and perhaps to the end of the year. The purpose would be to strengthen the international liquidity of the Central Bank and its ability to perform its mandatory tasks. We cannot at this point say under what circumstances we might use this additional liquidity. However, we think that additional international liquidity, based on an agreement with the Bank of England and perhaps other major central banks, would in and of itself increase confidence in the Central Bank and the financial system in general.

On March 26, David Oddsson sent a formal request to ECB Governor Jean-Claude Trichet asking for a 2 billion euro currency swap agreement with the Central Bank of Iceland.[14]

No formal response was received from the ECB, but in an email sent on April 1, 2008, by Francesco Papadia, Director General for Market Operations at the ECB, it was conveyed that the executive board of the ECB had not come to any conclusion regarding this matter. Papadia also asked whether the Icelandic authorities had approached the IMF,

BIS, or other central banks, besides the Bank of England, regarding financial support.[15]

Oddsson's letter to Jean-Claude Trichet and Mervyn King vividly describes how the Central Bank of Iceland viewed the matter:[16]

> By this letter, I wish to follow up on recent contacts about establishing a swap facility between the Central Bank of Iceland and the Bank of England.
>
> While concerns about Iceland subsided somewhat last week, the Icelandic banks have remained in the spotlight and questions continue to be raised in the press about their position and that of Iceland. In view of the delicate situation and global nature of the Icelandic banking system, the Central Bank of Iceland continues to seek to strengthen its position. Following the establishment of a swap facility, the Sovereign would promptly seek term funding in the global financial market to further bolster Central Bank reserves.
>
> On Thursday, April 10th, the Central Bank is scheduled to publish its Monetary Bulletin and announce a policy rate decision. Markets will clearly focus on the meeting on Thursday and it would provide an important venue for any further announcements.
>
> It should be emphasized that the Icelandic banks have not requested liquidity assistance from the Central Bank other than routine liquidity provision in the Icelandic Krona. The solvency of Icelandic banks is not in question. The objective of establishing swap facilities with other central banks should be seen as a precautionary arrangement to change expectations and allay concerns in the market about the Central Bank's ability to weather the storm. Moreover, such facility would serve as a deterrent against "unscrupulous" forces.
>
> If the Icelandic banking system were to be hit hard, the contagion effect could be widespread, especially given the current fragile state of international financial markets. As an example in recent history, in the first quarter of 2006 a brief interruption in the funding of the Icelandic banks sent ripples of fear through financial markets.
>
> In view of the current state of financial markets it [is] likely that the repercussions would be considerably stronger now. Icelandic bank paper is believed to be included in more than half of all CDO structures created in recent years. Our international banking contacts have underlined that a credit event stemming from a large scale liquidation of Icelandic bank obligations would have a serious impact on global asset markets. Similar concerns have been expressed about potential effects on emerging market economies, especially in Europe.
>
> The objective of the Central Bank of Iceland is to engage at least five central banks in swap agreements. I have already been in contact with some of the Nordic Central Banks, the Bank of England, the ECB as well as the BIS. The preliminary response has been positive.
>
> I look forward to your favorable consideration.

To follow up with the bank's request, Deputy Governor Fridriksson and Sturla Palsson, Director of Market Operations at the Central Bank of Iceland, met with leaders of several central banks at the spring meeting of the IMF on April 11, 2008.[17]

In a letter to the SIC, Stefan Ingves, governor of the Swedish central bank, Riksbank, described his experience at the meeting with the Icelandic delegation: "[M]y own impression was that the Icelandic representatives were stressed, not particularly well prepared, and [did] not fully appreciate the risk at hand."[18]

In the minutes of meeting with Mervyn King and Phil Evans on the same occasion, it was emphasized that King considered it necessary for the Central Bank of Iceland to lay out a credible plan on how it intended to use the money it requested.[19]

The Icelandic delegation received similar messages in a meeting with representatives of the Federal Reserve Bank of New York. According to unconfirmed minutes of the meeting, Timothy Geithner, governor of the Federal Reserve Bank of New York, said after his meeting with the governors of the central banks of Sweden, the UK, and Europe, that he felt that such a swap arrangement needed to be very big in order to have the intended impact, over USD 10 billion. Otherwise, financial markets would interpret it as weakness. He told the Icelandic delegation that his colleagues at the other central banks shared his skepticism.[20]

Slapping a Helping Hand

On April 15, David Oddsson sent another formal request for a 3–4 billion euro swap agreement, this time to five central banks: Sweden, Norway, and Denmark, as well as the Bank of England and the ECB.[21] With such a swap agreement, the Central Bank of Iceland hoped to show the financial markets that it would be able to provide liquidity to the Icelandic banks in all the currencies in which the banks operated.[22]

As noted in an earlier chapter, in a background memorandum, sent out with the letter to the five central banks, it was pointed out that the equity ratios of the banks were high, and nonperforming loans were low. Furthermore, the memorandum stated that the CDSs quoted in the market could easily be misleading, since two of the banks had recently issued new debt instruments at much more favorable rates than indicated by the CDS quotes.[23]

Already on April 17 the swap agreement with the three Nordic banks was being drafted, but no response had been received from the Bank of England. Deputy Governor Fridriksson sent Paul Tucker an email asking about the status of the request. Tucker replied the next day: "We are actively discussing with the other central banks."[24]

In an attempt to get an answer, David Oddsson sent a letter to Mervyn King on April 22 stating that he had hopes that King would be in a position to respond to the request from April 17, now that the swap agreement with the Nordics was well on its way.[25] An answer from King arrived the following day:[26]

It is clear that the balance sheet of your three banks combined has risen to the level where it would be extremely difficult for you effectively to act as a lender of last resort. International financial markets are becoming more aware of this position and increasingly concerned about it. In my judgment, the only solution to this problem is a programme to be implemented speedily to reduce significantly the size of the Icelandic banking system. It is extremely unusual for such a small country to have such a large banking system. It would not be sensible for me to suggest the precise way in which this might be achieved. But the sale of one or more banks or significant proportions of their assets overseas, to foreign banks must surely be high on your list of possible policy instruments. To design and implement such a programme is not easy. I would very much like to discuss how the international community could offer help to Iceland in respect of designing such a solution by raising the matter at the dinner of G10 Central Bank Governors to be held in Basel on 4 May. I have spoken about this with Stefan Ingves, Governor of the Riksbank in Sweden, and we shall both be requesting a discussion at the dinner.

The amount of money is very small relative to the potential need for funds should a problem arise with one or more of your banks. Indeed, the announcement of a swap, especially if restricted to a group of countries with which Iceland has good political relations, might well trigger concern in financial markets about the extent to which you and ourselves perceived a problem in the Icelandic banking system, and then attention would be drawn to the inadequate scale of financial resources available to you to deal with the problem. The swap might look rather like a political gesture rather than a credible financial strategy.

I know you will be disappointed. But among friends it is sometimes necessary to be clear about what we think. We have given much consideration to your proposal. In my judgment, only a serious attempt to reduce the size of the banking system would constitute a solution to the current problem. I would like to think that the international central banking community could find a way to offer effective help to enable you more easily to construct a programme to reduce the size of the banking system. I shall be willing to do all in our power to help you achieve that.

David Oddsson promptly responded the same day, saying:[27]

> Thank you for your letter of April 23, 2008. I very much value the attention that you have given to our situation and your expression of goodwill. I note from your response that I have not been able to explain clearly enough how the arrangement for a swap would help in strengthening confidence in Iceland and the Icelandic financial system.
>
> I remain convinced that a swap arrangement with several central banks would indeed help and very significantly reduce the likelihood of serious occurrences. In fact, I have grave concerns that the absence of a swap arrangement in the current circumstances could have very severe consequences. I must emphasize my belief that this is not an isolated Icelandic concern. Difficulties in Iceland could have serious contagious effects in other countries.

Oddsson's letter never addressed King's offer of help to reduce the size of the Icelandic banking system, but further insisted:[28]

> You strongly emphasize in your letter the necessity of the banks reducing in size. I fully agree with you. As I have explained, our intention with the swap arrangement was among other things to create a window of opportunity to pressure the banks to downsize. A swap arrangement would in our view greatly improve the conditions for the liquidation of assets.
>
> The Icelandic banks are well capitalized but they are dealing with a problem of perception. The signals we receive from the markets are that a swap facility for the Central Bank would contribute immeasurably to the alleviation of the problem.
>
> I hereby kindly ask you to reconsider this matter.

The Central Bank of Iceland received no official reply to this letter.[29]

Relinquishing Part of Sovereignty

During a dinner discussion at a meeting of central bank governors of the G10 in Basel on May 4, a new tone was struck toward the Icelandic request, leaving little room for further exploration of the possibility of a swap arrangement.[30] The only ones still willing to discuss it were Iceland's Scandinavian neighbors, the central banks of Denmark, Norway, and Sweden. David Oddsson followed up on May 7, urging that the arrangement be set up.[31]

On May 15, the Scandinavian central banks agreed on the terms, opening up a currency swap of 1.5 billion euros in total; 500 million euros from each central bank in exchange for Icelandic krona.

Those 1.5 billion euros came at a cost of surrendering part of Iceland's sovereignty. Fundamental macroeconomic management was now to be decided under the terms of the swap agreement, from restructuring the Housing Finance Fund, to avoiding further net borrowing and spending of the government, to addressing real wage increases in labor market settlements between unions and employers.[32]

The swap agreement was signed by three ministers, Prime Minister Geir H. Haarde, Foreign Minister Ingibjorg Solrun Gisladottir, and Finance Minister Arni M. Mathiesen, along with the three governors of the Central Bank of Iceland.[33]

Strictly Confidential[34]

To the Governors of Sveriges Riksbank, Danmarks Nationalbank, and Norges Bank

The purpose of the swap facility is to strengthen confidence in the Icelandic economy in the short term, thereby providing a window for addressing fundamental issues. The swap facility is not intended to be drawn upon.

If the swap facility is drawn on, it will be used to increase available liquid foreign exchange reserves. If drawn on, the facility will be used pro rata and not for exchange market intervention, nor will the funds be used for recapitalization of banks. Should recapitalization become necessary, the Government, while not subsidizing the banks or shareholders, will use other funds for that purpose.

In order to build confidence and to ensure stability in the financial sector and at the macro level, we intend to support the suggested precautionary swap facility by taking the following measures:

1. To increase available foreign exchange reserves, the Government will, with urgency raise EUR 1–2 bn. If the swap facility is drawn on, the Government will borrow an amount commensurate to the total amount of swap transactions.
2. The Central Bank and the Supervisory Authority will use their powers to pressure the banks to reduce the overall size of their balance sheets, in line with the measures suggested by the IMF.
3. In order to increase the effectiveness of monetary policy and to remove distortions, a credible plan for the restructuring and reform of the Housing Finance Fund system will, with urgency, be formulated and made public.
4. To maintain fiscal prudence and to avoid further net-borrowing our intention is to keep the public debt level at its current low level

as well as to strengthen the fiscal framework along the lines suggested by the IMF. We will consider how to address the concerns
on real wage clauses in the wage settlements.

5. Given the vulnerabilities of the financial system, an IMF FSAP up
date is welcome to assess the situation in more detail. The forth-
coming Article IV consultation discussions also provide a welcome
opportunity to assess the overall situation.

6. The Central Bank of Iceland will keep participating central banks
fully and promptly informed of the measures listed above

The Central bank sent two memos to its counterparties in
Scandinavia, one in July and the other in September 2008, giving
updates on the progress of the items stipulated in the agreement.
According to those memos, no progress had been made on those items,
apart from the increasing of the foreign exchange reserves by 1 billion
euros in the form of short-term borrowing from 1 to 3 months.[35]

The lack of urgency, sensed by Iceland's counterparties, did not
strengthen Iceland's position when the banks finally collapsed. The
Scandinavians were then reluctant to support the Icelandic state
unless under the leadership and surveillance of the IMF.[36] Iceland
was left increasingly isolated in the international forum of central
bankers, and in particular was left out of the swap agreement made
by the New York Fed with the Scandinavian countries in September
2008.[37]

Special Court on Minister's Accountability Issues Its Judgment

Despite the emphasis by the governors of the Scandinavian central
banks on swift policy change,[38] as stipulated in the swap agreement
and the necessary public announcement thereof, the full contents of
the swap agreement were not introduced to the rest of the cabinet,
nor were other stakeholders informed, such as the labor unions or
leaders of the Housing Finance Fund, who would surely have been
affected if the agreement had been honored.

On April 23, 2011, Prime Minister Geir H. Haarde was found
guilty as charged on this single count out of four before a special high
court, Landsdomur, for having failed to hold cabinet meetings on
matters of vital importance to the Republic of Iceland, as stipulated
in Article 17 of the Constitution of Iceland.[39]

In the view of the prosecution, such meetings would have been vital
after the meetings with the governors of the Central Bank of Iceland,

on February 14 and April 1, 2008, and after the announcement of the swap agreement with the Scandinavian central banks on May 15. The judges agreed with the prosecution's case in this regard.[40]

The Landsdomur ruling of 2011 was the first by this special high court since its establishment in 1905 to handle cases involving members of the Icelandic cabinet.[41]

Chapter 16

Putting a Poodle on Watch

Understaffed Oversight

When privatization of the Icelandic banks was completed in 2003, the Icelandic Financial Supervisory Authority (FME)—responsible for supervising not only the banking system, but also pension funds, mutual funds, insurance companies, and several other types of financial institutions—had a budget of just 265 million kronas (roughly USD 3.4 million at the time) and just 36 employees.[1] As the Icelandic banking system grew in size and became increasingly complex, financial oversight stagnated or got even weaker. While the number of employees in the financial industry grew from 6,100 in 2002 to 8,700 in 2007,[2] the number of FME employees only increased from 36 to 47.[3]

The rise of bank assets per FME employee gives an even better indication of the disparity in growth. In 2002 every FME staff member had on average 300 million euros under supervision, but close to 2 billion euros in 2007.[4] In just two years, from 2005 to 2007, Icelandic bank branches abroad increased from 4 to 21, and foreign subsidiaries of the banks from 21 to 31.[5] This growth of the Icelandic banking system beyond Iceland itself also called for increased cooperation with financial supervisors in the host countries.

The FME received around 4,000 reports per year from companies under supervision but, when the SIC began its investigation, no data warehouse or functioning database had been set up to house all these reports or analyze all this data.[6]

One of the main shortcomings of the FME, as concluded by the SIC, was lack of consistency and responsibility.[7] A good example of this is the collection of information on delinquent payments in the banking system. This information had been reported by the agency every quarter from 2001 to 2006, but no such information was reported in 2007 or the first quarter of 2008.[8] Statistics on non-performing loans (NPLs) were also not collected on a regular basis, despite the fact that NPLs are among the best barometers of the health of a banking system.

In a memo dated March 1, 2007, employees of the FME aired their concerns about the inability of the FME to identify risks in the financial system in general. They complained that the FME had no central database where key financial indicators could be monitored for the entire system. They further stressed that proper overview of the system was impossible since data archiving had not taken place: Old reports collected from individual financial institutions had not been properly stored. The employees suggested that a special statistics division be established within the agency to assemble and archive data for analytical purposes. Despite these employee suggestions, no changes were made to the agency.[9]

See No Evil, Hear No Evil

For trained statisticians, not to mention those who value financial stability, no further evidence is needed to understand the low quality and ineffectiveness of Icelandic financial supervision in the run-up to the collapse of the banks. The lack of data-archiving processes and an IT infrastructure for analysis together meant that effective supervision of the banking system was practically impossible.

Lack of effective supervision by the FME can also be seen in the incredibly low number of cases reported by the agency to police authorities. In 2006 there were just three cases reported, then only one in 2007, and just two in 2008 before the banks collapsed.[10]

The SIC was decisive when it comes to the effectiveness of the FME in the run up to the collapse of the banks. It reached a clear conclusion that the FME's inability to effectively supervise the banking system could mainly be attributed to the wrong prioritization of both policy-makers and FME leadership in regard to its supervisory and regulatory activities.[11]

The FME was not just understaffed. It also lacked the necessary experience and competence for effective oversight.[12] New recruits were mainly young and inexperienced, while more experienced supervisors left at the very height of the boom.[13] Average employment experience fell from roughly 10 years in 2000\ to roughly 4 years in 2008.[14]

In addition, the agency was marked by lack of authority and follow-up. Cases were kept informal for too long,[15] violations of the law went unnoticed, and, even when violations were detected, the law was not enforced.[16]

The Central Bank—No Plan to Avert Detected Risk

By law, the two primary responsibilities of the Central Bank of Iceland are to ensure price stability and financial stability.[17] In addition, the bank supervises the liquidity of financial institutions.

From 2001 to 2008, employee turnover was low and the competence of its roughly 100 employees was much higher than that of the FME, except for one division: the division in charge of financial stability. This division had four employees in 2001, rising to eight in 2008, but only one member of the division remained on the job during the entire period—the managing director.[18]

By law, the Central Bank of Iceland had a multitude of regulatory tools at its disposal with which to react to the astonishing growth of credit and bring it under control. It used none of them.[19] Instead it acted to enhance the growth of credit, by not including reserve requirements on foreign exchange deposits in branches abroad, reducing reserve requirements domestically, and leaving increasing foreign exchange imbalances untreated. It could have increased equity requirements, which would have significantly hampered credit growth while hedging against fluctuations of the krona, which was the main reason for allowing foreign exchange imbalances.

While the bank communicated some concern for the overheating economy, and acted to alleviate it, by raising interest rates, it did not respond even to its own assessment of increasing risk in the banking system. It continued to lower collateral requirements, and increased its lending to the banks through short-term collateralized lending facilities. The bank had full authority to establish better collateral rules in its lending to the financial system, but did not do so.[20]

Central Bank concerns about the risk of financial instability first got serious in November 2007, and the bank communicated that concern to the government. However, neither formally nor informally did it ever communicate to the government what it could and should do to prevent possible collapse. Had the governors of the Central bank felt that they did not have the necessary means, by law, to intervene, they never communicated that fact, neither to the cabinet, nor to the leaders of Parliament.[21]

And in fact the Central Bank seems to have thought it was doing fine. In an assessment on its own quality of work in the *Financial Stability Report* in 2006, it said (p. 5): "In recent years, the [Icelandic] authorities have built a strong framework of law, regulations, and supervision in the financial market, which matches the best that can be found in our neighboring countries."[22]

More Roman than Greek

Icelanders seem more Roman than Greek when it comes to interpreting the law. Thorarinn G. Petursson, senior economist at the Central Bank of Iceland, in testimony before the SIC, described how that creates a handicap for those responsible for financial oversight in Iceland. "I think there is a fundamental misunderstanding of what financial supervision is all about here in Iceland, not only at the FME but also at the Central Bank. They thought that the role of these institutions was to follow up on whether the letter of the law was met by those under supervision. So you are watching the entire financial system falling off a cliff, and as long as you follow the law, you're fine!"[23]

This is similar to one of the main conclusions of the Turner Review, the British investigative report into financial supervision by British authorities in the run-up to the collapse. "Regulatory and supervisory coverage should follow the principle of economic substance not legal form."[24]

Depreciation of Assets

In only four months, from June to October 2008, the assets of the Icelandic banking system were written down by 62 percent (Table 16.1).[25]

In June 2008, the three banks reported their half-year financial results showing combined total assets of 11,764 billion ISK, or

Table 16.1 Write-downs of assets of the three banks from June to October 2008 (billion ISK)

Amounts	Assets before value adjustment	Adjusted value	Write-down	Write-down as percentage of assets
Landsbanki Íslands hf.	4,353	1.994	2.359	54%
Kaupthing banki hf.	3,505	1.073	2.432	69%
Glitnir banki hf.	3,906	1.360	2.546	65%
Total	11,764	4.427	7.337	62%

Source: Special Investigation Commission, Press Conference Material April 12, available at: www.sic.althingi.is.

roughly USD 165 billion.[26] After write-downs, the total assets of the three banks amounted to 4,427 billion ISK, about USD 62 billion, still five times the GDP of Iceland.[27] In 2009, the combined balance sheet of the three banks, which were established from the ruins namely Arion Bank, Islandsbanki and New Landsbanki, amounted 150% of Iceland's GDP. The rest of the bank assets adhere to the bankrupt estates that are in a winding up process.

The SIC Verdict: Negligence in the Highest Places

The SIC was required by law to determine if mistakes or negligence had occurred in enforcement of laws and regulations relating to supervision of financial operations in Iceland. The law specifically stated that, in addition to actions that failed to fulfill legal requirements, actions that failed to take into consideration necessary information, including failure to react to information about a looming threat, could also be considered negligence.[28]

The SIC explained the position of the banks in Icelandic society by analogy to the famous example about the bank customer who had borrowed too much. The problem of the customer then turns into a serious problem for the bank, and, the bank's relationship with the customer undergoes a fundamental change. By the same token, when a country's financial system has grown to ten times the country's GDP, the authorities no longer hold the necessary power to discipline the players in the system. According to the SIC, Icelandic authorities were therefore at the mercy of the banks, putting all their energy into keeping them going at all cost.[29]

In its report, the SIC described how elected representatives and government officials, in testimony to the SIC, continuously pointed a finger at one another. As the SIC pushed for explanations as to why they had not taken action to mitigate the risk of financial collapse, the ministers and directors of public agencies repeatedly claimed that the subject at hand had been the responsibility of another government agency, not their own. None of them ever admitted responsibility for what happened.[30]

Nevertheless, the SIC concluded that the following people showed negligence within the meaning of article 1(1) of Act. No. 142/2008, the law on the Special Investigation Commission:[31]

Geir H. Haarde, Prime Minister.
Arni M. Mathiesen, Minister of Finance.

Bjorgvin G. Sigurdsson, Minister of Commerce.
Jonas Fr. Jonsson, Director General of FME.
David Oddsson, Governor of the Central Bank of Iceland.
Eirikur Gudnason, Deputy Governor of the Central Bank of Iceland.
Ingimundur Fridriksson, Deputy Governor of the Central Bank of Iceland.

Chapter 17

What Have We Learned?

The Importance of Equity

Countless lessons can be drawn from the Icelandic story, as described in the report of the Special Investigation Commission (SIC), upon which this book is based. Iceland has already benefited from many of them, with numerous policy reforms, especially relating to the financial system, implemented after the banking collapse.

First of all, corporations are no longer allowed to fund purchases of their own shares. The financial supervisory authority, FME, has increased from 47 employees to roughly 120, while the size of the banking system has been reduced from 10 times to about 1.7 times the GDP of Iceland. The financial stability division of the Central Bank has been strengthened significantly, and the governor of the Central Bank is now recruited by a professional selection committee, instead of being appointed politically. Legal provisions for the Central Bank have been strengthened, with rules on collateral accepted in its short-term liquidity facilities, as well as rules on liquidity requirements and the foreign exchange balances of financial institutions.

A monetary policy committee has been established, which sets the Central Bank's interest rate. The committee is chaired by the new Central Bank governor and includes the new deputy governor, the new chief economist of the Central Bank, and two outside economists. These are just a few of the changes, but many suggested reforms still remain to be implemented.

Ironically, Iceland is now widely viewed as the poster child of successful economic recovery. According to Statistics Iceland, unemployment has fallen from about 9 percent following the collapse to 4.9 percent in May 2013, and GDP has turned a corner from 6.6 percent decline in 2009 to almost 2.9 percent growth in 2011, although growth slowed to 1.6 percent in 2012. The fiscal deficit has been reduced from 13.5 percent of GDP in 2008 to just 3.4 percent in 2012.

Besides policy improvements in Iceland, another contribution of the Icelandic SIC to the world of finance stands out above all others. The diagram on the cover of this book—the cross-ownership structure in the Icelandic economy in 2008, revealed using network data analysis performed by Margret Bjarnadottir and Gudmundur Hansen, contractors to the SIC—makes it possible for the rest of us to visualize the cause of the collapse of the Icelandic banks.

After Bjarnadottir and Hansen identified related parties in the Icelandic system, the rest of the quantitative analyst team of the SIC was able to map out how credit was distributed among a handful of people, whatever we decide to call them—perhaps oligarchs, as Louis Brandeis did a century ago, or "impunitists," as I have chosen to call them, since they were seemingly able to act with impunity in the run-up to the collapse.[1]

The web of ownership constructed by these impunitists consisted of hundreds of special purpose vehicles (firms), most likely established for the sole purpose of tunneling money out of the Icelandic banking system. The impunitists managed to risk next to nothing of their own money at the outset, creating a system where the upside of their bets was surely theirs, while downside risk was put upon the rest of society.

There are several ways to prevent this risk from occurring in the future, whether in Iceland or elsewhere. The primary responsibility lies in the hands of policy-makers, who need to make it clear that extensive lending against shaky collateral, or even without any, undermines not just the interests of minority shareholders but also the entire banking system. Such lending practices should in all banking systems be punishable by law. Taxing dividends in such a way that they essentially evaporate as chains of holding companies get longer might also reduce the incentive to build up a web of holding companies in cross-ownership.

Policy-makers looking toward liberalizing their financial system need to make sure they build strong supervision alongside it, to be able to enforce the law. If they expect rapid credit growth to emerge, it needs to be managed, given the enormous risks that such episodes entail.

Bankers who extend credit to holding companies need to understand that such loans are subordinated. That is, loans to holding companies are a claim on the residual claim and should therefore be priced accordingly. If correctly priced, it is highly unlikely that individuals could become wealthy by risking only other people's money, and none of their own, simply because the financial cost would eat up most, if not all, of the benefits of such transactions.

Banking supervisors have an enormous responsibility. The complexity of modern financial systems puts higher demand on their shoulders to make use of modern information technology, recruit the best data analysts, and monitor the formation of correlation in their system. Institutions under supervision, as well as politicians, need to accept that such talent costs money, since it is time consuming and expensive for individuals to gain the training needed to be able to perform the necessary analyses. Financial supervision is, therefore, expensive. Lack of supervision, on the other hand, is much more expensive, as Icelanders can so painfully testify.

It is the regulator's responsibility to monitor whether bankers are incentivized to underestimate the risk they take on behalf of the bank. The regulator must also set a common legal framework, including caps on incentive pay for the entire banking industry, so that competitive forces will not lead to a race to the bottom, as experienced in Iceland.

Similarly, in the same spirit, if banks are owned by holding companies, it is the regulator's responsibility to monitor whether the holding companies are leveraged or not. If leveraged, the equity requirements of the banks need to be higher, since such banks are more risky. Holding companies have incentive to influence the management of banks to take more risk, grow faster, and pay out dividends to meet their obligations at the other end. This is contrary to the interests of deposit holders, who place money in the bank because they do not want to take it to the stock or the bond market. They're looking for low risk.

Financial supervisors also need to ascertain that a bank's equity in fact exists. If the reported equity is nowhere to be found, the law on minimum equity requirements needs to be enforced. Similarly, it is the responsibility of auditors to ensure that equity has been paid into each bank.

Should our politicians decide to expose the rest of the society to the risk of allowing holding companies—as opposed to individuals—to own banks, those holding companies need to be subjected to the same financial supervision as banks. Only then can we be sure that the equity ratios of banks are for real.

The SIC provides empirical evidence supporting the theory, developed by John Geanakoplos, on leverage cycles. Once the "corporate veil" was pierced so we could see who owned what the SIC report shows that credit was extended to and through structures that allowed for excessive leverage to the point where equity was just a tiny fraction of the firms' balance sheets, and the rest was borrowed money. This leads to a lesson for central bankers, who should monitor the overall level of leverage in a financial system and establish rules for managing it.

Economists and business managers can learn from psychologists. By understanding our inherent bounded rationality we may improve our decision making and decrease the likelihood of harmful mistakes. But we can never overcome cognitive biases and avoid mistakes altogether. Banking supervisors can also benefit from understanding these biases, in order to better anticipate how those under supervision are likely to behave.

But, having studied the fall of the Icelandic banking system for over five years now, I believe that the lessons learned, and the remedies, boil down to a few simple things taught in the first classes of economics, statistics, and finance: pricing, correlation, and incentives.

The equity of each firm is the shareholders' contribution to the business, whether in the form of capital contributed up front or unpaid hours worked for the company. But in addition there is credit, which can help make the company grow faster than only revenues would allow for, thereby also contributing more to the economic well-being of the rest of society.

Credit must be accurately priced so that those who provide it are compensated in line with the risk they take. But if the shareholder has placed leveraged funds into the firm as equity, creditors can never appropriately assess the risk involved in lending money to the firm. They will therefore not receive a yield reflecting the true risk. Equity thus needs to be transparent and truly paid into the firm.

Long chains of interrelated (correlated) and leveraged firms must be abolished so that incentives can be aligned and risk can be borne by those who potentially reap the benefits from it. Only then can our capitalist system provide the outcome it is intended to do.

An economy without equity is essentially an economy without its pillars, and hence will eventually collapse. Entrepreneurs such as Petur Snaeland, the one described at the very beginning of this book, are the ones who form those pillars. They are willing to make the sacrifice, bear the risk, and, if all goes well, enjoy the benefits.

Gardabaer, June 4, 2013
Gudrun Johnsen

Notes

1 Illusion of Prosperity

1. P. Hilbers, I. Otker-Robe, C. Pazarbasiglou, and G. Johnsen, 2005, "Assessing and Managing Rapid Credit Growth—and the Role of Supervisory and Prudential Policies," IMF Working Paper no. 05/151, Washington DC.
2. Evergreening refers to bank lending to stressed borrowers, indirectly, to assist them in paying off other loans.
3. P. O. Gourinchas, P.O., R. Valdés, R., and O. Landerretche, O., 2001, "Lending Booms: Latin America and the World," *Economia*, 1, no. 2 (Spring 2001): 47–99. Spring 2001
4. Hilbers, et al. "Assessing and Managing Rapid Credit Growth."
5. Hilbers et al. "Assessing and Managing Rapid Credit Growth."
6. Hilbers et al. "Assessing and Managing Rapid Credit Growth."
7. Bob Harris, 2009, "A Startling Revelation: What the IMF and Central Bankers Knew—and didn't Tell Us," weblog about the Trade Union Advisory Committee meeting at the OECD in May 2009, http://fundingeducation.blogspot.com/2009_05_01_archive.html (accessed May 29, 2013).
8. Hilbers et al., "Assessing and Managing Rapid Credit Growth."

2 Collapse

1. Special Investigation Commission (SIC), 2008, *Background and Causes of the Collapse of the Icelandic banks in 2008 and Related Events*, Vol. 7, Chapter 20, p. 48 (Report of the Special Investigation Commission, Reykjavik).
2. Speech of the prime minister of Iceland, Geir H. Haarde on October 6, 2008, translated from Icelandic. http://www.forsaetisraduneyti.is/radherra/raedurGHH/nr/3034
3. In Icelandic "upplausnarástand" and "þjóðargjaldþrot," respectively.
4. "Guð blessi Ísland"
5. "Guð blessi Ísland" is also the title of a documentary film about the collapse of the three Icelandic banks and the Kitchenware revolution that followed.

3 Panic

1. Special Investigation Commission (SIC), 2008, *Background and Causes of the Collapse of the Icelandic banks in 2008 and Related Events*, Vol. 2, Chapter 7, p. 15. (Report of the Special Investigation Commission, Reykjavik).
2. Author's calculation, 550 million euro payment amounted 94.6 billion ISK on September 25, 2008, when the exchange rate reached 172.1 ISK/EUR. Glitnir's equity base, as reported in the bank's half-year results in 2008, was 200 billion ISK (Special Investigation Commission (SIC), 2008, *Background and Causes of the Collapse of the Icelandic banks in 2008 and Related Events*, Vol. 2, Chapter 8, p. 323. (Report of the Special Investigation Commission, Reykjavik).s.
3. Glitnir's total bonds outstanding in 2008 were 17.8 billion euros (Mark Flannery, 2010, *Iceland's Failed Banks: A Post Mortem*, SIC Report, Vol. 9 (Reykjavik: Special Investigation Commission), Appendix 3.
4. Special Investigation Commission (SIC), 2008, *Background and Causes of the Collapse of the Icelandic banks in 2008 and Related Events*, Vol. 7, Chapter 20, p. 8. (Report of the Special Investigation Commission Reykjavik).
5. SIC Report, Vol. 7, Chapter 20, p. 12.
6. SIC Report, Vol. 7, Chapter 20, p. 9.
7. SIC Report, Vol. 7, Chapter 20, p. 10.
8. SIC Report, Vol. 7, Chapter 20, p. 11.
9. SIC Report, Vol. 7, Chapter 20, p. 10.
10. Gudni Th. Johannesson, 2009, *Hrunið: Ísland á barmi gjaldþrots og upplausnar* [E. The Collapse: Iceland on the Brink of Bankruptcy and Chaos] (Reykjavik, Iceland: JPV), endnote 76.
11. SIC Report, Vol. 7, Chapter 20, p. 25.
12. SIC Report, Vol. 7, Chapter 20, p. 25.
13. SIC Report, Vol. 7, Chapter 20, p. 25.
14. SIC Report, Vol. 7, Chapter 20, p. 25.
15. SIC Report, Vol. 7, Chapter 20, p. 13.
16. SIC Report, Vol. 7, Chapter 20, p. 13.
17. SIC Report, Vol. 7, Chapter 20, p. 41.
18. SIC Report, Vol. 7, Chapter 21, p. 249.
19. SIC Report, Vol. 7, Chapter 20, p. 41.
20. SIC Report, Vol. 7, Chapter 20, p. 14.
21. SIC Report, Vol. 7, Chapter 20, p. 15.
22. SIC Report, Vol. 7, Chapter 20, p. 15.
23. SIC Report, Vol. 7, Chapter 20, p. 16.
24. SIC Report, Vol. 7, Chapter 20, p. 16.
25. SIC Report, Vol. 7, Chapter 20, p. 17.
26. SIC Report, Vol. 7, Chapter 20, p. 17.
27. SIC Report, Vol. 7, Chapter 20, p. 22.
28. SIC Report, Vol. 7, Chapter 20, p. 44.

29. SIC Report, Vol. 7, Chapter 20, p. 24.
30. SIC Report, Vol. 7, Chapter 20, p. 24.
31. SIC Report, Vol. 7, Chapter 20, p. 45.
32. SIC Report, Vol. 7, Chapter 20, p. 26.
33. SIC Report, Vol. 7, Chapter 20, p. 26.
34. SIC Report, Vol. 7, Chapter 20, p. 26.
35. SIC Report, Vol. 7, Chapter 20, p. 28.
36. SIC Report, Vol. 7, Chapter 20, p. 47.
37. SIC Report, Vol. 7, Chapter 20, p. 34.
38. SIC Report, Vol. 7, Chapter 20, p. 29.
39. SIC Report, Vol. 7, Chapter 20, p. 29.
40. SIC Report, Vol. 7, Chapter 20, p. 29.
41. SIC Report, Vol. 7, Chapter 20, p. 29.
42. SIC Report, Vol. 7, Chapter 20, p. 31.
43. SIC Report, Vol. 7, Chapter 20, p. 31.
44. SIC Report, Vol. 7, Chapter 20, p. 30.
45. SIC Report, Vol. 7, Chapter 20, p. 30.
46. SIC Report, Vol. 7, Chapter 20, p. 34.
47. SIC Report, Vol. 7, Chapter 20, p. 33.
48. SIC Report, Vol. 7, Chapter 20, p. 35.
49. SIC Report, Vol. 7, Chapter 20, p. 35.
50. SIC Report, Vol. 7, Chapter 20, p. 14.
51. SIC Report, Vol. 7, Chapter 20, p. 14.
52. SIC Report, Vol. 7, Chapter 20, p. 48.
53. http://www.visir.is/simarnir-raudgloandi-hja-glitni-i-morgun
    /article/2008298116706
54. http://www.vb.is/frettir/13102/
55. Johannesson, 2009, *Hrunið: Ísland á barmi gjaldþrots og upplausnar*
    (E. *The Collapse: Iceland on the Brink of Bankruptcy and Chaos*), p. 75.
56. http://www.visir.is/simarnir-raudgloandi-hja-glitni-i-morgun
    /article/2008298116706
57. SIC Report, Vol. 7, Chapter 20, p. 49.
58. SIC Report, Vol. 7, Chapter 20, p. 49.
59. Johannesson, 2009, *Hrunið: Ísland á barmi gjaldþrots og upplausnar*
    (E. *The Collapse: Iceland on the Brink of Bankruptcy and Chaos*), p. 71.
60. SIC Report, Vol. 7, Chapter 20, p. 48.
61. SIC Report, Vol. 7, Chapter 20, p. 162.
62. SIC Report, Vol. 7, Chapter 20, p. 77.
63. SIC Report, Vol. 7, Chapter 20, p. 80.
64. SIC Report, Vol. 7, Chapter 20, p. 77.
65. SIC Report, Vol. 7, Chapter 20, p. 77.
66. SIC Report, Vol. 7, Chapter 20, p. 49.
67. SIC Report, Vol. 7, Chapter 20, p. 78.
68. SIC Report, Vol. 7, Chapter 20, p. 79.
69. SIC Report, Vol. 7, Chapter 20, p. 49.
70. SIC Report, Vol. 7, Chapter 20, p. 80.

71. SIC Report, Vol. 7, Chapter 20, p. 162.
72. SIC Report, Vol. 7, Chapter 20, p. 87.
73. SIC Report, Vol. 7, Chapter 20, p. 87.
74. SIC Report, Vol. 7, Chapter 20, p. 160.
75. SIC Report, Vol. 7, Chapter 20, p. 163.
76. Johannesson, 2009, *Hrunið: Ísland á barmi gjaldþrots og upplausnar (E. The Collapse: Iceland on the Brink of Bankruptcy and Chaos),* p. 77.
77. SIC Report, Vol. 7, Chapter 20, p. 87.
78. SIC Report, Vol. 7, Chapter 20, p. 49.
79. SIC Report, Vol. 7, Chapter 20, p. 82.
80. SIC Report, Vol. 7, Chapter 20, p. 81.
81. SIC Report, Vol. 7, Chapter 20, p. 163.
82. SIC Report, Vol. 7, Chapter 20, p. 163.
83. SIC Report, Vol. 7, Chapter 20, p. 83.
84. SIC Report, Vol. 7, Chapter 20, p. 162.
85. SIC Report, Vol. 7, Chapter 20, pp. 87–88.
86. SIC Report, Vol. 7, Chapter 20, p. 88.
87. SIC Report, Vol. 7, Chapter 20, p. 164.
88. Johannesson, 2009, *Hrunið: Ísland á barmi gjaldþrots og upplausnar* (E. The collapse: Iceland on the brink of bankruptcy and chaos), p. 86.
89. Author's calculation, 1100 million euro payment amounted 189.2 billion ISK on September 25, 2008, when the exchange rate reached 172.1 ISK/EUR. Glitnir's equity base, as reported in the bank's half-year results in 2008, was 200 billion ISK (SIC Report, Vol. 2, Chapter 8, p.323).
90. SIC Report, Vol. 9, Appendix 3, p. 99.
91. SIC Report, Vol. 7, Chapter 20, p. 164.
92. Johannesson, 2009, *Hrunið: Ísland á barmi gjaldþrots og upplausnar* (E. The Collapse: Iceland on the Brink of Bankruptcy and Chaos), p. 120.
93. SIC Report, Vol. 7, Chapter 20, p. 49.
94. SIC Report, Vol. 7, Chapter 20, pp. 88–89.
95. SIC Report, Vol. 7, Chapter 20, p. 90.
96. SIC Report, Vol. 7, Chapter 20, p. 142.
97. SIC Report, Vol. 7, Chapter 20, p. 91.
98. SIC Report, Vol. 7, Chapter 20, p. 91.
99. SIC Report, Vol. 7, Chapter 20, p. 92.
100. SIC Report, Vol. 7, Chapter 20, p. 92.
101. SIC Report, Vol. 7, Chapter 20, p. 143.
102. SIC Report, Vol. 7, Chapter 20, p. 50.
103. SIC Report, Vol. 7, Chapter 20, p. 50.
104. SIC Report, Vol. 7, Chapter 20, pp. 86 and 102.
105. SIC Report, Vol. 7, Chapter 20, p. 145.
106. SIC Report, Vol. 7, Chapter 20, pp. 93–94.

107. SIC Report, Vol. 7, Chapter 20, p. 145.
108. SIC Report, Vol. 7, Chapter 20, p. 94.
109. SIC Report, Vol. 7, Chapter 20, p. 95.
110. SIC Report, Vol. 7, Chapter 20, p. 100.
111. SIC Report, Vol. 7, Chapter 20, p. 95.
112. SIC Report, Vol. 7, Chapter 20, p. 101.
113. SIC Report, Vol. 7, Chapter 20, p. 101.
114. SIC Report, Vol. 7, Chapter 20, pp. 98–99.
115. SIC Report, Vol. 7, Chapter 20, p. 104.
116. SIC Report, Vol. 7, Chapter 20, p. 104
117. SIC Report, Vol. 7, Chapter 20, p. 105.
118. SIC Report, Vol. 7, Chapter 20, p. 105.
119. SIC Report, Vol. 6, Chapter 19, p. 161.
120. SIC Report, Vol. 7, Chapter 20, pp. 105 and pp. 114–117.
121. The author witnessed the chief justice say this during the Landsdomur trial. The transcripts of the trial have not been made public, but the audio recordings of the hearings are available on www.landsdomur.is/adalmedferd/
122. SIC Report, Vol. 7, Chapter 20, p. 123.
123. SIC Report, Vol. 7, Chapter 20, p. 165.
124. SIC Report, Vol. 7, Chapter 20, p. 124.
125. SIC Report, Vol. 7, Chapter 20, p. 126.
126. SIC Report, Vol. 7, Chapter 20, p. 147.
127. SIC Report, Vol. 7, Chapter 20, p. 147.
128. SIC Report, Vol. 7, Chapter 20, p. 147.
129. SIC Report, Vol. 7, Chapter 20, p. 147.
130. SIC Report, Vol. 7, Chapter 20, p. 148.
131. SIC Report, Vol. 7, Chapter 20, p. 148.
132. SIC Report, Vol. 7, Chapter 20, p. 129.
133. Johannesson, 2009, *Hrunið: Ísland á barmi gjaldþrots og upplausnar (E. The Collapse: Iceland on the Brink of Bankruptcy and Chaos)*, p. 159.
134. SIC Report, Vol. 7, Chapter 20, p. 161.
135. SIC Report, Vol. 7, Chapter 20, p. 161.
136. SIC Report, Vol. 7, Chapter 20, p. 165.
137. SIC Report, Vol. 7, Chapter 20, p. 166.
138. SIC Report, Vol. 7, Chapter 21, p. 256.
139. SIC Report, Vol. 7, Chapter 21, p. 256.
140. SIC Report, Vol. 7, Chapter 20, p. 165.
141. SIC Report, Vol. 7, Chapter 20, p. 148–149.
142. SIC Report, Vol. 7, Chapter 20, p. 165.
143. SIC Report, Vol. 7, Chapter 20, p. 166.
144. SIC Report, Vol. 7, Chapter 20, p. 166.
145. SIC Report, Vol. 7, Chapter 20, p. 167.
146. SIC Report, Vol. 7, Chapter 20, p. 51.
147. SIC Report, Vol. 7, Chapter 20, p. 168.

148. SIC Report, Vol. 7, Chapter 20, p. 168.
149. SIC Report, Vol. 7, Chapter 20, p. 168.
150. SIC Report, Vol. 7, Chapter 20, p. 168.
151. SIC Report, Vol. 7, Chapter 20, p. 149.
152. SIC Report, Vol. 7, Chapter 20, p. 169.
153. SIC Report, Vol. 7, Chapter 20, p. 150.
154. SIC Report, Vol. 7, Chapter 20, p. 150.
155. SIC Report, Vol. 7, Chapter 20, p. 151.
156. SIC Report, Vol. 7, Chapter 20, p. 171.
157. SIC Report, Vol. 7, Chapter 21, p. 257.
158. Statistics Iceland, Public Finance, Central Government Financial Assets and Liabilities, www.statice.is (accessed October 1, 2013).
159. Johannesson, 2009, *Hrunið: Ísland á barmi gjaldþrots og upplausnar (E. The Collapse: Iceland on the Brink of Bankruptcy and Chaos)*, p. 216.
160. Johannesson, 2009, *Hrunið: Ísland á barmi gjaldþrots og upplausnar (E. The Collapse: Iceland on the Brink of Bankruptcy and Chaos)*, p. 216.

4   Investigation

1. Article (1), Icelandic legal act nr. 142/2008
2. Article (2), Icelandic Legal act nr. 142/2008.
3. Special Investigation Commission (SIC), 2008, *Background and Causes of the Collapse of the Icelandic banks in 2008 and Related Events*, Vol. 1, Chapter 1, p. 40 (Report of the Special Investigation Commission, Reykjavik).
4. Nick Harré, Susan Foster, and Maree O'Neill, 2005, Self-enhancement, Crash-risk Optimism and the Impact of Safety Advertisements on Young Drivers. *British Journal of Psychology* 96, no. 2: 215–230. They show, for example, that automobile drivers tend to think of themselves as above average when asked about their driving skills.
5. Special Investigation Commission (SIC), 2008, *Background and Causes of the Collapse of the Icelandic banks in 2008 and Related Events*, Vol. 9, Appendix 2, pp. 64–65 (Report of the Special Investigation Commission, Reykjavik).
6. Gallup survey on May 5, 2010. Available at www.capacent.is/Frettir-og-frodleikur/Frettir/Frett?NewsID=ae92494d-1b53–4772-a039-a149d01b7108
7. SIC report, Vol. 7, Chapter 21, p. 178, Records the combined bank balance sheets, according to half year results in June 2008, to be 14,437 bln. ISK, while Statistics Iceland reports GDP for 2008 to be 1,483 bln. ISK, see National Accounts available at https://hagstofa.is/lisalib/getfile.aspx?ItemID=12205
8. SIC report, Vol. 7, Chapter 21, p. 177.

5   Financial Liberalization

1. Special Investigation Commission (SIC), 2008, *Background and Causes of the Collapse of the Icelandic Banks in 2008 and Related Events*, Vol. 1, Chapter 6, p. 228. (Report of the Special Investigation Commission, Reykjavik).
2. SIC Report, Vol. 1, Chapter 5, p. 209.
3. SIC Report, Vol. 1, Chapter 6, p. 230.
4. SIC Report, Vol. 1, Chapter 6, p. 229.
5. SIC Report, Vol. 1, Chapter 6, p. 231.
6. SIC Report, Vol. 1, Chapter 6, p. 231.
7. SIC Report, Vol. 1, Chapter 6, p. 231.
8. SIC Report, Vol. 1, Chapter 6, p. 231.
9. SIC Report, Vol. 1, Chapter 6, p. 229.
10. SIC Report, Vol. 1, Chapter 6, p. 232.
11. SIC Report, Vol. 1, Chapter 6, p. 235.
12. SIC Report, Vol. 1, Chapter 6, p. 235.
13. SIC Report, Vol. 1, Chapter 6, p. 235.
14. SIC Report, Vol. 1, Chapter 6, pp. 236–237.
15. SIC Report, Vol. 1, Chapter 6, pp. 236–237.
16. SIC Report, Vol. 1, Chapter 6, p. 237.
17. SIC Report, Vol. 1, Chapter 6, p. 237.
18. SIC Report, Vol. 1, Chapter 6, p. 239.
19. SIC Report, Vol. 1, Chapter 6, p. 238.
20. SIC Report, Vol. 1, Chapter 6, p. 239.
21. SIC Report, Vol. 1, Chapter 6, p. 239.
22. SIC Report, Vol. 1, Chapter 6, p. 242.
23. SIC Report, Vol. 1, Chapter 6, pp. 242–243.
24. SIC Report, Vol. 1, Chapter 6, p. 242.
25. SIC Report, Vol. 1, Chapter 6, p. 242.
26. SIC Report, Vol. 1, Chapter 6, p. 243.
27. SIC Report, Vol. 1, Chapter 6, p. 246.
28. SIC Report, Vol. 1, Chapter 6, p. 246.
29. SIC Report, Vol. 1, Chapter 6, p. 247.
30. SIC Report, Vol. 1, Chapter 6, p. 261.
31. SIC Report, Vol. 1, Chapter 6, p. 248.
32. SIC Report, Vol. 1, Chapter 6, p. 272.
33. SIC Report, Vol. 1, Chapter 6, p. 266.
34. SIC Report, Vol. 1, Chapter 6, p. 266.
35. SIC Report, Vol. 1, Chapter 6, p. 266.
36. SIC Report, Vol. 1, Chapter 6, p. 263.
37. SIC Report, Vol. 1, Chapter 6, p. 263.
38. SIC Report, Vol. 1, Chapter 4, p. 109.
39. SIC Report, Vol. 1, Chapter 6, p. 250.
40. SIC Report, Vol. 1, Chapter 6, p. 250.
41. SIC Report, Vol. 1, Chapter 6, p. 254.

42. SIC Report, Vol. 1, Chapter 6, p. 254.
43. SIC Report, Vol. 1, Chapter 6, p. 255.
44. SIC Report, Vol. 1, Chapter 6, p. 256.
45. SIC Report, Vol. 1, Chapter 6, p. 256.
46. SIC Report, Vol. 1, Chapter 6, p. 257.
47. SIC Report, Vol. 1, Chapter 6, p. 258.
48. SIC Report, Vol. 1, Chapter 6, p. 258.
49. SIC Report, Vol. 1, Chapter 6, p. 258.
50. SIC Report, Vol. 1, Chapter 6, p. 259.
51. SIC Report, Vol. 1, Chapter 6, p. 259.
52. SIC Report, Vol. 1, Chapter 6, p. 259.
53. SIC Report, Vol. 1, Chapter 6, p. 259, footnote no. 115.
54. SIC Report, Vol. 1, Chapter 6, p. 273.
55. SIC Report, Vol. 1, Chapter 6, p. 273.
56. SIC Report, Vol. 1, Chapter 6, p. 272.
57. SIC Report, Vol. 1, Chapter 6, p. 272.
58. SIC Report, Vol. 1, Chapter 6, p. 275.
59. SIC Report, Vol. 1, Chapter 6, p. 275.
60. SIC Report, Vol. 1, Chapter 6, p. 276.
61. SIC Report, Vol. 1, Chapter 6, p. 277.
62. SIC Report, Vol. 1, Chapter 6, p. 277.
63. SIC Report, Vol. 1, Chapter 6, p. 279.
64. SIC Report, Vol. 1, Chapter 6, p. 277.
65. SIC Report, Vol. 1, Chapter 6, p. 279.
66. SIC Report, Vol. 1, Chapter 6, pp. 276 and 281.
67. SIC Report, Vol. 1, Chapter 6, p. 283.
68. SIC Report, Vol. 1, Chapter 6, p. 306.
69. SIC Report, Vol. 1, Chapter 6, p. 293.
70. SIC Report, Vol. 1, Chapter 6, p. 306.

6   Funding the Banks

1. Special Investigation Commission (SIC), 2008, *Background and Causes of the Collapse of the Icelandic Banks in 2008 and Related Events*, Vol. 2, Chapter 7, p. 9. (Report of the Special Investigation Commission, Reykjavik).
2. Figure 5, SIC Report, Vol. 2, Chapter 8, p. 89.
3. SIC Report, Vol. 2, Chapter 7, p. 11.
4. SIC Report, Vol. 2, Chapter 7, p. 11.
5. SIC Report, Vol. 2, Chapter 7, p. 12.
6. SIC Report, Vol. 2, Chapter 7, p. 14.
7. SIC Report, Vol. 2, Chapter 7, p. 15.
8. SIC Report, Vol. 2, Chapter 7, p. 35.
9. SIC Report, Vol. 2, Chapter 7, p. 36.
10. SIC Report, Vol. 2, Chapter 7, p. 14.
11. SIC Report, Vol. 2, Chapter 7, p. 18.

12. SIC Report, Vol. 4, Chapter 12, p. 14.
13. SIC Report, Vol. 2, Chapter 7, p. 12.
14. SIC Report, Vol. 2, Chapter 7, p. 12.
15. Richard Thomas,2006, *Icelandic Banks—Not What You Are Thinking*, European Credit Research Report, Merrill Lynch, March 7, 2006, www.scribd.com/doc/19606822/Merrill-Lynch-Icelandic -Banks-Not- What- You- Are-Thinking
16. Carsten Valgreen, Lars Christensen, Peter Possing Andersen, and Rene Kallestrup, 2006, *Iceland: Geyser Crisis*, Economic Research Report, Danske Bank, March 21, 2006, www.mbl.is/media /98/398.pdf (accessed May 2, 2013).
17. SIC Report, Vol. 2, Chapter 7, p. 12.
18. SIC Report, Vol. 2, Chapter 7, p. 13.
19. SIC Report, Vol. 2, Chapter 7, p. 36.
20. SIC Report, Vol. 2, Chapter 7, p. 37.
21. SIC Report, Vol. 2, Chapter 7, p. 14.
22. SIC Report, Vol. 2, Chapter 7, p. 18.
23. SIC Report, Vol. 2, Chapter 7, p. 18.
24. SIC Report, Vol. 2, Chapter 7, p. 13; Richard Barley, 2007, "Moody's Upgrades Raft of Banks, Surprises Analysts," *Reuters, Online Edition*, February 26, 2007, http://www.reuters.com/article /2007/02/26/banks-moodys-idUSL2638561520070226 (accessed July 4, 2012).
25. John Glover, 2007, "Moody's Blasted for Giving Icelandic Banks Top Rating." *Bloomberg* February 26, 2007, http://www.bloomberg. com/apps/news?pid=newsarchive&sid=ailqCAI6I8Nk&refer=hom e (accessed July 4, 2012).
26. Gudrun, Johnsen, 2007, Lánshæfi til blessunar eða bölvunar? [English: Credit rating: A blessing or a curse?], *Vidskiptabladid*, March 7, 2007.
27. SIC Report, Vol. 2, Chapter 7, p. 13.
28. SIC Report, Vol. 2, Chapter 7, p. 13.
29. SIC Report, Vol. 2, Chapter 7, p. 13.
30. SIC Report, Vol. 2, Chapter 7, p. 36.
31. SIC Report, Vol. 2, Chapter 7, p. 36.
32. SIC Report, Vol. 2, Chapter 7, p. 14.
33. SIC Report, Vol. 2, Chapter 7, p. 13.
34. SIC Report, Vol. 2, Chapter 7, p. 42.
35. SIC Report, Vol. 2, Chapter 7, p. 18.
36. SIC Report, Vol. 2, Chapter 7, p. 40.
37. SIC Report, Vol. 2, Chapter 7, p. 36.
38. SIC Report, Vol. 2, Chapter 7, p. 20.
39. SIC Report, Vol. 2, Chapter 7, p. 43.
40. SIC Report, Vol. 2, Chapter 7, p. 43.
41. SIC Report, Vol. 2, Chapter 7, p. 20.
42. Richard Thomas, 2006, *Icelandic Banks—Not What You Are Thinking*, European Credit Research Report, Merrill Lynch, March 7, 2006,

http://www.scribd.com/doc/19606822/Merrill-Lynch-Icelandic
-Banks-Not- What- You- Are-Thinking, p. 2 "More Emerging Market
than Western Europe: When looking at relative value, we think the
banks should be compared less with other European banks and more
with emerging market banks, since the systemic risks we see in Iceland
have much more in common with emerging markets than the stability that is typical of most Western European banking markets.
Chart 2 therefore shows the Icelandic banks when compared with
some selected emerging market banks and their sovereigns. In our
opinion, neither the Moody's nor even Fitch has been able to factor
the systemic risk into their ratings for the Icelandic banks adequately.
We therefore do not take much comfort from these agencies' mid-to
high – A ratings. The only agency we are aware of who factors economic and industry risk into their ratings on a consistent basis is S&P
and of course it results in lower ratings, though not always notably so.
In any case, the market is pricing the Icelandic banks' credit risk as
'BBB', which is precisely our opinion of where S&P's ratings would
come out, if they were public."

43. SIC Report, Vol. 2, Chapter 7, p. 19.

7   The Geyser Crisis

1. Special Investigation Commission (SIC), 2008, *Background and
   Causes of the Collapse of the Icelandic Banks in 2008 and Related
   Events*, Vol. 2, Chapter 7, p. 32. (Report of the Special Investigation
   Commission, Reykjavik).
2. SIC Report, Vol. 2, Chapter 7, p. 12.
3. Carsten Valgreen, Lars Christensen, Peter Possing Andersen, and
   Rene Kallestrup, 2006, *Iceland: Geyser Crisis*, Economic Research
   Report, Danske Bank. Research paper, March 21, 2006, www.mbl
   .is/media/98/398.pdf (accessed May 2, 2013).
4. Carsten Valgreen, Lars Christensen, Peter Possing Andersen, and
   Rene Kallestrup, 2006, *Iceland: Geyer Crisis*.
5. Carsten Valgreen, Lars Christensen, Peter Possing Andersen, and
   Rene Kallestrup, 2006, *Iceland: Geyer Crisis*.
6. Credit default swap (CDS) is a term insurance contract written on
   the notional value of a bond issue. It is designed to reallocate the
   credit risk between different parties. Those that hold bonds and are
   exposed to the borrower not paying back or defaulting can engage
   in a swap by handing over cash to a third party, which in turn promises to pay the debt of the borrower if she defaults. The CDS spread
   is the quote on how much it costs to insure against a default of the
   bond issuer.
7. Speech given by Jonas Fr. Jonsson, Director General of FME, at
   an annual meeting of the Icelandic Financial Services Association,
   April 10, 2008, SIC Report, Vol. 2, Chapter 7, p. 20, available in

Icelandic,   http://www.sff.is/media/frettir/Avarp_forstjora_FME
_-_Jonas_Fr._Jonasson.pdf (accessed July 10, 2012).

8. SIC Report, Vol. 2, Chapter 7, p. 22.
9. SIC Report, Vol. 2, Chapter 7, p. 22.
10. see Credit Derivatives Handbook 2006. Merrill Lynch, February
    14, 2006, http://www.nuclearphynance.com/User%20Files/5542
    /Guida%20ML%201.pdf (accessed July 10, 2012).
11. A naked CDS is a credit default swap bought by someone who has
    no prior interest to be insured by the CDS instrument. Since the
    CDS holder receives the insured amount in the event of a default of
    the institution or instrument in question, CDSs were used to short
    or bet against the fall of the Icelandic banks since shorting their
    stocks was difficult.
12. SIC Report, Vol. 2, Chapter 7, p. 21.
13. Frederic S. Mishkin and Tryggvi Thor Herbertsson, 2006, *Financial
    Stability in Iceland* (Report of the Iceland Chamber of Commerce,
    Reykjavik), http://www.vi.is/files/555877819Financial%20Stability
    %20in%20Iceland%20Screen%20Version.pdf (accessed July 10, 2012).
14. Speech by Valgerdur Sverrisdottir, Minister of Commerce on
    September 27, 2006, at the Icelandic-American Chamber of
    Commerce included the following remarks:

> As many of you will know, the Icelandic economy came under
> the harsh spotlight of the international press last spring.
> Instability in Iceland's stock market raised concerns about
> the stability of the economy in general, and Icelandic banks
> in particular. The attention in the international media and
> among international investors and financial institutions was
> new to us. Unfortunately, it is not always true that all public-
> ity is good publicity. Many of the reports were factually inac-
> curate, conclusions were based on false assumptions and the
> special characteristics and strengths of the Icelandic economy
> were not recognized. This negative coverage resulted in tem-
> porary turbulence in the Icelandic Stock Market and the
> Icelandic Krona came under fire as well.
>
> This was a hard lesson for us. It was clear that a strong and
> healthy economy was not enough on its own. People needed to
> know about it too. By a concentrated effort involving both the
> Icelandic authorities and relevant industries, we managed to
> demonstrate that Iceland's economic fundamentals are strong
> and that there is no imminent threat to the Icelandic economy
> or financial stability. Indeed, ratings this year by major
> agencies have confirmed this view, and Icelandic banks have
> been able to refinance through US banks with no difficulty.
>
> A key event in this process was the presentation here in
> New York of a report by Professors Fred Mishkin and
> Tryggvi Þór Herbertsson on Financial Stability in Iceland.

However, even if we might have won this round, there is no room for complacency. The volatility of the Icelandic Krona, and its openness to negative coverage and external shocks, show the difficulties for a small currency in the free flow of financial markets. We are, after all, by far the smallest single currency area in the world.
The speech is available at http://www.mfa.is/news-and-publications /nr/3194
Prime Minister Geir H. Haarde attended a public meeting on May 4, 2006, at the Icelandic-American Chamber of Commerce along with Tryggvi Herbertsson and Frederick Mishkin. The title of the meeting was *Financial Crisis or Economic Opportunity: The Real Story about Iceland"* (Arnason, Vilhjálmur, Salvör Nordal, and Kristín Asgeirsdottir, 2010, *Ethics and Governance: In Relations with the Fall of the Icelandic Banks 2008*, SIC Report, Vol. 8, Appendix 1, p. 215).

15. SIC Report, Vol. 2, Chapter 7, pp.37 and 41.
16. Statistics Iceland, 2008, *Gross Domestic Product 2007*, Statistical Series—National Accounts, Statistics Iceland.
17. "Iceland gets $4.6 billion USD bailout from IMF, Nordics" *Bloomberg*, November 20, 2008, http://www.bloomberg.com/apps /news?pid=newsarchive&sid=anS9Ze0bmXmM (accessed February 18, 2013).

8   Love Letters to the Rescue

1. Fabozzi, Modigliani, and Jones provide an excellent overview of short-term liquidity facilities provided by central banks in their textbook *Foundations of Financial Markets and Institutions*, published by Prentice Hall in 2009.
2. Special Investigation Commission (SIC), 2008, *Background and Causes of the Collapse of the Icelandic Banks in 2008 and Related Events*, Vol. 1, Chapter 4, p. 165. (Report of the Special Investigation Commission, Reykjavik).
3. SIC Report, Vol. 6, Chapter 19, p. 207.
4. SIC Report, Vol. 6, Chapter 19, p. 207.
5. SIC Report, Vol. 6, Chapter 19, p. 207.
6. SIC Report, Vol. 2, Chapter 7, p. 44.
7. SIC Report, Vol. 2, Chapter 7, p. 45.
8. SIC Report, Vol. 2, Chapter 8, p. 326 and SIC Report, Vol. 2, Chapter 7, p. 45.
9. SIC Report, Vol. 2, Chapter 7, pp. 29–30.
10. SIC Report, Vol. 2, Chapter 7, pp. 29–30.
11. SIC Report, Vol. 2, Chapter 7, pp. 28–30.
12. SIC Report, Vol. 2, Chapter 7, p. 30.
13. SIC Report, Vol. 2, Chapter 7, p. 30.

14. SIC Report, Vol. 6, Chapter 19, p. 206.
15. SIC Report, Vol. 6, Chapter 19, p. 206.
16. SIC Report, Vol. 1, Chapter 4, p. 100.
17. The Icelandic National Audit Office, Report on Bailout Cost of the Icelandic State in Relations with the Banking Collapse (*Title in Icelandic: Fyrirgreiðsla ríkisins við fjármálafyrirtæki og stofnanir í kjölfar bankahrunsins*) p. 6.

9 Playing Tricks on the European Central Bank

1. Special Investigation Commission (SIC), 2008, *Background and Causes of the Collapse of the Icelandic Banks in 2008 and Related Events*, Vol. 2, Chapter 7, p. 46. (Report of the Special Investigation Commission, Reykjavik).
2. SIC Report, Vol. 2, Chapter 7, p. 46.
3. Hreidar Mar Sigurdsson report to the SIC on July 21, 2009, SIC Report, Vol. 2, Chapter 7, p.47.
4. SIC Report, Vol. 2, Chapter 7, p. 45.
5. SIC Report, Vol. 2, Chapter 7, p. 45.
6. SIC Report, Vol. 2, Chapter 7, p. 46.
7. SIC Report, Vol. 2, Chapter 7, footnote 88: "The Irish and the Spanish banks increased their borrowing from the ECB during similar period. From August 2007 till July 2008 the proportion of Spanish banks borrowing as share of total borrowing of European banks from the ECB went from 4% to 10,5%, and the share of borrowing on part of the Irish banks went from 4,5% to 9,5% '[a]nother measure of the increase in the scale of the Eurosystem's lending to the Spanish banks since the beginning of the crisis in August 2007, is the value of the monthly loans extended to Spanish banks by the Banco de España. This went from a low of about €23 billion in August 2007 to a high of more than €75bn in December 2007.'" (Willem H. Buiter, September 2008, *Central Banks and Financial Crises.* Discussion Paper no. 619. (London: Financial Markets Group, London School of Economics and Political Science)."
8. SIC Report, Vol. 2, Chapter 7, p. 46.
9. SIC Report, Vol. 2, Chapter 7, p. 46.
10. SIC Report, Vol. 2, Chapter 7, p. 46.
11. SIC Report, Vol. 2, Chapter 7, p. 46.
12. SIC Report, Vol. 2, Chapter 7, p. 46.
13. SIC Report, Vol. 2, Chapter 7, p. 46, & Background Memorandum, Central Bank of Iceland, 15th of April 2008, doc. nr. SI40299.
14. SIC Report, Vol. 2, Chapter 7, p. 46.
15. SIC Report, Vol. 2, Chapter 7, p. 47.
16. SIC Report, Vol. 2, Chapter 7, p. 47.

17. SIC Report, Vol. 2, Chapter 7, p. 47, footnote 92: "Draft of the minutes of the meeting. Executive Board meeting and the FME with Bank Managers April 25, 2008, at 15.00–15.45. SI 47404."
18. SIC Report, Vol. 2, Chapter 7, p. 47.
19. SIC Report, Vol. 2, Chapter 7, p. 47, footnote 92: "Draft of the minutes of the meeting. Executive Board meeting and the FME with Bank Managers April 25, 2008, at 15.00–15.45. SI 47404."
20. SIC Report, Vol. 2, Chapter 7, p. 47.
21. SIC Report, Vol. 2, Chapter 7, p. 47.
22. SIC Report, Vol. 2, Chapter 7, p. 47, footnote 92: "Draft of the minutes of the meeting. Executive Board meeting and the FME with Bank Managers April 25, 2008, at 15.00–15.45. SI 47404."
23. SIC Report, Vol. 2, Chapter 7, p. 47.
24. SIC Report, Vol. 2, Chapter 7, p. 47.
25. SIC Report, Vol. 2, Chapter 7, p. 48.
26. SIC Report, Vol. 2, Chapter 7, p. 48, footnote 94.
27. SIC Report, Vol. 2, Chapter 7, p. 48, footnote 97: "Description of refinancing facilities between Kaupthing hf., Kaupthing Singer & Friedlander and Kaupthing Bank Luxembourg." Memo, June 21, 2009. Signy Sif Sigurdardottir and Eva Soley Gudbjornsdottir.
28. SIC Report, Vol. 2, Chapter 7, p. 48, figure 61.
29. SIC Report, Vol. 2, Chapter 7, p. 52, footnote 110: "David Oddsson's report to the SIC on August 7th 2009, p. 45."
30. SIC Report, Vol. 2, Chapter 7, p. 52, footnote 111: "David Oddsson's report to the SIC on August 7th 2009, p. 45."
31. SIC Report, Vol. 2, Chapter 7, p. 53, footnote 112: "David Oddsson's report to the SIC on August 7th 2009, p. 46."
32. SIC Report, Vol. 2, Chapter 7, p. 53.
33. SIC Report, Vol. 2, Chapter 7, p. 53: footnote 113: "According to draft of the minutes, from the Central Bank, of the meeting with Yves Mersch, Nicolas Weber and Frank Bisdorff, on July 4th."
34. SIC Report, Vol. 2, Chapter 7, p. 53.
35. SIC Report, Vol. 2, Chapter 7, p. 53.
36. SIC Report, Vol. 2, Chapter 7, p. 53.
37. SIC Report, Vol. 2, Chapter 7, p. 53, footnote 113: "According to draft of the minutes, from the Central Bank, of the meeting with Yves Mersch, Nicolas Weber and Frank Bisdorff, on July 4th."
38. SIC Report, Vol. 2, Chapter 7, p. 53.
39. SIC Report, Vol. 2, Chapter 7, p. 54.
40. SIC Report, Vol. 2, Chapter 7, p. 54.
41. SIC Report, Vol. 2, Chapter 7, p. 54.
42. SIC Report, Vol. 2, Chapter 7, p. 54.
43. SIC Report, Vol. 2, Chapter 7, p. 54.
44. SIC Report, Vol. 2, Chapter 7, p. 54, footnote 117: "David Oddsson's report to the SIC on August 7, 2009, p. 46."

45. SIC Report, Vol. 2, Chapter 7, p. 54, footnote 117: "David Oddsson's report to the SIC on August 7th 2009, p. 46."
46. SIC Report, Vol. 2, Chapter 7, p. 55, footnote 121: "A letter from Yves Mersch to Bjorn Jonsson at Kaupthing, dated June 30, 2008."
47. SIC Report, Vol. 2, Chapter 7, p. 55, footnote 121: "A letter from Yves Mersch to Bjorn Jonsson at Kaupthing, dated June 30, 2008."
48. SIC Report, Vol. 2, Chapter 7, p. 55.
49. SIC Report, Vol. 2, Chapter 7. p. 48.
50. SIC Report, Vol. 2, Chapter 7, p. 51.
51. SIC Report, Vol. 2, Chapter 7, p. 52.
52. SIC Report, Vol. 2, Chapter 7, p. 52.
53. SIC Report, Vol. 2, Chapter 7. p. 49.
54. *Annual Report*, 2010, p. 19. Icelandic Central Bank, Reykjavik.

10 The Web of Ownership

1. Table 1, Special Investigation Commission (SIC), 2008, *Background and Causes of the Collapse of the Icelandic Banks in 2008 and Related Events*, Vol. 7, Chapter 21, p. 91. (Report of the Special Investigation Commission (SIC). Reykjavik: Special Investigation Commission) and Mark Flannery, 2009, *Iceland's Failed Banks: A Post-Mortem*, SIC Report, Vol. 9. (Reykjavik: Special Investigation Commission).
2. Table 4, SIC Report, Vol. 2, Chapter 8, p. 92
3. IFS (International Finance Statistics), Lines 22D and 147, for bank credit to private sector in 2001. For credit to households and corporations in 2008 see IMF Staff Report of Second Review under Stand by Arrangement, April 2010, p. 13.
4. Gylfi Magnusson, 2010, *Lessons from a Small Country in a Financial Crisis or Dr. Minsky and Mr. Ponzi in Iceland*. Insititute of Economic Studies. Working Paper Series, W10:03, Reykjavik: University of Iceland, http://hhi.hi.is/sites/hhi.hi.is/files/W-series/2010/WP1003.pdf (accessed May 12, 2013).
5. SIC Report, Vol. 2, Chapter 8, p. 84
6. SIC Report, Vol. 2, Chapter 8, p. 96
7. SIC Report, Vol. 2, Chapter 8, p. 93.
8. SIC Report, Vol. 2, Chapter 8, pp. 191–199
9. SIC Report, Vol. 2, Chapter 8, pp. 191–199
10. SIC Report, Vol. 2, Chapter 8 p. 194
11. See, for example, SIC Report, Vol. 2, Chapter 8, p. 192
12. SIC Report, Vol. 2, Chapter 8, p. 192
13. Bjarnadottir and Hansen, 2010, *Investigation into the Cross Ownership and Bank Credit to Related Parties*. (Report of the Special Investigation Commission (SIC), Vol. 9, p.15. [Title in

Icelandic: Rannsókn á krosseignartengslum og útlánum bankanna til tengdra aðila] Reykjavik: Special Investigation Commission).

14. Bjarnadottir and Hansen, 2010, SIC Report, Vol. 9, p. 11.
15. Bjarnadottir and Hansen, 2010, SIC Report, Vol. 9, p. 22.
16. Bjarnadottir and Hansen, 2010, SIC Report, Vol. 9, p. 74.
17. Amendments to the Law on Financial Undertakings have been put into force by Parliament via legal bill nr. 75/2010.
18. Bjarnadottir and Hansen, 2010, SIC Report, Vol. 9, p. 75.
19. The SIC team assigned an unbiased rule of thumb (also built on David P. Ellerman, 1991, "Cross Ownership of Corporations: A New Application for Input-Output Theory," *Metroeconomica* 42, no. 1: 33–46) that a firm is considered to be in a particular business group when the ultimate owner (individual) owns at least 20 percent in the subsidiaries or the sub-subsidiaries. Furthermore, entities that are included in the business group are the ones that are financially dependent on the group, such that if the equity of one entity collapses, the financially dependent entity will also collapse as a consequence.
20. Bjarnadottir and Hansen, 2010, SIC Report, Vol. 9, p. 32.
21. Icelandic legal act No. 161/2002 art. 30. on financial institutions states that large exposures of individual borrower or related parties cannot exceed 25 percent of the bank's equity base.
22. SIC Report, Vol. 1, Chapter 2, p. 33.

11 Tunneling Money through Related-Party Lending

1. Special Investigation Commission (SIC), 2008, *Background and Causes of the Collapse of the Icelandic Banks in 2008 and Related Events*, Vol. 2, Chapter 8, p. 86. (Report of the Special Investigation Commission (SIC). Reykjavik: Special Investigation Commission).
2. SIC Report, Vol. 2, Chapter 8, p. 85.
3. Admati, Anat & Martin Hellwig, 2013, *Banker's New Clothes: What's Wrong with Banking and What to Do about It?* Princeton, NJ: Princeton University Press.
4. Basel Committee on Banking Superivision, 1991, *Measuring and Controlling Large Credit Exposures.* (Basel: Basel Committee on Banking Supervision).
5. Board of Governors of the Federal Reserve System, 1993, *Risks of Concentration of Credit and Nontraditional Activities, Board of Governors.* Washington, DC: Board of Governors, March 26, 1993.
6. SIC Report, Vol. 2, Chapter 8, p. 86.
7. O. Benda, 1999, "Privitization Guru Foresaw Tunneling," Prague Post, Entry posted on January 6, 1999, http://www.praguepost.com /archivescontent/29782-privatization-guru-foresaw-tunneling .html (accessed on October 1, 2013).

8. According to Johnson et al., tunneling occurs mainly through two means:

First, a controlling shareholder can simply transfer resources from the firm for his own benefit through self-dealing transactions. Such transactions include outright theft or fraud, which are illegal everywhere though often go undetected or unpunished, but also asset sales, contracts such as transfer pricing advantageous to the controlling shareholder, excessive executive compensation, loan guarantees, expropriation of corporate opportunities, and so on. Second, the controlling shareholder can increase his share of the firm without transferring any assets through dilutive share issues, minority freezeouts, insider trading, creeping acquisitions, or other financial transactions that discriminate against minorities.

Johnson, S, La Porta, R., Lopez-de-Silanes, and Andrei Sleifer, 2000, "Tunneling," *American Economic Review* 90 no. 2 (May 2000).

9. SIC Report, Vol. 2, Chapter 8, pp. 137–138.
10. SIC Report, Vol. 2, Chapter 8, pp. 137–138.
11. SIC Report, Vol. 2, Chapter 8, p. 137.
12. Since 2009, the mandatory takeover rule is activated at 33 percent ownership of listed shares in Iceland.
13. News release from Baugur Group titled "Baugur completes restructuring as a pure Retail investor and builds new investment pool," http://web.archive.org/web/20090210015129/http://www.baugur.com/Pages/407?NewsID=1318#nav (accessed on March 24, 2013).
14. Bjarnadottir and Hansen, 2010, *Investigation into the Cross Ownership and Bank Credit to Related Parties.* Report of the Special Investigation Commission (SIC), Vol. 9, p. 64. [Title in Icelandic: Rannsókn á krosseignartengslum og útlánum bankanna til tengdra aðila] Reykavik: Special Investigation Commission.
15. 66.23 ISK/USD exchange rate on March 22, 2007, according to the Icelandic Central Bank.
16. Bjarnadottir and Hansen, 2010, SIC Report, Vol. 9, p. 55.
17. Bjarnadottir and Hansen, 2010 SIC Report, Vol. 9, pp. 63–65.
18. SIC Report, Vol. 2, Chapter 8, 145–146.
19. Bjarnadottir and Hansen, 2010, SIC Report, Vol. 9, p. 59.
20. 62 ISK/USD exchange rate on December 30, 2007, according to the Icelandic Central Bank.
21. Bjorgolfur Thor Bjorgolfsson, 2013, *Ardur af Landsbanka afram inn i Samson* [e. Dividends from Landsbanki paid on to Samson]. btb—Bjorgolfur Thor Bjorgolfsson Weblog. Entry posted on March 24, 2013, http://www.btb.is/landsbankinn-02–08/ardgreidslur/
22. A list of Bjorgolfur Thor Bjorgolfsson's investments can be found on his own website, in Icelandic at: www.btb.is
23. SIC Report, Vol. 2, Chapter 8, p. 150.

24. SIC Report, Vol. 2, Chapter 8, p. 144.
25. Foreign exchange rates as quoted by the Central Bank of Iceland on May 20, 2008.
26. SIC Report, Vol. 2, Chapter 8, p. 143.
27. Foreign exchange rates as quoted by the Central Bank of Iceland on May 20, 2008.
28. SIC Report, Vol. 2, Chapter 8, p. 143.
29. http://www.institutionalinvestor.com/Article/2097595 /Kaupthing-Sues-Oscatello-For-643M.html#.UUnM9kL7WYo and http://london-gazette.vlex.co.uk/vid/oscatello-invest ments-limited-216021847 (http://www.london-gazette.co.uk /issues/59511/notices/1179911)
30. Board of Governors, 2011, *Annual Report of the Federal Reserve System*, http://www.federalreserve.gov/publications/budget-review /files/2011-budget-review.pdf (accessed March 26, 2013).
31. Net expenditure of law enforcement, judicial, and prison systems 17.3 billion ISK in 2011, according the *Icelandic State Annual Report*, Budget Review, http://www.fjs.is/upload/files /R%C3%ADkisreikningur%202011%20%C3%A1rsreikningar%20 r%C3%ADkiisa%C3%B0ila.pdf (accessed March 26, 2013).
32. See, for example, Pierre-Olivier Gourinchas, Rodrigo Valdes, and Oscar Landerretche, 2001, "Lending Booms: Latin America and the World," *Economía* 1, no. 2: 47–99 and Paul Hilbers, Inci Otker-Robe, Ceyla Pazarbasioglu, and Gudrun Johnsen, 2005, *Assessing and Managing Rapid Credit Growth and the Role of Supervisory and Prudential Policies*. Working Paper 05/151, Washington, DC: International Monetary Fund (IMF)., also Cottarelli, Dell'Ariccia, and Ivanna Vladkova-Hollar, 2005, "Early Birds, Late Risers, and Sleeping Beauties: Bank Credit Growth to the Private Sector in Central and Eastern Europe and in the Balkans," *Journal of Banking & Finance* 29, no. 1: 83–104, to name a few.
33. John Geanakopolos, 1997, "Promises, Promises," in *The Economy as an Evolving Complex System, II*. ed., W. B. Arthur, S. Durlauf and D. Lane (Reading, MA: Addison-Wesley, 1997), 285–320. [CFDP 1143 and CFP 1057]
34. John Geanakoplolos, 2010, "The Leverage Cycle," in D. Acemoglu, K. Rogoff and M. Woodford, eds., *NBER Macroeconomic Annual 2009* 24: 1–65, University of Chicago Press, 2010]
35. Such as Nobuhiro Kiyotaki, and John Moore, 1997, Credit Cycles, *Journal of Political Economy* 105, no. 2: 211–248, see also Evan Kraft, and Ljubinko Jankov, 2005, "Does Speed Kill? Lending Booms and Their Consequences in Croatia," *Journal of Banking and Finance* 29: 105–21.
36. S. Schaffer, 1998, "Winners Curse in Banking." *Journal of Financial Intermediation,* 7, no. 4 (1998): 359–392.
37. SIC Report, Vol. 2, Chapter 8, p. 102.

38. SIC Report, Vol. 2, Chapter 8, figure 22, p. 98.
39. SIC Report, Vol. 2, Chapter 8, figure 23, p. 99.
40. SIC Report, Vol. 2, Chapter 8, figure 22, p. 100.
41. SIC Report, Vol. 2, Chapter 8, figure 34–36, pp. 102–103.
42. SIC Report, Vol. 2, Chapter 8, figure 37, p. 103.

12 Market Manipulation and Falsification of Equity

1. Special Investigation Commission (SIC), 2008, *Background and Causes of the Collapse of the Icelandic Banks in 2008 and Related Events*, Vol. 2, Chapter 8, p. 103. (Report of the Special Investigation Commission (SIC). Reykjavik: Special Investigation Commission).
2. SIC Report, Vol. 2, Chapter 8, p. 103.
3. SIC Report, Vol. 2, Chapter 8, p. 103.
4. Iceland's GDP in 2007 amounted 1279 billion ISK according to *Statistics Iceland* Report https://hagstofa.is/lisalib/getfile.aspx?ItemID=7925 (accessed April 11, 2013).
5. SIC Report, Vol. 2, Chapter 8, p. 107.
6. Article 55, Icelandic Corporate Law nr. 2/1995.
7. See International Accounting Standard (IAS) 32
8. Combining monthly trades from January 2004 to October 2008, when Kaupthing sold more than it bought each month, the accumulated shares sold amounted to 21 million shares on the stock exchange compared with 164 million shares sold over the counter. Combining monthly trades where Kaupthing bought more than it sold each month, Kaupthing bought over 200 million shares net on the exchange compared with 54 million shares bought net over the counter in after-hours trades. See Figure 12.6.
9. SIC Report, Vol. 4, Chapter 12, p. 30.
10. Frettabladid, August 28, 2010, Interview with Sigurdur Einarsson, Frmr. Chairman of Board of Directors of Kaupthing, "I have nothing to hide" [Title translated from Icelandic: "Ég hef ekkert að fela", pp. 24–28, Reykjavik, Iceland
11. The indictments of the Special Prosecutor against the former Kaupthing management and staff are available on in Icelandic at: The indictments against the former management and staff of Landsbanki are available in Icelandic at: http://eyjan.pressan.is/frettir/wp-content/uploads/2013/03/72cba2177b-x_o.pdf (accessed April 8, 2013).
12. The indictments of the Special Prosecutor against the former Kaupthing management and staff are available on in Icelandic at: The indictments against the former management and staff of Landsbanki are available in Icelandic at: http://eyjan.pressan.is/frettir/wp-content/uploads/2013/03/72cba2177b-x_o.pdf (accessed April 8, 2013).
13. SIC Report, Vol. 4, Chapter 12, p. 35.
14. SIC Report, Vol. 4, Chapter 12, p. 38.
15. SIC Report, Vol. 4, Chapter 12, p. 51.

16. SIC Report, Vol. 2, Chapter 8, pp. 173–177.
17. SIC Report, Vol. 2, Chapter 8, pp. 173–177.
18. SIC Report, Vol. 2, Chapter 8, pp. 175–177.
19. SIC Report, Vol. 3, Chapter 9, p. 11, see also 5th paragraph of 84th article of Act 161/2002 on Financial Undertaking.
20. SIC Report, Vol. 3, Chapter 9, p. 22.
21. Minimum CAD requirement was at the time 8 percent according to Article 84 of Act 161/2002 on Financial Undertaking.
22. *Landsbanki Annual Report*, 2007, http://www.lbi.is/library/Opin -gogn/pdf/landsbanki_annual_report_2007.pdf (accessed April 21, 2013).

13 Wages of Failure

* The title of the chapter is inspired by the work of Lucian Bebchuck, Alma Cohen, and Holger Spamann from their paper on CEO compensation of the failed banks in the United States, Bear Sterns and Lehman Brothers; Lucian A. Bebchuk, Alma Cohen, and Holger Spamann, 2009, "The Wages of Failure: Executive Compensation at Bear Stearns and Lehman 2000–2008 (November 24, 2009)." *Yale Journal on Regulation* 27 (2010): 257–282; *Harvard Law and Economics* Discussion Paper No. 657; ECGI—Finance Working Paper No. 287. Available at SSRN: http://ssrn.com/abstract=1513522

1. Lin Peng, and Ailsa A. Röell, 2008, "Executive Pay and Shareholder Litigation (2008)." *Review of Finance* 12, no. 1: 141–184, http: //ssrn.com/abstract=1159298
2. A famous social psychology study conducted by Stanley Milgram in the 1960s reveals that two-thirds of subjects are obedient to authority, even though the action commanded by authority involves an apparent physical harm to another human being.
3. Special Investigation Commission (SIC), 2008, *Background and Causes of the Collapse of the Icelandic Banks in 2008 and Related Events*, Vol. 3, Chapter 10, p. 32. (Report of the Special Investigation Commission (SIC). Reykjavik: Special Investigation Commission).
4. SIC Report, Vol. 3, Chapter 10, p. 32.
5. SIC Report, Vol. 3, Chapter 10, p. 32.
6. Michael C. Jensen, Kevin J. Murphy, and Eric G. Wruck, 1976, *Remuneration: Where We've Been, How We Got to Here, What are the Problems, and How to Fix Them* (2004). Harvard NOM Working Paper No. 04–28; ECGI—Finance Working Paper No. 44/2004, http://ssrn.com/abstract=561305 or http://ssrn.com /abstract=561305 or http://dx.doi.org/10.2139/ssrn.561305
7. SIC Report, Vol. 3, Chapter 10, pp. 39–42.
8. SIC Report, Vol. 3, Chapter 10, p. 39.
9. Mark Flannery, 2009, *Iceland's Failed Banks: A Post-Mortem*, SIC Report, Vol. 9, p. 94. (Reykjavik: Special Investigation Commission), Table 2.

10. SIC Report, Vol. 3, Chapter 10, p. 40.
11. According to Landsbanki's analyst report on Glitnir, http://www.landsbankinn.is/uploads/documents/English/1Q_2006_GLB_ENG.pdf (accessed April 29, 2013).
12. SIC Report, Vol. 3, Chapter 10, p. 40.
13. SIC Report, Vol. 3, Chapter 10, p. 40.
14. SIC Report, Vol. 3, Chapter 10, p. 40.
15. SIC Report, Vol. 3, Chapter 10, p. 42.
16. Figure 22, SIC Report, Vol. 3, Chapter 10, p. 45.
17. Oyer, Paul, 2004, Why Do Firms Use Incentives that Have No Incentive Effects? *Journal of Finance* 59: 1619–1649.
18. IFRS 2 Share Based Payment, Paragraph 43 b) http://ec.europa.eu/internal_market/accounting/docs/arc/ifrs2/ifrs2_en.pdf
19. SIC Report, Vol. 3, Chapter 10, p. 60.
20. SIC Report, Vol. 3, Chapter 10, p. 64.
21. SIC Report, Vol. 3, Chapter 10, p. 69.
22. SIC Report, Vol. 3, Chapter 10, p. 69.
23. SIC Report, Vol. 3, Chapter 10, p. 61.
24. SIC Report, Vol. 3, Chapter 10, p. 60.
25. SIC Report, Vol. 3, Chapter 10, p. 68.
26. SIC Report, Vol. 3, Chapter 10, pp. 60–61.
27. Also stipulated by Icelandic law 3rd paragraph, article 83, of law 161/2002 on financial undertakings.
28. SIC Report, Vol. 3, Chapter 9, p. 16.
29. Available, with subscription at: www.moodys.com/credit-ratings/Landsbanki-Islands-hf-credit-rating-600021838
30. SIC Report, Vol. 3, Chapter 9, p. 16.
31. All entities, independent or formed through managerial ties, and can be considered related parties, who own 10 percent or more or intend to acquire 10 percent or more in a financial institution subject to financial supervision, are under legal obligation to file for an approval of the FME to become controlling stakeholder and as a consequence are subdued to elevated disclosure obligation according to law on Financial Undertakings nr. 161/2002, articles 41 and 42.
32. SIC Report, Vol. 3, Chapter 10, p. 72.
33. SIC Report, Vol. 3, Chapter 10, p. 68.
34. SIC Report, Vol. 3, Chapter 10, p. 51.
35. SIC Report, Vol. 3, Chapter 10, p. 71.
36. SIC Report, Vol. 3, Chapter 10, p. 69.
37. SIC Report, Vol. 3, Chapter 10, p. 68.
38. SIC Report, Vol. 3, Chapter 10, pp. 70–72 and pp. 95–98 and pp. 46–49.
39. *Kaupthing Annual Report 2006*, available on April 30, 2013 at: www.euroland.com/arinhtml/is-kaup/2006/AR_ENG_2006/
40. SIC Report, Vol. 3, Chapter 10, figure 62, p. 78.
41. SIC Report, Vol. 3, Chapter 10, p. 77.

42. SIC Report, Vol. 3, Chapter 10, p. 78.
43. SIC Report, Vol. 3, Chapter 10, p. 79.
44. SIC Report, Vol. 3, Chapter 10, p. 45.
45. Jensen, Michael C., and William H. Meckling, 1976, Theory of the Firm: Managerial Behavior, Agency Costs and Ownership Structure, *Journal of Financial Economics* 3, no. 4; Eric Talley, and Gudrun Johnsen, 2005, *Corporate Governance, Executive Compensation and Securities Litigation.* CLEO and Law & Economics Research Paper Series, University of Southern California Law School; Lin Peng, and Ailsa Röell, 2008, Executive Pay and Shareholder Litigation, *Review of Finance* 12, no. 1: 141–184; and others.
46. SIC Report, Vol. 2, Chapter 7, pp. 65–67.
47. SIC Report, Vol. 2, Chapter 7, pp. 65–67.
48. SIC Report, Vol. 2, Chapter 7, pp. 65–67.
49. SIC Report, Vol. 2, Chapter 7, p. 67.
50. SIC Report, Vol. 2, Chapter 7, p. 66.
51. SIC Report, Vol. 3, Chapter 10, pp. 30–31 and pp. 49–50 and pp. 72–73.
52. SIC Report, Vol. 3, Chapter 10, pp. 30–31 and pp. 49–50 and pp. 72–73.
53. SIC Report, Vol. 3, Chapter 10, pp. 30–31 and pp. 49–50 and pp. 72–73.
54. SIC Report, Vol. 3, Chapter 10, figure 7, p. 32, figure 54 p. 74.
55. SIC Report, Vol. 3, Chapter 10, p. 87. Translated from Icelandic:
    "Hæ Magnús, Við gengum ekki frá bónus fyrir síðasta ár. Ég legg til 1 millj evrur. Hvað segir þú. Kv. Se."
    Tölvubréf Sigurðar Einarssonar til Magnúsar Guðmundssonar, dags. 9. júlí 2008.
    "Takk Meira en nog: -)."
    Svar Magnúsar Guðmundssonar, dags. 9. júlí 2008, við tilvitnuðu tölvubréfi Sigurðar Einarssonar.
56. SIC Report, Vol. 8, Appendix 1, Table 1, p. 43. Remuneration in USD is calculated by using average exchange rate provided by the Central Bank of Iceland, during each year 2004–2008; 2004:70.1 ISK/USD, 2005: 62.8 ISK/USD, 2006: 69.7 ISK/USD, 2007: 64 ISK/USD, 2008, Jan-Oct.: 79.6 ISK/USD.
57. News alert from the Glitnir-estate December 11, 2009 on Bjarni Armansson's reimbursement: www.glitnirbank.com/press-room/358-statement-from-the-resolution-committee-of-glitnir-hf.html

14   Funded by the Ill-Informed

1. Special Investigation Commission (SIC), 2008, *Background and Causes of the Collapse of the Icelandic Banks in 2008 and Related Events*, Vol. 2, Chapter 7, p. 36. (Report of the Special Investigation Commission (SIC). Reykjavik: Special Investigation Commission).

2. SIC Report, Vol. 6, Chapter 18, p. 5.
3. SIC Report, Vol. 6, Chapter 18, p. 5.
4. SIC Report, Vol. 2, Chapter 7, p. 36.
5. SIC Report, Vol. 2, Chapter 7, p. 39.
6. SIC Report, Vol. 2, Chapter 7, p. 39.
7. SIC Report, Vol. 6, Chapter 18, p. 8.
8. SIC Report, Vol. 6, Chapter 18, p. 8.
9. SIC Report, Vol. 6, Chapter 18, p. 9.
10. SIC Report, Vol. 6, Chapter 18, p. 8.
11. SIC Report, Vol. 6, Chapter 18, p. 5.
12. SIC Report, Vol. 6, Chapter 18, p. 10. It is incorrectly stated in the SIC report that the parent company and the FME in Iceland were responsible for liquidity oversight. According to article 12 of law nr. 36/2001 on the Central Bank of Iceland also correctly stated by the SIC in Vol. 2, Chapter 7, p. 68.
13. SIC Report, Vol. 6, Chapter 18, p. 45.
14. SIC Report, Vol. 2, Chapter 7, p. 36.
15. *The Daily Telegraph*, February 5, 2008, and SIC Report, Vol. 6, Chapter 18, p. 10.
16. *Sunday Times*, February 10, 2008, and SIC Report, Vol. 6, Chapter 18, p. 10.
17. SIC Report, Vol. 6, Chapter 18, p. 10.
18. SIC Report, Vol. 6, Chapter 18, pp. 11–12.
19. SIC Report, Vol. 6, Chapter 18, p. 17, figure 4, at the time, stock of deposits in the Icesave accounts in the UK was in the amount of 600–700 billion ISK. Iceland's GDP in 2007 was 1,308 billion ISK according to *Statistics Iceland*.
20. SIC Report, Vol. 6, Chapter 18, pp. 12 and 53.
21. SIC Report, Vol. 6, Chapter 18, p. 12.
22. SIC Report, Vol. 6, Chapter 18, p. 53.
23. SIC Report, Vol. 6, Chapter 18, p. 13.
24. SIC Report, Vol. 6, Chapter 18, p. 13.
25. SIC Report, Vol. 6, Chapter 18, p. 14.
26. SIC Report, Vol. 6, Chapter 18, p. 14 and undated memo written by Ingibjorg Solrun Gisladottir recording the events during the meeting of the governors of the Central Bank with the leaders of the government on April 1, 2008.
27. Through the emergency bill installed on October 6, 2008, deposits became a primary claim. The primary claims into Landsbanki amounted to 1,323 billion ISK in May 2012 roughly 11 billion. The asset portfolio of Landsbanki's estate exceeded primary claims by 1 billion USD at that time. (Announcement from Landsbanki's Winding Up Committee available at: http://www.lbi.is/home/news/news-item/2012/05/31/Announcement-from-Landsbanki-Islands-hf.--Creditors-Meeting/)
28. SIC Report, Vol. 6, Chapter 18, p. 44.

29. EFTA Court, Case E-16/11. Judgement of the Court, January, 28, 2013. The court ruled in favor of Iceland, explaining that the European Directive on deposit-guarantee schemes "does not envisage that the defendant itself must ensure payments to depositors in the Icesave branches" given the "systemic crisis of the magnitude experienced in Iceland."

30. SIC Report, Vol. 6, Chapter 18, p. 24.

31. SIC Report, Vol. 6, Chapter 18, pp. 34–40.

32. http://www.hm-treasury.gov.uk/8659.htm

33. The freezing order of the UK government coming into force at 10.10 a.m. October 8, 2010 http://www.legislation.gov.uk/uksi/2008/2668/pdfs/uksi_20082668_en.pdf (accessed May 4. 2013).

34. SIC Report, Vol. 6, Chapter 18, p. 54.

35. Morgunbladid, 11th of October, Námsmenn í vanda (English: Students in trouble), http://www.mbl.is/greinasafn/grein/1249404/?item_num=3&searchid=a959cab1db6c22a70dce89d34feb2acf4a10f82a (accessed June 4, 2013).

36. SIC Report, Vol. 7, Chapter 20, p. 160.

37. SIC Report, Vol. 7, Chapter 20, pp. 169 and 175.

38. SIC Report, Vol. 7, Chapter 20, p. 169.

39. SIC Report, Vol. 7, Chapter 20, p. 172.

40. The Queen (on the application of Kaupthing bank hf.) and her Majesty's Treasury. Statement of facts and grounds, p. 13. And the SIC report, Vol. 7, Chapter 20, p. 161.

41. SIC Report, Vol. 7, Chapter 20, p. 160.

42. A famous in-house campaign geared toward Kaupthing's staff to create team spirit in the company, Kaupthing's management advocated "Kaupthinking," which among other things entailed outwitting bureaucracy. One of those videos http://www.youtube.com/watch?v=Rkz-hjpch38 (accessed on May 4, 2013).

43. SIC Report, Vol. 7, Chapter 20, pp. 160–161.

44. SIC Report, Vol. 7, Chapter 20, p. 161.

45. Testimony of FSA staff member, Sheila Nicoll, before the The High Court of Justice, Chancery Divison, 8th of October, p. 9, during the case of Kaupthing Resolution Committee against HM's Treasury, and SIC report, Vol. 7, Chapter 20, p. 161.

46. SIC Report, Vol. 7, Chapter 20, p. 162.

47. SIC Report, Vol. 7, Chapter 20, p. 163.

48. SIC Report, Vol. 7, Chapter 20, p. 165.

49. SIC Report, Vol. 7, Chapter 20, p. 160.

50. SIC Report, Vol. 2, Chapter 7, p. 19.

15 A Debt-Free State; Isolated and without Credit

1. According to the Ministry of Finance, the outstanding debt of the Icelandic state at year-end 2007 amounted 23.5 percent of

GDP. Net debt of the Icelandic state amounted to 4.4 percent of GDP. Ministry of Finance, Oct. 2008, *The Icelandic Economy*, Autumn 2008, table 13, http://www.ministryoffinance.is/media /Thjodarbuskapurinn/The_Icelandic_Economy_Autumn_2008. pdf (accessed June 4, 2013).

2. Moody's, 2008, Iceland's Aaa Ratings at "Crossroads," *Moody's Investor Service—Global Credit Research, Online Announcement*, January 28, http://www.moodys.com/research/Moodys-Icelands-Aaa-ratings-at-a-crossroads – PR_148360 (accessed May 15, 2013).

3. According to a Central Bank memo dated February 4, 2008, SI-38808 on Moody's Credit rating report, that in their report the rating agency pointed out that the Central Bank of Iceland should search for ways to increase its foreign currency reserves through borrowing in the international market. The memo emphasizes the importance of discussing such borrowings with representatives of the credit agencies to assess its impact on the countries' credit rating. The memo further discusses ways to do this, including co-operation with the Nordic Central Banks and in particular the Bank of England, since that was the main hub of the Icelandic banks outside of Iceland. (SIC Report, Vol. 1, Chapter 4, p.167).

4. As a general rule, the Central Bank of Iceland kept its currency reserve close to the value of imported goods over three months (short of imports of airplanes and ships) according to Palsson and Benediktsson, 2005, Monetary Bulletin, 2005/3, Benediktsson, Haukur C., and Sturla Palsson, 2005, "Central Bank Foreign Reserves." *Central Bank of Iceland—Monetary Bulletin* no. 3 (2005): 79–86.Central Bank of Iceland, see also SIC Report, Vol. 1, Chapter 4, p. 167.

5. SIC Report, Vol. 1, Chapter 4, p. 77.

6. SIC Report, Vol. 1, Chapter 4, p. 168 and Minutes of the meeting with the Bank of England—memo nr. SI-39476 of the Central Bank of Iceland, dated March 5, 2008.

7. SIC Report, Vol. 1, Chapter 4, p. 168.

8. SIC Report, Vol. 1, Chapter 4, p. 168.

9. SIC Report, Vol. 1, Chapter 4, p. 168 and Memo SI-39555 of the Central Bank of Iceland, dated March 18, 2008.

10. SIC Report, Vol. 1, Chapter 4, p. 168 and Memo SI-39555 of the Central Bank of Iceland, dated March 18, 2008.

11. SIC Report, Vol. 1, Chapter 4, p. 168 and Memo SI-39555 of the Central Bank of Iceland, dated March 18, 2008.

12. SIC Report, Vol. 1, Chapter 4, p. 168.

13. SIC Report, Vol. 1, Chapter 4, p. 169.

14. SIC Report, Vol. 1, Chapter 4, p. 169. Letter to Jean-Claude Trichet from David Oddsson on March 26, 2008.

15. SIC Report, Vol. 1, Chapter 4, p. 169.

16. SIC Report, Vol. 1, Chapter 4, p. 169.

17. SIC Report, Vol. 1, Chapter 4, p. 170.

18. SIC Report, Vol. 1, Chapter 4, p. 170.
19. SIC Report, Vol. 1, Chapter 4, p. 171 and minutes from the meeting, undated and unreviewed, written by Sturla Palsson.
20. SIC Report, Vol. 1, Chapter 4, p. 171 and unreviewed minutes of the meeting written by Sturla Palsson, 14, of April 2008.
21. Sturla Palsson's testimony to the SIC on July 20, 2009, SIC Report, Vol. 1, Chapter 4, p. 171
22. SIC Report, Vol. 1, Chapter 4, p. 172.
23. "Background memorandum," SI-40299, Central Bank of Iceland April 15, 2009 and SIC Report, Vol. 1, Chapter 4, p. 172.
24. SIC Report, Vol. 1, Chapter 4, p. 172.
25. SIC Report, Vol. 1, Chapter 4, p. 172. Letter from David Oddsson to Mervyn King, dated April 22, 2008.
26. SIC Report, Vol. 1, Chapter 4, p. 173, Letter from Mervyn King to David Oddsson, dated April 23, 2008.
27. SIC Report, Vol. 1, Chapter 4, p. 173.
28. SIC Report, Vol. 1, Chapter 4, p. 174.
29. SIC Report, Vol. 1, Chapter 4, p. 174.
30. SIC Report, Vol. 1, Chapter 4, p. 174 and testimony of David Oddsson to the SIC on August 7, 2009 p. 50.
31. SIC Report, Vol. 1, Chapter 4, p. 174.
32. SIC Report, Vol. 1, Chapter 4, p. 175.
33. SIC Report, Vol. 1, Chapter 4, p. 176.
34. SIC Report, Vol. 1, Chapter 4, p. 177.
35. SIC Report, Vol. 1, Chpater 4, p. 178.
36. SIC Report, Vol. 1, Chapter 2, p. 42.
37. SIC Report, Vol. 1, Chapter 4, p. 179.
38. SIC Report, Vol. 1, Chapter 4, p. 176.
39. Landsdomur judgment in the case against former prime minister, Geir H. Haarde, p. 1, available in Icelandic on May 15, 2013 at: http://www.xn – landsdmur-b7a.is/domar-og-urskurdir
40. Landsdomur judgment in the case against former prime minister, Geir H. Haarde, available in Icelandic on May 15, 2013 at: http://www.xn--landsdmur-b7a.is/domar-og-urskurdir
41. Landsdomur is a special court assembled to rule on alleged breaches of ministers in their duties. The court's organization is stipulated by law on ministers' accountability nr. 4/1963 and in the constitution of the Icelandic Republic, law nr. 33/1944. Althingi, the Parliament, is the prosecutor in the cases brought to Landsdomur and elects 8 of the 15 judges at a 6-year interval. Five Supreme Court judges take a seat in Landsdomur. The Chief Justice of Reykjavik Court District and professor of constitutional law at the University of Iceland also have a seat at Landsdomur as stipulated by law 3/1963. Chief Justice of the Supreme Court is appointed Chief Justice to Landsdomur.

16   Putting a Poodle on Watch

1. Special Investigation Commission (SIC), 2008, *Background and Causes of the Collapse of the Icelandic Banks in 2008 and Related Events*, Vol. 5, Chapter 16, p. 130. (Report of the Special Investigation Commission (SIC). Reykjavik: Special Investigation Commission).
2. *Statistics Iceland, Labor Market Statistics, Activity Rate* www .statice.is (accessed May 20, 2013).
3. SIC Report, Vol. 5, Chapter 16, p. 130
4. This statistic is arrived at by dividing the total assets of the three failed banks in the run up to their collapse by a number of FME staff. It leaves out all the other responsibilities of the FME staff such as oversight over pension funds, mutual funds, savings, and loans cooperations. It also leaves out the fact that only a handful of FME staff are supervisors.
5. SIC Report, Vol. 5, Chapter 16, p. 129.
6. SIC Report, Vol. 5, Chapter 16, p. 66.
7. SIC Report, Vol. 5, Chapter 16, p. 71.
8. SIC Report, Vol. 5, Chapter 16, p. 71.
9. SIC Report, Vol. 5, Chapter 16, p. 71.
10. SIC Report, Vol. 5, Chapter 16, p. 65.
11. SIC Report, Vol. 1, Chapter 2, p. 45.
12. SIC Report, Vol. 1, Chapter 2, p. 45.
13. SIC Report, Vol. 5, Chapter 5, p. 145–146.
14. SIC Report, Vol. 5, Chapter 16, p. 143.
15. SIC Report, Vol. 5, Chapter 5, p. 117–120.
16. SIC Report, Vol. 1, Chapter 2, p. 45, SIC Report, Vol. 5, Chapter 16, p. 95 and Presentation of the SIC at the press conference held announcing the publication and conclusion of the SIC investigation on April 12, 2010, available in Icelandic at: http://www.rna. is/media/skjol/KynningRannsoknarnefnd.pdf (accessed May 21, 2013).
17. Article 3 & 4 of Law 36/2001 on the Central Bank of Iceland.
18. SIC Report, Vol. 5, Chapter 16, p. 182.
19. SIC Report, Vol. 1, Chapter 4, p. 164.
20. SIC Report, Vol. 5, Chapter 16, p. 177.
21. SIC Report, Vol. 1, Chapter 2, p. 38.
22. SIC Report, Vol. 5, Chapter 16, p. 186.
23. SIC Report, Vol. 1, Chapter 16, p. 156.
24. Financial Services Authority (FSA), 2009, *The Turner Review: A Regulatory Response to the Global Banking Crisis—March 2009*, FSA Review. (The Financial Services Authority), London, UK.
25. SIC presentation on April 12, 2010, on the main findings of the Report, available in Icelandic at www.rna.althingi.is
26. Average exchange rate was 71 kronas to the dollar between January 1 and June 30 according to Central Bank of Iceland.

27. SIC presentation on April 12, 2010, on the main findings of the Report, available in Icelandic at www.rna.althingi.is
28. SIC Report, Vol. 1, Chapter 1, p. 28.
29. SIC Report, Vol. 1, Chapter 2, p. 46.
30. SIC presentation on April 12, 2010, on the main findings of the Report, available at www.rna.althingi.is
31. SIC Report, Vol. 1, Chapter 2, pp. 46 and 47.

17   What Have We Learned?

1. The word impunitist is derived from the Latin word "impunitus," which has the following meanings: Scott-free, unrestrained, unpunished, safe

References

Admati, Anat and Martin Hellwig, 2013, *Banker's New Clothes: What's Wrong with Banking and What to Do about It?* Princeton, NJ: Princeton University Press.

Althingi, 2008, Act 142/2008: *Lög um rannsókn á aðdraganda og orsökum falls íslensku bankanna 2008 og tengdra atburða* (e. Act on the Investigation of the Background and Causes of the Collapse of the Icelandic Banks in 2008 and Related Events), Icelandic Legal Act, Althingi, Reykjavik.

Althingi, 2008, Act 161/2002: *Log um fjarmalafyrirtaeki* (e. Act on Financial Undertaking), Icelandic Legal Act, Althingi, Reykjavik.

Althingi, 2008, Act 36/2001: *Log um Sedlabanka Islands* (e. Act on the Central Bank of Iceland), Icelandic Legal Act, Althingi, Reykjavik.

Arnason, Vilhjálmur, Salvör Nordal, and Kristín Asgeirsdottir, 2010, *Ethics and Governance: In Relations with the Fall of the Icelandic Banks 2008.* Report of the Special Investigation Commission (SIC), Vol. 8, App. 1. Reykjavik: Special Investigation Commision.

Barley, Richard, 2007, "Moody's Upgrades Raft of Banks, Surprises Analysts," *Reuters, Online Edition*, February 26.

Basel Committee on Banking Superivision, 1991, *Measuring and Controlling Large Credit Exposures.* Basel: Basel Committee on Banking Supervision.

Baugur Group, 2008, "Baugur Completes Restructuring as a Pure Retail Investor and Builds New Investment Pool," *Baugur Group, Online Archives,* April 8.

Bebchuk, Lucian A., Cohen, Alma, and Spamann, Holger, 2009, "The Wages of Failure: Executive Compensation at Bear Stearns and Lehman 2000–2008 (November 24, 2009)." *Yale Journal on Regulation* 27 (2010): 257–282. Benediktsson, Haukur C., and Sturla Palsson, 2005, "Central Bank Foreign Reserves." *Central Bank of Iceland—Monetary Bulletin* no. 3: 79–86.

Bjarnadottir, Margret and Gudmundur A. Hansen, 2010, *Investigation into the Cross Ownership and Bank Credit to Related Parties.* Report of the Special Investigation Commission (SIC), Vol. 9 (Title in Icelandic: Rannsókn á krosseignartengslum og útlánum bankanna til tengdra aðila). Reykavik: Special Investigation Commission.

Bjorgolfsson, Bjorgolfur Thor, 2013, *Ardur af Landsbanka afram inn i Samson* [e. Dividends from Landsbanki paid on to Samson]. Btb— Bjorgolfur Thor Bjorgolfsson Weblog. Entry posted on March 24.

Black, William, 2005, *The Best Way to Rob a Bank Is to Own One: How Corporate Executives and Politicians Looted the S&L Industry*. Austin: University of Texas Press.

Board of Governors of the Federal Reserve System, 1993, *Risks of Concentration of Credit and Nontraditional Activities*, Board of Governors. Washington, DC: March 26,1993.

Board of Governors of the Federal Reserve System, 2011, *Annual Report: Budget Review*, Federal Reserve Board, Washington DC.

Bowers, Simon, Nick Mathiason, David Teather, and Julia Finch, 2009, "Kaupthing Sues Tchenguiz Firm for £643m," *The Guardian, Online Edition*, February 7.

Benda, O., 1999, "Privitization guru foresaw tunneling", Prague Post, Entry posted on January 6th 1999, available on October 1st 2013 at: http://www.praguepost.com/archivescontent/29782-privatization-guru-fore saw-tunneling.html

Brogger, Tasneem and Helga Kristin Einarsdottir, 2006, "Iceland Gets $4.6 Billion Bailout from IMF, Nordics," *Bloomberg, Online Edition*, November 20.

Buiter, Willem H., 2008, *Central Banks and Financial Crises*. Discussion Paper no 619. London: Financial Markets Group, London School of Economics and Political Science.

Capacent Gallup, 2010, Ánægja með skýrslu rannsóknarnefndar Alþingis [e. Satisfaction with SIC's Report], *Capacent, Online Edition*, May 5.

Central Bank of Iceland Annual Report 2010, Central Bank of Iceland, Reykjavik

Collapse of the Icelandic Banks in 2008 and Related Events, Vol. 6. Report of the Special Investigation Commission (SIC), Reykjavik: Special Investigation Commission.

Cottarelli, Dell'Ariccia, and Ivanna Vladkova-Hollar, 2005, "Early Birds, Late Risers, and Sleeping Beauties: Bank Credit Growth to the Private Sector in Central and Eastern Europe and in the Balkans," *Journal of Banking & Finance* 29, no. 1: 83–104.

European Commission, 2004, *International Financial Reporting Standard 2—Share-Based Payment*. Accounting Report. Brussels: European Commission.

"Executive Compensation at Bear Stearns and Lehman 2000–2008 (November 24, 2009)." *Yale Journal on Regulation* 27 (2010): 257–282.

Fabozzi, Frank J., Franco P. Modigliani and Frank J. Jones, 2009, *Foundations of Financial Markets and Institutions*. New York: Prentice Hall.

Financial Services Authority (FSA), 2009, *The Turner Review: A Regulatory Response to the Global Banking Crisis*—March 2009, FSA Review, The Financial Services Authority, London, UK.

Fjarsysla Rikisins (e. Government Accounting Office), 2011, *Annual Report 2011—Annual Financial Statement of Government Entities*. Icelandic State Annual Report. Iceland: Ministry of Finance.

Flannery, Mark, 2009, *Iceland's Failed Banks: A Post-Mortem*, SIC Report, Vol. 9 (Reykjavik: Special Investigation Commission), Appendix 3.

Fostel, Ana, and John Geanakoplos, 2008, "Leverage Cycles and the Anxious Economy," *American Economic Review*, 98, no. 4: 1211–1244.

Geanakopolos, John, 1997, "Promises, Promises." In, *The Economy as an Evolving Complex System, II*, edited by W. B. Arthur, S. Durlauf and D. Lane, 285–320. Reading, MA: Addison-Wesley.

Geanakplolos, John, 2010, "The Leverage Cycle." In D. Acemoglu, K. Rogoff and M. Woodford, eds., *NBER Macroeconomic Annual 2009* 24: 1–65, University of Chicago Press, 2010.

Glitnir Bank, 2009, "Statement from the Resolution Committee of Glitnir hf.," *Glitnir Bank, Online Edition*, December 11.

Glover, John, 2007, "Moody's Blasted for Giving Icelandic Banks Top Rating," *Bloomberg, Online Edition*, February 26.

Gourinchas, Pierre-Olivier, Rodrigo Valdes, and Oscar Landerretche, 2001, "Lending Booms: Latin America and the World," *Economía* 1, no. 2: 47–99.

Haarde, H. Geir, 2008, "Address by the Prime Minister due to Unusual Conditions in Financial Markets," *Prime Minister's Office, Online Edition*, October 6, Reykjavik.

Harré, Nick, Susan Foster, and Maree O'Neill, 2005, "Self-enhancement, Crash-risk Optimism and the Impact of Safety Advertisements on Young Drivers," *British Journal of Psychology* 96, no. 2: 215–230.

Harris, Bob, 2009, "A Startling Revelation: What Did the IMF and Central Banks Know—and Didn't Tell Us," *Weblog about the Trade Union Advisory Committee meeting at the OECD in May, 2009.* http://fundingeducation. blogspot.com/2009_05_01_archive.html (accessed May 29, 2013).

Hilbers, Paul, Inci Otker-Robe, Ceyla Pazarbasioglu, and Gudrun Johnsen, 2005, *Assessing and Managing Rapid Credit Growth and the Role of Supervisory and Prudential Policies*. Working Paper 05/151. Washington, DC: International Monetary Fund (IMF).

House of Commons, Treasury Committee, 2009, *Banking Crisis: The Impact of the Failure of the Icelandic Banks, Fifth Report of Sessions 2008–09, House of Commons*. London: Stationary Office Limited, http://www.hm-treasury .gov.uk/8659.htm.

Icelandic National Audit Office, 2012, *Fyrirgreiðsla ríkisins við fjármála-fyrirtæki og stofnanir í kjölfar bankahrunsins* [e. Government Lending to Financial Institutions and Agencies in the Wake of the Banking Collapse]. Report to the Parliament, Reykjavik: Icelandic National Audit Office.

International Monetary Fund (IMF), 2010, *Iceland: Staff Report for Second Review Under Stand-By Arrangement and Request for Extension of the*

Arrangement, Rephasing of Access and Establishment of Performance Criteria. Staff Report. Washington, DC: International Monetary Fund.

Jensen, Michael C., and William H. Meckling, 1976, "Theory of the Firm: Managerial Behavior, Agency Costs and Ownership Structure," *Journal of Financial Economics* 3, no. 4.

Jensen, Michael C., Kevin J. Murphy, and Eric G. Wruck, 2004, *Remuneration: Where We've Been, How We Got to Here, What Are the Problems, and How to Fix Them.* Harvard NOM Working Paper No. 04–28; ECGI—Finance Working Paper No. 44/2004, Harvard Business School, European Corporate Governance Institute (ECGI).

Johannesson, Guðni Th., 2009, *Hrunið: Ísland á barmi gjaldþrots og upplausnar (e. The Collapse: Iceland on the Brink of Bankruptcy and Dissolution)* Reykjavik, Iceland: JPV.

Johnsen, Gudrun, 2007, Lánshæfi til blessunar eða bölvunar? [e. Credit Rating: A Blessing or a Curse?], *Vidskiptabladid*, March 7, p. 14, Reykjavik

Johnson, Simon, Rafael La Porta, Florencio Lopez-de-Silanes and Andrei Shleifer, 2000. "Tunneling," *American Economic Association* 90, no. 2 (May): 22–27.

Kakodkar, Atish, Stefano Galiani, Jon G. Jonsson, and Alberto Gallo, 2006, *Credit Derivatives Handbook 2006*, Vol. 1. Credit Derivatives Strategy Report, Merrill Lynch, New York.

Kaupthing Bank, 2006, *Annual Report 2006*, Kaupthing Bank, Reykjavik, Iceland.

Kiyotaki, Nobuhiro, and John Moore, 1997, "Credit Cycles," *Journal of Political Economy* 105, no. 2: 211–248.

Kraft, Evan, and Ljubinko Jankov, 2005, "Does Speed kill? Lending Booms and Their Consequences in Croatia," *Journal of Banking and Finance* 29: 105–121.

Landsbanki, 2007, *Annual Report 2007*, Reykjavik: Landsbanki.

Landsdomur Trial, 2012, Audio Recordings of Hearings, http://www.landsdómur.is/adalmedferd

Landsdomur, 2012, Verdict 4/23/2012 in National Proceedings no. 3/2011: Althingi Against Geir Hilmar Haarde, Judgements and Rulings, Landsdomur.

Magnusson, Gylfi, 2010, *Lessons from a Small Country in a Financial Crisis or Dr. Minsky and Mr. Ponzi in Iceland.* Working Paper, Reykjavik: University of Iceland.

Milgram, Stanley, 1963, "Behavioral Study of Obedience," *Journal of Abnormal Social Psychology* 67, no. 4: 371–378.

Ministry of Finance, October 2008, *The Icelandic Economy*, Autumn 2008

Mishkin, Frederic S., and Tryggvi Thor Herbertsson, 2006, *Financial Stability in Iceland.* Report by Iceland Chamber of Commerce. Reykjavik: Iceland Chamber of Commerce.

Moody's, 2007, Landsbanki Islands hf Credit Rating, *Moody's Investor Service, Online Edition*, June 28.

Moody's, 2008, Iceland's Aaa Ratings at "Crossroads," *Moody's Investor Service—Global Credit Research, Online Announcement*, January 28.

Oyer, Paul, 2004, Why Do Firms Use Incentives that Have No Incentive Effects? *Journal of Finance* 59: 1619–1649.

Peng, Lin, and Ailsa Röell, 2008, "Executive Pay and Shareholder Litigation," *Review of Finance* 12, no. 1: 141–184.

Schaffer, S., 1998, "Winners Curse in Banking." *Journal of Financial Intermediation*, Vol. 7, No. 4: pp. 359–392.

Sedlabanki Islands (Central Bank of Iceland)—Exchange Rate, 2007–2008.

Sedlabanki Islands (Central Bank of Iceland)—Exchange Rate, 2008.

Shakespeare, William, 1600, *Merchant of Venice*, printed in London by I. E. for Thomas Heyes. http://shakespeare.mit.edu/merchant/full.html (accessed June 1, 2013).

Special Investigation Commission (SIC), 2008, *Background and Causes of the Collapse of the Icelandic Banks in 2008 and Related Events*, Vol. 1. Report of the Special Investigation Commission (SIC). Reykjavik: Special Investigation Commission.

Special Investigation Commission (SIC), 2008, *Background and Causes of the Collapse of the Icelandic Banks in 2008 and Related Events*, Vol. 2. Report of the Special Investigation Commission (SIC). Reykjavik: Special Investigation Commission.

Special Investigation Commission (SIC), 2008, *Background and Causes of the Collapse of the Icelandic Banks in 2008 and Related Events*, Vol. 3. Report of the Special Investigation Commission (SIC). Reykjavik: Special Investigation Commission.

Special Investigation Commission (SIC), 2008, *Background and Causes of the Collapse of the Icelandic Banks in 2008 and Related Events*, Vol. 4. Report of the Special Investigation Commission (SIC), Reykjavik: Special Investigation Commission.

Special Investigation Commission (SIC), 2008, *Background and Causes of the Collapse of the Icelandic Banks in 2008 and Related Events*, Vol. 5. Report of the Special Investigation Commission (SIC). Reykjavik: Special Investigation Commission.

Special Investigation Commission (SIC), 2008, *Background and Causes of the Collapse of the Icelandic Banks in 2008 and Related Events*, Vol. 6. Report of the Special Investigation Commission (SIC). Reykjavik: Special Investigation Commission.

Special Investigation Commission (SIC), 2008, *Background and Causes of the Collapse of the Icelandic Banks in 2008 and Related Events*, Vol. 7. Report of the Special Investigation Commission (SIC). Reykjavik: Special Investigation Commission.

Special Investigation Commission (SIC), 2008, *Background and Causes of the Collapse of the Icelandic Banks in 2008 and Related Events*, Vol. 8. Report of the Special Investigation Commission (SIC). Reykjavik: Special Investigation Commission.

Special Investigation Commission (SIC), 2008, *Background and Causes of the Collapse of the Icelandic Banks in 2008 and Related Events*, Vol. 9. Report of the Special Investigation Commission (SIC). Reykjavik: Special Investigation Commission.

Special Investigation Commission (SIC), 2010, *Report of the Special Investigation Commission on the Collapse of the Banks in 2008*. Press Conference Presentation, Special Investigation Commission.

Statistics Iceland—Labor Market Statistics: Activity Rate, 2002–2007.

Statistics Iceland—Main Economic Variables for the Public Sector 1980–2011.

Statistics Iceland, 2008, Gross Domestic Product 2007, Statistical Series— National Accounts, Statistics Iceland, Reykjavik.

Stephen, John Akers, 2010, Notice: 1179911 (Issue: 59511)—Oscatello Investments Limited, *The London Gazette, Online Edition*, London, August 9.

Sverrisdottir, Valgerdur, 2006, Luncheon, Icelandic-American Chamber of Commerce, New York, *Ministry for Foreign Affairs, Online Edition*, September 27.

Talley, Eric, and Gudrun Johnsen, *2005, Corporate Governance, Executive Compensation and Securities Litigation*. CLEO and Law & Economics Research Paper Series, University of Southern California Law School, Los Angeles.

Thomas, Richard, 2006, *Icelandic Banks–Not What You Are Thinking*, European Credit Research Report, Merrill Lynch. London, UK.

Thorisson, Hermann Mar, and Ingi Sturla Thorisson, 2006, Álit á uppgjöri (e. Analysis of Quarterly Results)—Glitnir Bank, Investment Research Report, Landsbanki, Reykjavik.

U.K. Parliament, 2008, *No. 2668—Banks and Banking—The Landsbanki Freezing Order 2008*, Statutory Instrument, U.K. Parliament.

Valgreen, Carsten, Lars Christensen, Peter Possing Andersen, and Rene Kallestrup, 2006, *Iceland: Geyser Crisis*, Economic Research Report, Danske Bank, Copenhagen, Denmark.

Viðskiptablaðið, 2008, Glitnir opnar fyrir viðskipti með sjóði á ný [e. Glitnir Reopens for Trading in Funds), *Viðskiptablaðið, Online Edition*, September 30.

Vísir, 2008, Símarnir rauðglóandi hjá Glitni í morgun (e. The Phones Glowing Red at Glitnir This Morning), *Vísir, Online Edition*, September 30, Reykjavik.

Index

Printed and bound in Great Britain by
CPI Group (UK) Ltd, Croydon, CR0 4YY